VITAMIN POWER

VITAMIN POWER

A User's Guide to Nutritional Supplements
& Botanical Substances That Can
Change Your Life

RITA AERO and STEPHANIE RICK

Foreword by ELSON M. HAAS, M.D.

Illustrations by Elizabeth Garsonnin

HARMONY BOOKS/NEW YORK

Publisher's Note: This book contains instructions concerning
the use of nutritional supplements within the context of an overall
health program. However, not all supplements should be used by
all individuals. Before commencing any health program a
physician should be consulted. The instructions in this book are
not intended as a substitute for professional medical advice.

*Published by Harmony Books, a division of
Crown Publishers, Inc., 225 Park Avenue South,
New York, New York 10003 and represented in
Canada by the Canadian MANDA Group.*

*HARMONY and colophon are trademarks of
Crown Publishers, Inc.
Manufactured in the United States of America*

Library of Congress Cataloging-in-Publication Data

Aero, Rita
    Vitamin power.

    Bibliography: p.
    Includes index.
    1. Vitamin therapy. 2. Vitamins. 3. Minerals in
human nutrition. 4. Materia medica, Vegetable.
I. Rick, Stephanie. II. Title. [DNLM: 1. Medicine,
Herbal—popular works. 2. Minerals—popular
works. 3. Nutrition—popular works. 4. Vitamins—
popular works. QU 160 A252v]
RM259.A35   1987   615'.328   87-8
ISBN 0-517-56428-9

10   9   8   7   6   5   4   3   2   1

FIRST EDITION

CONTENTS

CHAPTER SIX — PROBLEM SOLVING

ACKNOWLEDGMENTS

Our approach to the information in this book was, initially, a divided one. One of your authors is an enthusiast, the other a skeptic — a combination that created much heated discussion, scrambling for journal articles, and frequent (sometimes frantic) calls and letters to nutritionists, physicians, herbalists, and other researchers who were all extraordinarily patient and helpful. We are especially grateful to Bethany Argisle; Patricia Cooper, Ph.D.; Penelope Edwards, M.P.H.; Debbie Fletcher; Elson M. Haas, M.D.; Maribeth Riggs; Betsy Small; and to Elizabeth Garsonnin for her wonderful botanical drawings.

In writing a book that explores a field in which information changes constantly and important new findings appear virtually overnight, we were fortunate to have friends, family, and allies who were supportive in so many wonderful ways. Our heartfelt thanks go to Pamela Allen, Jean Caldwell, Paul Challacombe, Tan Chang, Dona Christianson, Robin Clauson, John Connolly, Nadine Cutwright, Leslie Fuller, Jan Gallagher, Don Girard, Steve Haight, Mary Hutchison, Jean Kelton, Henryk Kramek, Lorna Kriss, Ann Leeds, Irene Leffler, Peg Lucerne, Judy Maas, John Main, Jerry Mander, Anthony Ramos, Howard Rheingold, DeLores Rick, Richard Rosenberg, and James Webb.

And finally, we are deeply indebted to our editor, Esther Mitgang, who, with great wit and insight, showed us the way.

FOREWORD

by Elson M. Haas, M.D.

Director of the Marin Clinic of Preventive Medicine and author of
Staying Healthy with the Seasons and *Staying Healthy with American Medicine*

Nutrition, immunology, stress management, preventive medicine, and self-care are the leading issues at the threshold of American medicine — and, I believe, we stand at the gateway to a new health-care system, a system that will really support the health of the individual. Modern illness, especially the rapidly increasing rate of degenerative diseases, can be postponed or totally prevented by changing the way we live and by using supportive nutritional and herbal supplements when we are well. Doctors and patients alike share the responsibility for educating themselves about how to stay healthy and how to prevent potential disease.

Many doctors still discount the importance of nutrition and the use of supplements and herbs, but times are changing, and more and more of my fellow physicians are beginning to bring nutritional medicine into their practices. The field of nutritional medicine is advancing rapidly, and with recent strides in valuable research, nutritional practitioners have increased background support available to them. It is now possible to evaluate people medically for diet and vitamin/mineral deficiencies. This makes it possible to create an individualized-supplement program that can support health and prevent disease.

In my experience, nutritional supplements and dietary changes are effective in the treatment of many diseases and their symptoms. There is a definite advantage when all the necessary nutrients are available for the body's cells to use, right when they are needed. For example, there are a number of new studies showing that the use of vitamin A, vitamin C, and zinc will speed the healing of tissue in wounds, injuries, and surgical procedures. Increasing one's intake of these nutrients before and after surgical procedures can shorten the hospital stay, reduce morbidity, and speed recovery.

In today's world of special diets, chemical foods, environmental stress, and immune-system insults, everyone can benefit from nutrient support. Millions of Americans currently use vitamins; but without an understanding of the basic principles of nutrition, it is difficult to get the best value and results from supplement programs. I believe the easy-to-use text in *Vitamin Power* will make it possible for the reader to create an effective nutrition program based on individual health requirements.

A great deal of work and research has gone into creating *Vitamin Power*, and the result is a medically responsible approach to the use of nutritional supplements. I have spent many years reading and writing on this topic, and, let me tell you, it is not always easy to differentiate between theory and reality. The authors have gone to great lengths to explore the world literature and to extract what is scientifically accurate and medically helpful. I believe that following the nutritional guidelines suggested in this book can enhance the quality and vitality of life. More important, the application of the *Vitamin Power* principles can help prevent disease and save lives.

11

INTRODUCTION

We live in a world that is going through a crisis of technological and physiological readjustment. One million years of evolutionary development did not prepare the human body for what has happened to the earth over the past fifty years. Rural or urban, we live in a polluted, stressful, artificially colored and flavored environment that has clearly demonstrated its ability to destroy our health. The faster our cells are damaged by chemicals and stress, the faster we age and the more likely we are to develop diseases such as arthritis, cancer, and atherosclerosis. Worse yet, we cannot avoid ingesting the substances that cause this cellular damage. They are present in our air, our water, our food, and even in our sunlight. Therefore, we must learn, as quickly as possible, how to neutralize these substances in our bodies and strengthen our immune systems against the world we live in. Until our bodies learn to adapt to the environment, and while technology catches up with itself and begins to clean up its mess, there are a number of health-protective measures we can take.

Tremendous scientific interest and funding is now focused on research into nutrition and the preventive technologies, with new studies published every day. Within the past twenty-four months, a number of available nutrients have been shown to achieve some remarkable protective and regenerative results. However, choosing from the vast commercial array of nutritional supplements can be confusing at best, even for the most knowledgeable health consumer. Because of this, we have compiled a tightly drawn dossier about each nutrient in order to give the reader an opportunity to examine the facts, the statistics, and the results of the most recent studies.

Our research led us in many unexpected directions, and one was toward the use of herbs as medicines. Herbs, of course, are not a new story in medicine — the vast majority of prescription drugs used today were synthesized from herbs. Now, new studies into the efficacy of herbs such as cayenne and ginseng are emerging, and some of the most recent research was impossible to overlook. These herbs and others are showing significant promise in controlling cardiovascular disease while protecting the body from toxins at the cellular level. Also, research into some of the plant-derived supplements, such as olive oil and fiber, demanded our attention. These supplements have been shown clearly to have an effect in the control of heart disease and the prevention of certain cancers, particularly colon cancer.

We have looked at every commercially available nutritional and botanical supplement that we could find, examined the most current research on each one, and included in this book all the nutrients that actually have a positive effect on the body's long-term health, along with the range of dosages used in the studies to achieve the desired effect. What has emerged from this, we believe, is a realistic view of the most recent and promising research into commercially available nutritional supplements — along with a no-nonsense guide to using them effectively.

CHOOSING THE RIGHT NUTRITIONAL SUPPLEMENT

Most Americans simply do not get the Recommended Daily Allowance (RDA) of some very important nutrients, especially vitamins A, B6, and C, and the minerals iron, zinc, calcium, and magnesium. These are all nutrients that the body needs to stay healthy. To reach RDA levels of all the essential nutrients through dietary sources means that your meals must be strategically planned and prepared, using the very freshest, most carefully grown ingredients. Most of the food should be eaten raw, since cooking destroys many important vitamins. This kind of labor- and time-intensive approach to nutrition is rarely feasible for the way most of us live and work.

The guidelines set out by both the American Heart Association and the American Cancer Society are forcing us to re-evaluate the way we eat. The very foods that health-conscious Americans are now avoiding because of their links to obesity, cancer, and cardiovascular disease (in particular, eggs, meat, and dairy products), contain high concentrations of nutrients that the body needs on a daily basis. To optimize health and prevent deficiency-related illnesses, these nutrients must be replaced from safer and more desirable sources. To make these intelligent dietary changes truly effective, those who restrict their intake of animal products should include nutritional supplements in their overall health strategy.

Within the past three years, a number of nutritional supplements have shown promise for many health benefits far beyond the prevention of deficiencies. Both in controlled laboratory studies and in epidemiological research, nutrients such as beta-carotene, selenium, and vitamin E have actually been shown to protect the body from the ravages of carcinogens — cancer-causing substances. Other nutrients such as calcium, chromium, niacin, and L-carnitine have demonstrated remarkable effectiveness in protecting the heart from cardiovascular disease, the nation's leading cause of death.

Once we accept the importance of supplemental nutrition in the long-term health of the human body, we are faced with the challenge of choosing the right multiple-vitamin/mineral formula. The vitamin counters in pharmacies and health food stores seem to contain an impossible and complicated selection of handsomely packaged (and esoteric) products. The main problem in choosing a formula lies in that very packaging. Vitamin companies are in the business of selling vitamins, and consumers should be in the business of choosing in an informed manner. Do not pay attention to vitamin names that promise specific results. If the words "stress," "brain power," or "fitness" are found in the name of the vitamin supplement, it does not mean that it is a bad formula, but since none of these achievements come through vitamins, it is important to look beyond the name.

Let's take a look at a typical label from a multiple vitamin/mineral supplement. Many of the nutrients listed, particularly the minerals, are in dosages so minimal that they can only be there for marketing purposes. Calcium — a mineral that has lately become a media star — is a good example. Some multiple formulas list less than 100 mg. of calcium, which is really not enough to make it worthwhile to swallow the pill. Again, it does not mean that the overall formula is bad, but when it contains less than a tenth of what the body requires, that nutrient should be considered missing from the formula.

Other nutrients listed on the label are in dosages that are far too high. The only consequence, in the case of most of the B vitamins, is some very pricey (and colorful) urine. Vitamin B6, however, commonly treated as just another nontoxic, water-soluble B vitamin, can cause serious neurological problems when taken in high dosages. Unfortunately, vitamin B6 has become an advertising sensation, touted as a "woman's vitamin," the solution to premenstrual syndrome (PMS). Many vitamin companies are scrambling to enter the market with "women's formulas" that feature this vitamin, so be certain to check that the dosage is in a safe range for long-term daily intake.

Too often, vitamin companies do not change their formulas when new research indicates that they should. For example, it's still hard to find a multiple-vitamin/mineral supplement that provides vitamin A in its beta-carotene form, which is now widely known to have anticarcinogenic properties. Instead, supplements continue to include vitamin A as fish oil, perhaps because vitamin manufacturers are able profit from beta-carotene's newfound popularity when they sell it only as an individual supplement. Unfortunately for the consumer, the body tends to satisfy its daily need for vitamin A from the fish oil in the multiple-vitamin/mineral first and may ignore the beta-carotene supplement altogether.

There are a number of nutrients that you will see listed on the label which are not included in this book. If the nutrient is not included, then current research indicates that it does not work very well — except to sell vitamins. PABA (para-aminobenzoic acid), for example, makes a frequent appearance on multiple-vitamin/mineral labels — but it cannot be metabolized by the human body, and therefore it contributes nothing nutritionally. Vitamin companies will add PABA and other newsworthy substances to their formulas in response to marketing studies that indicate a popular demand for a particular substance.

Among the nutrients we have not included are certain trace elements, most of the amino acids, the bioflavonoids, and substances such as inositol and lecithin. At the time of this book's publication, these substances fell into one of four categories: One — no conclusive studies have appeared to support their health benefit to humans; two — even an inadequate diet provides more than enough of the substance to achieve any nutritional benefit; three — the dosages required to provide unusual health benefits are either highly experimental, must be taken intra-venously, or are considered unsafe for use without medical supervision; four — research indicates that these substances have no effect in humans at all. Some of the popular supplements that fall into these categories are:

BIOFLAVONOIDS — Bioflavonoids such as rutin and hesperidin are predominantly the yellow pigments found in plants. They were originally called vitamin P, but this name was later discarded when a series of studies determined that they had no established role in human nutrition. Bioflavonoids caused a great stir in the medical world when several studies suggested that they might be useful for strengthening the walls of capillaries, perhaps helping to prevent their rupture. Yet the Food and Drug Administration (FDA), after a review of published studies on the subject, withdrew bioflavonoid drugs from the medical market because there was no therapeutic value demonstrated for them, even on capillaries. Other anecdotes about bioflavonoids, such as their ability to help the body utilize vitamin C, have turned out to be valid for guinea pigs but invalid for humans.

TRACE ELEMENTS — Some multiple-vitamin/mineral supplements contain trace amounts of elements such as silicon and vanadium. Silicon has been shown to be essential for rats and chicks: A deficiency in it causes these species to develop bone and connective-tissue abnormalities. However, silicon's role in human nutrition has not been established and, because silicon is so plentiful in our environment, human deficiency in it is considered highly unlikely to occur. Vanadium seems to be involved in bone and tooth development and the metabolism of fats. Animals deficient in vanadium develop elevated cholesterol levels. Human studies to date, however, have not determined any nutritional role for vanadium, and attempts to use doses of vanadium to lower cholesterol levels in humans have been unsuccessful.

AMINO ACIDS — The amino acids and their roles as supplemental nutrients have been the subject of considerable controversy over the past few years. The human body is in a state of constant flux and readjustment, synthesizing and secreting hormones and enzymes, repairing damaged cells, breaking down and discarding old tissues and building new ones. The amino acids are the basic building materials for all these adjustments. The body's amino-acid requirements are fairly specific — while it can synthesize adequate amounts of twelve to fourteen of them, eight of the amino acids, called the essential amino acids, must come from external sources such as dietary protein. Since the average American diet has double the amount of protein required by the body, amino-acid supplements are rarely needed, except in specific medical situations. In addition, even if certain amino acids have specific effects in the body, research to date indicates that the body must have adequate amounts of all the amino acids present in order to perform its routine housekeeping duties. These amounts are maintained in a fine balance that can be upset when an individual amino acid is taken in large amounts as a supplement without all the others, and the effect of disturbing this balance has the potential to disrupt many basic metabolic processes.

Most of the studies to date on therapeutic uses of supplemental amino acids have been conducted on animals, and those which have been done on humans have shown mostly disappointing results. While L-cysteine, L-arginine, and L-lysine are included and discussed in this book, along with L-carnitine, an amino-acid-like substance, none of the others are because claims about their efficacy, at safe dosages taken orally, have not been substantiated. For example, researchers in the field of mental health have been working on forming and regulating certain neurotransmitters that can affect such things as depression by "loading" the body with substances that are their precursors. Recent attempts to use supplemental amino acids such as tryptophan, phenylalanine, and tyrosine to "load" the body, however, have been, for the most part, a disappointment. Not only

17

did they fail to substantially alter neurotransmitter formation, they were often given intravenously, not orally, and involved such large doses that medical supervision was required. In addition, some unpleasant side effects appeared — tryptophan triggered nausea, phenylalanine elevated blood pressure, and tyrosine seemed to aggravate migraine problems. Some benefits have appeared as a result of these studies — large doses of tryptophan, for example, can help normalize sleep patterns in people with mild insomnia, but the substance does not induce sleep in those with normal sleep patterns or in those suffering from severe insomnia. More detailed and long-term research is needed on amino acids, especially in the area of the safety of long-term intake of these substances.

CHOLINE AND LECITHIN — Lecithin, found in the cells of all living organisms, is used in foods and cosmetics as an emulsifier and has been touted as a liver detoxifier and an aid in fighting atherosclerosis and elevated cholesterol levels. While lecithin in the body does remove excess fat from the liver, and studies have shown that supplemental lecithin can reverse some of the damage from alcohol to the liver in dogs, human studies have not supported this claim. There has also not been any good evidence that the supplemental oral intake of lecithin either helps atherosclerosis or reduces cholesterol levels. In addition, the lecithin used in the studies was about ninety percent pure: Most of the lecithin preparations available in health food stores, on the other hand, are rarely more than thirty to fifty percent pure, a level that has not been found to be worth using. Supplemental choline, which is actually a component of lecithin, has been studied for the same uses as lecithin, with the same lack of success. In addition, choline has also been studied because of its role in the body as the precursor for the neurotransmitter acetylcholine. Attempts to use supplemental choline for precursor "loading," however, particularly in patients with Alzheimer's disease, have not fulfilled the expectations of researchers. Since the liver can synthesize choline from carbohydrate molecules, and the average American diet provides 400 to 900 mg. of choline, supplemental choline seems to be unnecessary. In addition, some forms of choline, when taken orally, are changed in the intestine to trimethylamine, which gives the body a fishy odor.

INOSITOL — Inositol, or myoinositol (its biologically active form), is another substance found widely in plant and animal tissues and products. Like lecithin, inositol in the body works to remove fats from the liver. Supplemental inositol may help some diabetics with nerve problems in their hands and feet, although these reports are only from preliminary research. Some heart-protective effects in animals have been shown from the use of supplemental inositol, but none have yet been demonstrated in humans. Inositol has been shown to be of no help in preventing hair loss.

PABA — In the past two or three years, a new additive has appeared in many multiple-vitamin/mineral supplements — PABA (para-amino-benzoic acid). PABA is a substance required by bacteria to manufacture folic acid for their cell-replication needs. In effect, it is a nutrient, possibly even a vitamin, for bacteria; but humans have no known nutrient need for it. Taken internally, PABA can cause diarrhea and nausea in some people, perhaps because of effects it may have on intestinal bacteria. PABA is stored in the tissues, and long-term large doses of it have been suspected of being toxic to the liver, although studies have not been conclusive. Reports of its effects, when taken internally, as a skin-clearing agent, hair restorer, invigorator, cell-protecting agent, and cure for anemia have all been anecdotal and unsubstantiated. The only really valid use for PABA by humans is external and topical: As a sunscreen, PABA ranks as one of the best and is actually able to block many of the sun's destructive effects on the skin.

If your vitamins contain these supplements — as do some of the ones we recommend — it is not a cause for concern. Generally, the dosages of these supplements found in multiple-vitamin/mineral formulas have no effect in the body, good or bad. It is important to take those nutrients that *do* have scientifically established benefits — and to take them correctly. The general guidelines for taking nutritional supplements are:

1. Always take supplements on a full stomach unless you are specifically instructed otherwise.
2. Take your supplements every day, without fail, forever.
3. Keep it simple. Do not take an individual supplement when you can get it from a multiple formula.
4. Do not experiment on yourself. Let the scientists do it first, then read the results, or consult a nutrition specialist.

Nutritional supplements will not suddenly cure physical problems, and they are not meaningful to overall health if they are not taken regularly, year in, year out. For this reason, those who do begin taking supplements are not likely to discover suddenly that they feel better, unless a deficiency has been present. Nor are supplements a substitute for necessary medical treatment. In fact, individuals who are under medical care, and pregnant or breast-feeding women, should work with their physicians to evaluate the nutritional support system best for them.

Rational nutritional support is nutritional self-defense for those of us who want to compensate for the technical inadequacies in medicine, the low cure rates for cancer and cardiovascular disease, and the increased risk of disease from exposure to a dangerous environment. This self-defense approach is for the informed individual who is fighting for a life that is longer, better, and free of disease.

THE VITAMIN POWER FORMULA

Vitamin A (as beta-carotene)	15,000 to 25,000 IU
Vitamin B1 - Thiamin	10 mg.
Vitamin B2 - Riboflavin	10 mg.
Niacin (as niacinamide)	50 to 100 mg.
Pantothenic Acid	25 to 50 mg.
Vitamin B6 - Pyridoxine	25 to 50 mg.
Vitamin B12	6 to 30 mcg.
Folic Acid	400 mcg.
Biotin	100 to 300 mcg.
Vitamin C	250 to 1,000 mg.
Vitamin D	400 IU
Vitamin E	200 to 400 IU
Vitamin K	0 to 100 mcg.
Calcium	1,000 to 1,500 mg.
Chromium	100 to 200 mcg.
Copper	2 to 3 mg.
Iodine	150 mcg.
Iron	18 to 30 mg.
Magnesium	400 to 600 mg.
Manganese	5 to 10 mg.
Molybdenum	100 to 200 mcg.
Selenium	100 to 200 mcg.
Zinc	15 to 30 mg.

THE VITAMIN POWER FORMULA

The Vitamin Power Formula represents baseline nutritional support for optimum health protection. All the nutrients in the Formula are in dosages that are essential to good health. Six of the nutrients, however, have demonstrated significant protective functions when they are present in the body at high levels — higher than can be achieved through a normal diet or through most commercial one-per-day vitamin products. They are: the beta-carotene form of vitamin A, vitamin C, vitamin E, calcium, chromium, and selenium.

Research suggests that the nutrients in the Vitamin Power Formula, taken daily in the dosages indicated, will help the body achieve the goals of nutritional self-defense. Because of the sheer mass of certain nutrients, especially calcium and magnesium, it will be necessary to swallow several pills each day. The good news is that the current market price of this preventive technology costs no more than a cup of coffee — between thirty and seventy cents a day.

Make a copy of the Vitamin Power Formula on the facing page and carry it with you to use as a guide when you shop for a multiple-vitamin/mineral supplement. Not only does the Formula show the effective dosages of each nutrient, it also outlines a carefully structured balance, particulary among the minerals. For example, the dosage ratio between zinc and copper is roughly ten to one, which is an ideal balance between these essential minerals. When shopping for multiple-vitamin/mineral formulas, you will often find that the vitamin dosages they contain, especially the B vitamins, are higher than what you need, and that the minerals are lower. Calcium, for instance, is rarely found in a multiple formula at the recommended dosage range of 1,000 to 1,500 mg. This important mineral should be taken as a separate supplement in addition to your multiple, in order to reach Vitamin Power levels.

To help simplify your search for the ideal multiple-vitamin/mineral supplement, five commercially available products are reviewed, beginning on page 223. All of them have formulas that are either relatively close to our ranges or are easily supplemented with the addition of individual nutrients, such as calcium or beta-carotene. We were able to locate these products quite readily from a variety of sources — health food stores, grocery stores, pharmacies, and through mail order — and all are from established vitamin companies. These are not, by any means, the only companies with suitable formulas — a little shopping around will turn up other sources.

Some individuals will have nutritional needs that go beyond what is available in any particular formula. The Programs, which begin on page 137, can help those with specific physical concerns, such as stress and excess weight, to design their own nutritional strategies. For those suffering from physical disorders, the Problem Solving chapter, which begins on page 185, lists physical conditions that can show improvement through nutritional therapy.

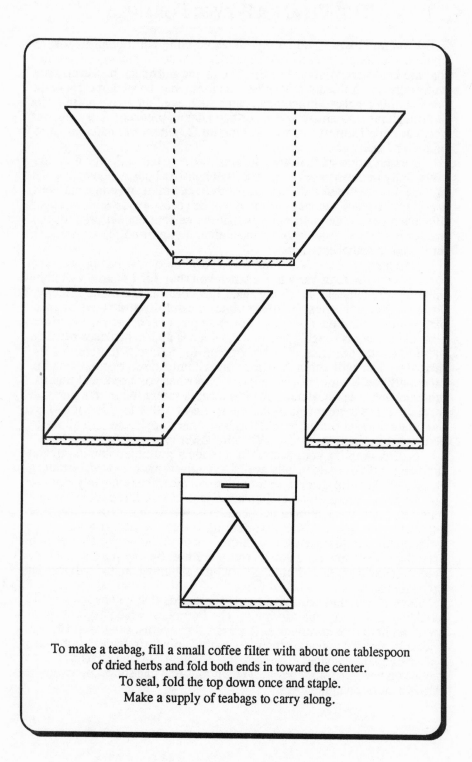

To make a teabag, fill a small coffee filter with about one tablespoon
of dried herbs and fold both ends in toward the center.
To seal, fold the top down once and staple.
Make a supply of teabags to carry along.

HOW TO USE THE BOTANICALS

Herbs and other botanicals have been used successfully for thousands of years as remedies for an assortment of ailments and disorders. In fact, until the beginning of the twentieth century, botanicals and plant-derived medicines made up the bulk of most of the world's official pharmacopoeias. Today, in our modern, scientific world, we have come to rely on nonbotanical, synthetic drugs and have forgotten or overlooked the fact that botanicals have a useful place in our lives. They can produce relief from many of the minor aches, pains, and illnesses that plague us, such as indigestion, stuffed sinuses, and cuts and bruises. Plant-derived medicines can also change our psychological attitudes and outlooks. They can relieve tension and anxiety and help revive and refresh flagging spirits. Most important, a number of botanicals are showing remarkable effects both as antioxidants, helping to protect the body against cellular damage from contaminants, and as agents that can help reduce the risk of developing cardiovascular disease.

The botanicals included in this book were selected on the basis of their efficacy, availability, and simplicity in preparation and application. Every herb listed can be found in a health food store. A number of them are also available in grocery stores. Most are available prepackaged in some form, as teabags or in capsules, but many can also be bought fresh or dried in bulk.

When buying fresh herbs, reject those which are wilted, brown, or otherwise unacceptable, just as you would any fruit or vegetable. When selecting dried herbs, inspect them carefully for the presence of mold, insects, or other undesirable elements. Be sure to smell them — in most cases, if the dried herbs have no smell, they have little, if any, efficacy. Most of the fresh herbs can be air-dried at home. Once they are dried, store them away from direct sunlight in glass jars, packed loosely. Be sure to label and date them, and replace them after one year.

Almost all the herbs come in capsule form, which is frequently the way you will want to take them. If swallowing capsules is a problem for you, many of them, such as ginseng, can be opened, emptied into hot water, and taken as a tea. For take-along convenience, make your own prepackaged herbal teabags as shown on the facing page. The active parts of the plants used for tea are usually either the root or the leaves. Tea prepared from roots is generally boiled in a glass or enameled pot. Tea prepared from leaves is steeped, not boiled, since boiling the leaves can destroy the active substances in them.

Formulas for preparing each herb will be found in Chapter Four, "The Botanicals." Techniques for using the herbs and botanicals for specific remedies are described in the Problem Solving chapter, page 185. Keep in mind that herbs are strong, fast-acting medicines. Individuals who are already taking medications should consult their physicians before using herbs internally. Also, pregnant or breast-feeding women should not use herbs or any medications without first consulting a health professional.

GLOSSARY OF TERMS

Alkaloid — A bitter substance in plants, such as morphine in opium poppies, that can have strong physiological effects in humans and animals. These effects can be medicinal or poisonous.

Amino Acid — An organic compound containing nitrogen. Amino acids, such as cysteine and lysine, are the building blocks for protein and are essential to human metabolism.

Antioxidant — A substance, such as vitamin E, that delays or prevents the oxidation processes that contribute to the breakdown of cells, as opposed to a pro-oxidant, which triggers oxidation.

Arteriosclerosis — The name for a group of cardiovascular diseases in which artery walls thicken and harden. Arteriosclerosis proper, one of the diseases, is the hardening of the arteries resulting from mineral and fatty deposits in the middle layer of the arterial wall.

Atherosclerosis — A cardiovascular disease characterized by the deposit of yellowish plaques, or atheromas, on the inner lining of arterial walls. These plaques can clog an artery and stop blood flow to organs such as the heart, resulting in a life-threatening situation.

Bioavailable — The amount of a nutrient that the body can actually absorb and use.

Carcinogen — A substance such as tobacco smoke that can induce the development of cancerous cells.

Chelated — A mineral that has been combined with another substance, ostensibly to increase its bioavailability. Bioavailability, however, can be affected by so many other factors that a chelated mineral is not necessarily better than a nonchelated one, just more expensive.

Cholesterol — A fat-related substance manufactured by the body that acts as a precursor for many of the hormones and is a part of such things as bile, nerve fibers, and brain tissue. The body produces the cholesterol it needs, so dietary intake often proves excessive, resulting in harmful effects. Too much dietary cholesterol, from such things as egg yolks and saturated animal fats and oils, is thought to be a factor in atherosclerosis.

DNA (deoxyribonucleic acid) — A molecule that is one of the major chemical constituents of chromosomes in the cells. DNA carries the instructions that govern the functions and normal reproduction of each cell. It also carries the genetic code that transmits hereditary patterns from generation to generation.

Dysplasia — The faulty development or growth of cells, which results in cellular abnormalities. Some forms of dysplasia, such as cervical dysplasia, are considered highly indicative of a risk for developing cancer.

Electrolyte — An electrolyte is a substance that, when added to a liquid like water, breaks apart into electrically charged atoms. These charged atoms, called ions, have either a positive or a negative charge and allow a current of electricity to pass through the liquid they occupy. In the body, potassium and sodium are positive ions, while chloride is a negative ion. Most of the potassium ions are found inside the cells, while most of the sodium and chloride ions are outside the cells in the liquids surrounding them. Electrolyte imbalances can affect conditions such as edema and hypertension.

Free Radical — A highly reactive molecule that can damage cells when it combines with oxygen in the process called oxidation. Although oxidation is a vital process in human metabolism, it can damage cells in the body and lead to their breakdown, just as the oxidation of a piece of iron, otherwise known as rusting, can cause a hard piece of metal to crumble and decompose. Antioxidants, such as vitamin E, work in the body to scavenge and disarm free radicals by bonding to them, thereby delaying or preventing damaging oxidation processes.

Gram (g.) — The basic unit of weight in the metric system equivalent to about one-twenty-eighth of an ounce (1 gram = 1,000 milligrams = 1,000,000 micrograms).

IU (International Units) — An internationally agreed-on unit of measure used to describe vitamins A, D, and E by the amount of their biological activity, rather than their weight. On vitamin product labels, dosages of these vitamins are listed in IUs rather than in milligrams.

Lipids — The name used to describe organic fatty substances that are not soluble in water, such as fats, oils, and triglycerides. Lipids, along with proteins and carbohydrates, are the primary materials that make up living cells. Some lipids, such as eicosapentaenoic acid (EPA), are beneficial to the overall health of the cardiovascular system, while others, such as saturated fats, are a threat to it.

Microgram (mcg.) — A unit of weight in the metric system equal to one-millionth of a gram (1,000 micrograms = 1 milligram).

Milligram (mg.) — A unit of weight in the metric system equal to one-thousandth of a gram (1,000 milligrams = 1 gram).

Mineral (essential mineral) — A chemical element that the body requires in daily amounts of 100 mg. or more. The minerals for humans are calcium, chlorine, magnesium, phosphorus, potassium, sodium, and sulfur. Dietary intake is the best source for chlorine, phosphorus, potassium, sodium, and sulfur. Elements needed in amounts under 100 mg. are referred to as trace elements.

pH — The letters pH stand for *power* of *H*ydrogen ion concentration. It is the abbreviation used to describe symbolically, on a scale of 1 to 14, whether a substance is acid or alkaline. The middle of the scale, 7, is considered neutral and is the value of distilled water. The lower end, 1 through 6, indicates acidity, and the upper end, 8 through 14, indicates alkalinity.

RDA (Recommended Daily Allowance) — The average daily amount of a nutrient that is recommended by the National Research Council of the National Academy of Sciences as necessary to maintain a person's health and prevent deficiencies. RDA tables are fairly detailed and are broken down by gender into ten specific age groups up to the age of fifty, and a general group for those over fifty. These tables differ from the U.S. RDA tables, which are more general and were established as a convenient and abbreviated labeling standard for nutrients such as vitamins and packaged foods.

RNA (ribonucleic acid) — A large molecule that is an essential part of all living cells. One form of RNA carries instructions from the DNA to areas in the cell where amino acids are strung together to form proteins. These instructions determine the type of protein to be formed.

Trace Element — A chemical element that the body requires in daily amounts under 100 mg. The trace elements for humans are chromium, copper, iodine, iron, manganese, molybdenum, selenium, and zinc. Elements needed in amounts greater than 100 mg. are referred to as minerals or essential minerals.

U.S. RDA — A convenient, simplified, and very general version of the RDA. The U.S. RDA is used as the standard for labeling amounts of nutrients in products such as vitamins or packaged foods. Unlike the RDA tables, which are quite detailed, the U.S. RDA tables do not distinguish by gender and only distinguish two age groups, older or younger than four years.

Vasodilator — A substance, such as the nicotinic acid form of niacin, that causes blood vessels to expand, increasing the amount of blood that flows through them.

Vegan — A strict vegetarian who avoids all forms of animal tissue, including poultry and seafood, as well as animal products such as milk and eggs.

Vitamin — An organic, or carbon-containing nutrient compound that meets two requirements: (1) the body cannot produce it, or cannot produce it in adequate amounts for its needs; and (2) a deficiency in a particular vitamin will trigger specific symptoms that can only be remedied by an intake of that vitamin. Vitamins are divided into two types according to solubility: The fat-soluble vitamins are A, D, E, and K; the water-soluble vitamins are B1 (thiamin), B2 (riboflavin), niacin, pantothenic acid, B6 (pyridoxine), B12, folic acid, biotin, and C.

— CHAPTER ONE —

THE VITAMINS

Vitamin A
Vitamin B1 — Thiamin
Vitamin B2 — Riboflavin
Niacin
Pantothenic Acid
Vitamin B6 — Pyridoxine
Vitamin B12 — Cobalamin
Folic Acid
Biotin
Vitamin C
Vitamin D
Vitamin E
Vitamin K

A

FORMS
*Retinol (fish liver oil),
beta-carotene (plant source),
retinyl palmitate (synthetic),
retinol acetate (synthetic).*

U.S. RDA
5,000 IU daily.

RECOMMENDED INTAKE
*15,000 to 25,000 IU daily of beta-carotene.
Include in a daily multiple-vitamin/mineral supplement, if possible.
Beta-carotene may be taken as an individual supplement.*

DIETARY SOURCES
*Beta-carotene: carrots, spinach, broccoli,
sweet potatoes, apricots, cabbage.
Retinol: liver, butter, egg yolks.*

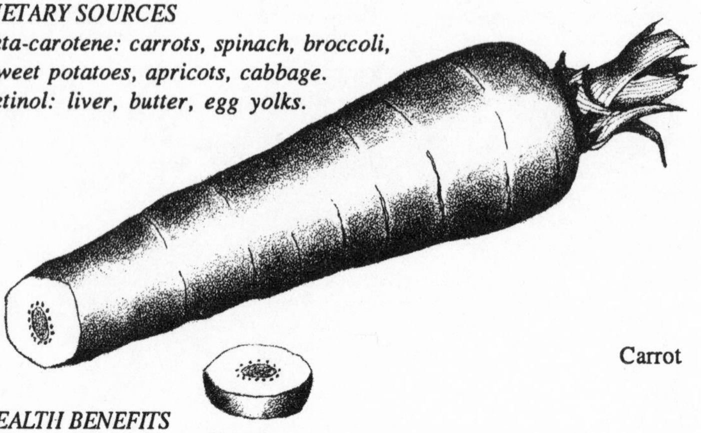

Carrot

HEALTH BENEFITS
*Vitamin A helps in the functioning of the immune system.
It may accelerate the healing of wounds.
Beta-carotene can help protect cells against environmental toxins.
It may have an anticarcinogenic
effect in the cells.*

INTERACTIONS
*Vitamin A helps the body use calcium.
Vitamin E and zinc help the body
use vitamin A.
Alcohol interferes with vitamin A.*

A

VITAMIN A

Vitamin A earned its name through the distinction of being the first vitamin to be discovered. It is used by the body to manufacture the building blocks of cells and is important in the health and formation of skin, bones, teeth, eyes, glands, and hair. An adequate vitamin A level in the body is critical for developing body cells that reproduce frequently, such as sperm in males and eggs that have been fertilized in females.

Vitamin A increases the body's resistance to infections, helps fight infections when they are present, and speeds up the healing of wounds and surgical incisions. Current studies also indicate that beta-carotene, a substance in plants that the body converts into vitamin A, is an antioxidant which seems to provide protection from certain cancer-causing agents.

Recent national surveys show that about one of every seven Americans is deficient in vitamin A. Such a deficiency has been linked to increased risks for cancer of the lung, throat, and bladder. Also, studies indicate that women whose daily vitamin A intake is lower than 3,500 IU triple their chances of developing serious cervical dysplasia or cervical cancer.

Signs of vitamin A deficiency include dry, rough skin, a lowered resistance to respiratory infections, and night blindness. Night blindness, the inability of the eye to adjust from lightness to darkness or discern shapes in low light, can usually be corrected by supplemental vitamin A. Anyone who eats a well-balanced diet will have an adequate vitamin A intake, but cigarette smokers, junk-food junkies, breathers of air pollution, consumers of processed foods (estimates are that many processed foods sacrifice up to forty percent of their vitamin A), and anyone undergoing surgery or fighting an infection would probably benefit from a vitamin A supplement.

Vitamin A is commonly found in two forms, retinol and beta-carotene. Retinol is found in meat and animal products and has a specific function in the retina of the eye, hence its name. Beta-carotene is found in plants such as carrots, sweet potatoes, and broccoli and is the substance that gives many fruits and vegetables their yellow orange color.

While retinol is the form of vitamin A that is most easily usable by the body, beta-carotene is the form that provides the most anticarcinogenic protection. Because the body accepts retinol as a "pure" substance, absorbing it even after all nutrient needs are supplied, it is ideal for therapeutic uses but can reach toxic levels with prolonged high dosages. Beta-carotene, however, is converted into retinol in the cells of the small intestine, a process that stops when the body's requirements are met. As a result, a high beta-carotene intake does not trigger toxic reactions.

The U.S. RDA for vitamin A is 5,000 IU, an amount that is adequately supplied in the form of beta-carotene by an average-sized carrot. Recent research suggests, however, that a higher daily intake of 15,000 to 25,000 IU of vitamin A, in beta-carotene form, may increase protective and beneficial effects on the body. It should be noted that repeated and lengthy exposure to summer sunlight can break down beta-carotene in people, particularly those of Caucasian and Asian extraction, possibly decreasing its protective benefits against many kinds of cancer.

B₁

FORMS
Thiamin hydrochloride (HCl),
thiamin mononitrate.

U.S. RDA
1.5 mg. daily.

RECOMMENDED INTAKE
10 mg. daily.
Include in a daily multiple-
  vitamin/mineral supplement.

DIETARY SOURCES
Whole wheat, sunflower seeds,
beans, peas, brown rice,
Brazil nuts,
oats.

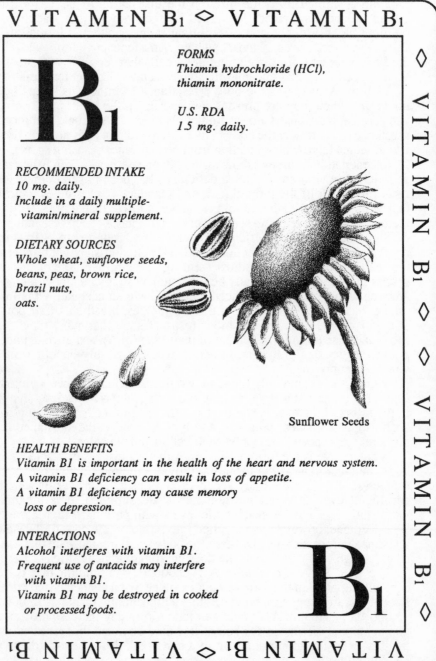

Sunflower Seeds

HEALTH BENEFITS
Vitamin B1 is important in the health of the heart and nervous system.
A vitamin B1 deficiency can result in loss of appetite.
A vitamin B1 deficiency may cause memory
  loss or depression.

INTERACTIONS
Alcohol interferes with vitamin B1.
Frequent use of antacids may interfere
  with vitamin B1.
Vitamin B1 may be destroyed in cooked
  or processed foods.

B₁

VITAMIN B1 — THIAMIN

Vitamin B1, a water-soluble vitamin, is one of a series of vitamins with a "B" designation. Vitamin B1 was the first of these B vitamins to be discovered and is commonly known as thiamin. It plays an indispensable role in breaking down carbohydrates and fats in order to release energy for the body's use. Thiamin is necessary for the proper functioning of the heart and other smooth muscles, such as the stomach and intestines. In addition, thiamin is essential to the processes that transmit nerve impulses throughout the body.

The earliest signs of thiamin deficiency are loss of appetite, insomnia, constipation, and irritability, often coupled with difficulty in concentrating, nausea, and rolling or jittery eyeballs. Severe thiamin deficiency results in the age-old disease beriberi, named after the Philippine words for "I can't, I can't." Beriberi is a debilitating condition, with pain and paralysis in the limbs, edema, weakening of the heart, and eventual death. The disease has been known since ancient times, but it was not until recently that the cause of beriberi was discovered. Near the turn of the century, there were large outbreaks of beriberi in the Orient, and later in Europe, that focused attention on the ways in which rice processing had changed. Instead of eating cheap, natural, unmilled rice, vast segments of the populations of China, Japan, and the Philippines switched their diet to polished rice, which was perceived as better and purer overall. This attitude also prevailed in European flour processing, and the pure white flour became preferable to whole wheat flour, resulting in large outbreaks of beriberi there. As it turned out, the rice and flour were overrefined, and the necessary thiamin had been discarded with the rice polishings and wheat hulls.

Thiamin is found in almost all plant and animal tissues, but usually in very small amounts. Laws in the United States (The Enrichment Act of 1942) and England now require that all processed grains be enriched with thiamin to prevent beriberi, making severe deficiencies uncommon in these countries. Marginal deficiencies do, however, appear in people with irregular and unbalanced diets and are particularly prevalent among alcoholics and the elderly. An estimated one-third of the adults in the United States over the age of fifty may not be getting enough dietary thiamin. People fighting fevers and infections, diabetics, and women who are pregnant, breast-feeding, or taking oral contraceptives will usually benefit from a supplemental thiamin intake.

The U.S. RDA for thiamin is 1.5 mg. To prevent deficiencies, thiamin intake is keyed to calorie intake of about 0.5 mg. of thiamin per thousand calories, with a minimum of 1 mg. per day. People on high-carbohydrate diets, in jobs involving heavy labor, or in athletic training will have greater thiamin needs. Recent studies indicate that a daily thiamin intake of 10 mg., incorporated into a multiple-vitamin/mineral formula, will adequately cover the body's needs for this important nutrient. At this time, there are no known toxic effects from too much thiamin, as any excess seems to be excreted in urine.

33

B₂

FORMS
Riboflavin.

U.S. RDA
1.7 mg. daily.

RECOMMENDED INTAKE
10 mg. daily.
Include in a daily multiple-vitamin/mineral supplement.

DIETARY SOURCES
Spinach, nuts, peas, beans,
whole wheat, milk,
dried fruits.

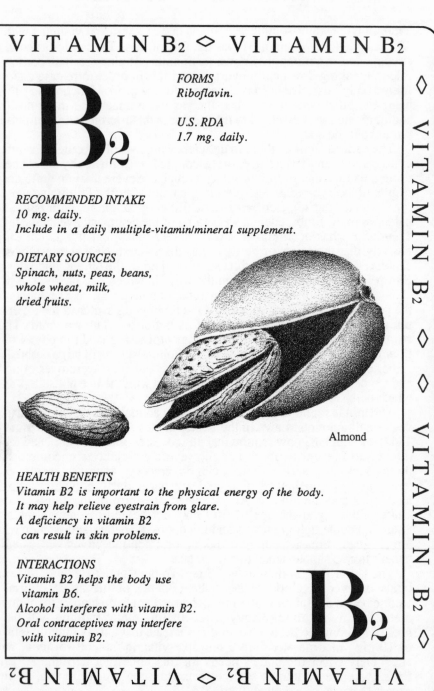

Almond

HEALTH BENEFITS
Vitamin B2 is important to the physical energy of the body.
It may help relieve eyestrain from glare.
A deficiency in vitamin B2
can result in skin problems.

INTERACTIONS
Vitamin B2 helps the body use
vitamin B6.
Alcohol interferes with vitamin B2.
Oral contraceptives may interfere
with vitamin B2.

B₂

VITAMIN B2 — RIBOFLAVIN

Vitamin B2 is found in every cell of the body. This yellow green, water-soluble vitamin is commonly called riboflavin, a name derived from its component sugar, D-ribose, and the Latin word for yellow, *flavus*. It is riboflavin that gives multiple vitamins their characteristic smell and taste. Riboflavin is essential for growth and tissue functions and for the metabolic processes that convert and release energy the body can use. It helps prevent the eyes from being oversensitive to light and glare and is particularly important for maintaining the health of mucous membranes such as those lining the mouth, nose, and stomach. In addition, riboflavin's activity as a coenzyme is being investigated carefully, as it may play a part in detoxifying the body after chemical and alcohol abuse.

Riboflavin is fairly stable when heated but breaks down when exposed to sunlight. In foods that have been bleached or refined, such as white flour, almost all the riboflavin has been destroyed and must be restored artificially. Since riboflavin is so widely available in a variety of foods, however, severe riboflavin deficiencies are quite rare, and marginal ones are not easy to recognize because they usually occur in combination with other nutrient deficiencies.

Symptoms of riboflavin deficiency are: "shark skin," a greasy, scaly rash, found especially where the nose joins the face; sores that refuse to heal on the lips, in the mouth, or at the corners of the mouth; a loss of color in the face; and glossitis, a magenta coloring of the tongue. More extreme symptoms include anemia, certain nerve diseases, and a sudden influx of red blood vessels into the normally clear cornea of the eye. The people most susceptible to marginal riboflavin deficiencies are those who have inadequate diets (particularly high-carbohydrate diets that are severely low in protein), teenagers who shun milk, and alcoholics. In addition, those taking thyroid hormones or tricyclic antidepressants (such a Elavil), senior citizens, and women who are pregnant, breast-feeding, or taking oral contraceptives often need supplemental riboflavin. At this time, there are no additional significant therapeutic uses for riboflavin.

The U.S. RDA for riboflavin is 1.7 mg. The actual amounts necessary to prevent deficiency, however, are dependent on individual caloric intakes and should be calculated at about 0.6 mg. of riboflavin for every thousand calories, with a minimum intake of at least 1 mg. every day. People who consume a very low protein diet or who expend a lot of physical energy in their jobs — farmers and athletes, for example — will have higher riboflavin needs than those with more sedentary professions. Many recent studies indicate that 10 mg. of riboflavin, incorporated into a multiple-vitamin/mineral formula, is a safe and effective way to meet the body's vitamin B2 requirements. Riboflavin toxicity appears to be very unlikely even at high doses, since any unused amounts are excreted in the urine, giving it a bright yellow orange color.

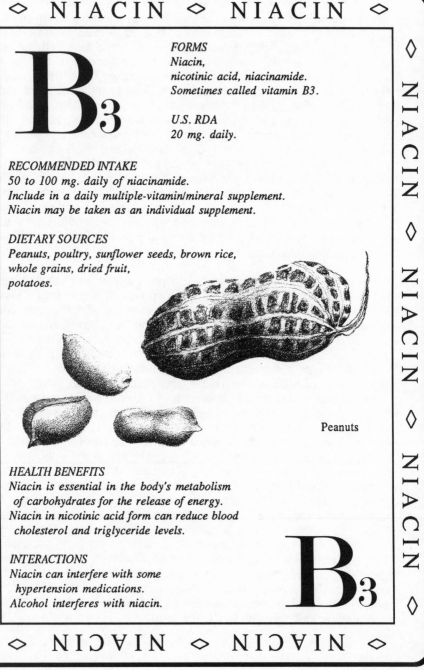

B₃

FORMS
Niacin,
nicotinic acid, niacinamide.
Sometimes called vitamin B3.

U.S. RDA
20 mg. daily.

RECOMMENDED INTAKE
50 to 100 mg. daily of niacinamide.
Include in a daily multiple-vitamin/mineral supplement.
Niacin may be taken as an individual supplement.

DIETARY SOURCES
Peanuts, poultry, sunflower seeds, brown rice,
whole grains, dried fruit,
potatoes.

Peanuts

HEALTH BENEFITS
Niacin is essential in the body's metabolism
of carbohydrates for the release of energy.
Niacin in nicotinic acid form can reduce blood
cholesterol and triglyceride levels.

INTERACTIONS
Niacin can interfere with some
hypertension medications.
Alcohol interferes with niacin.

B₃

NIACIN

Niacin is found in two basic water-soluble forms: nicotinic acid, which dilates the capillaries and increases blood flow, and niacinamide. Both forms have equal vitamin/nutritional activity and, unless there is a specific need for distinguishing them, they are usually referred to by the common term *niacin*. Niacin, sometimes called vitamin B3, acts as a catalyst to over one hundred and fifty different reactions in the body's cells. These reactions include processes that generate skin pigments, hormones, and insulin, as well as the oxidation of glucose, which releases energy for the body's use.

The nicotinic acid form of niacin, taken as a dietary supplement, has been known to reduce triglyceride and cholesterol levels in the blood. New studies show these reductions to be quite remarkable — blood triglyceride levels dropped by over half, while cholesterol levels dropped by about one-fifth — and there is evidence that nicotinic acid may even reverse atherosclerosis in some people.

Niacin was identified in 1937 in the wake of devastating epidemics of pellagra in the southern United States. Pellagra, the result of severe niacin deficiency, gets its name from the Italian words for one of its more visible signs, "rough skin." Its symptoms are designated the three D's — diarrhea, dermatitis, and dementia. Left untreated, pellagra results in the fourth D, death. The addition of niacin to corn and refined wheat products virtually eliminated pellagra in the South in one generation, but it is still prevalent in parts of the world where corn is the main source of dietary protein.

The human body is able to form small amounts of niacin on its own; yet marginal niacin deficiencies are not uncommon, with symptoms of headache, diarrhea, extreme nervousness, and a swollen, red tongue. Alcoholics and drug addicts are among those most susceptible to a niacin deficiency, as are individuals with a very poor diet or with overactive thyroid glands. Also at risk are people in stressful situations — particularly in physical stress — such as those suffering from burns or recovering from surgery. Those who frequently contract infections, and women who are pregnant, breast-feeding, or taking oral contraceptives, may also need supplemental niacin.

The U.S. RDA for niacin is 20 mg. To prevent deficiency, daily niacin intake is calculated on a ratio of about 6.6 mg. for every thousand calories consumed, with a minimum of 13 mg. According to recent findings, a multiple-vitamin/mineral formula that contains 50 to 100 mg. of niacin will take advantage of its health benefits. Larger doses are not recommended without the supervision of a nutrition specialist; and individuals with arrhythmia, or irregular heartbeat, should consult their physicians before taking supplemental niacin, particularly the nicotinic acid form. Many people taking this form of niacin experience a rapid flush and burning sensation in the face and hands, sometimes accompanied by sudden nausea. These effects are temporary and usually occur with a dose of 75 mg. or more. They can be avoided by starting with smaller doses and building up slowly or by taking the niacinamide form.

B5

FORMS
Calcium pantothenate,
d-panthenol,
d-calcium pantothenate.
Sometimes called vitamin B5.

U.S. RDA
10 mg. daily.

RECOMMENDED INTAKE
25 to 50 mg. daily.
Include in a daily multiple-vitamin/mineral supplement.

DIETARY SOURCES
Corn, lentils, egg yolks, nuts, soybeans,
sunflower seeds,
whole wheat.

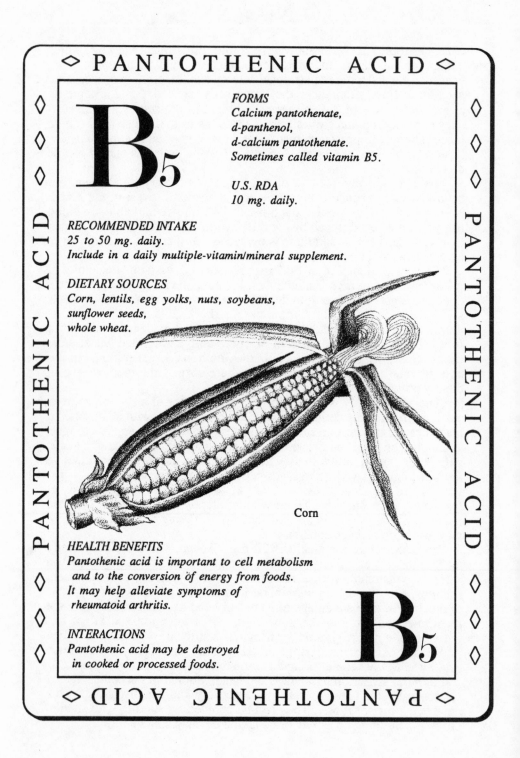

Corn

HEALTH BENEFITS
Pantothenic acid is important to cell metabolism
and to the conversion of energy from foods.
It may help alleviate symptoms of
rheumatoid arthritis.

INTERACTIONS
Pantothenic acid may be destroyed
in cooked or processed foods.

B5

PANTOTHENIC ACID

Pantothenic acid, sometimes called vitamin B5, derives its name from the Greek word *pantothen,* "from all sides," since it is found in almost all living tissue. It is the major component of royal jelly, a white, gooey substance secreted by worker bees which stimulates the development and growth of queen bees. In the human body, pantothenic acid, a water-soluble vitamin, is essential for catalyzing many metabolic functions. It contributes to the breakdown of carbohydrates and fatty acids, as well as to the release of stored energy to meet the body's needs. Pantothenic acid is also involved in triggering the production of sex hormones and in the formation of heme, the iron-containing and oxygen-carrying part of hemoglobin.

Pantothenic acid helps synthesize acetylcholine, a particularly important neurotransmitter for many of the brain's functions. Recent studies have uncovered acetylcholine deficiencies in people suffering from Alzheimer's disease, and many of the mental problems associated with growing old seem to be due, in part, to the decrease in acetylcholine production that occurs as the body ages.

Pantothenic acid is so prevalent in foods that it stands out among the vitamins: A severe deficiency of it in humans has not been known to occur naturally. Marginal deficiencies may occur, but at this time there are no tests available that indicate a specific pantothenic acid deficiency. Under experimental conditions in which pantothenic acid was rendered unusable to the body, symptoms of deficiency appeared after a few weeks. These included nausea, stomach pains, numbness in the hands and feet, insomnia, headache, and muscle spasms. In addition, there were fewer antibodies present in the blood to ward off invading microorganisms, indicating a weakened immune system.

There are no significant therapeutic uses at this time for pantothenic acid except to prevent its deficiency. Recent studies have indicated that megadoses of pantothenic acid can be effective in alleviating several of the symptoms of rheumatoid arthritis: The disease was less debilitating, morning stiffness lasted for shorter periods of time, and the severity of pain was diminished when daily doses of 2 g. (2,000 mg.) were taken. While current evidence suggests that pantothenic acid is nontoxic in doses as large as 10 g. (10,000 mg.) a day for up to six weeks, there has been no substantial research about long-term effects of megadoses. Amounts of 1,000 mg. or more are not recommended without the supervision of a nutrition specialist.

The U.S. RDA for pantothenic acid is 10 mg., easily available from the average Western diet of twenty-five hundred to three thousand calories daily. People on low-calorie diets or who are fasting for long periods of time, and those who are fighting infections, will probably benefit from supplemental pantothenic acid. Recent research indicates that a daily multiple-vitamin/mineral supplement that includes 20 to 50 mg. of pantothenic acid will provide adequate insurance that the body's needs are met.

B₆

FORMS
Pyridoxal,
pyridoxamine,
pyridoxine hydrochloride (HCl).

U.S. RDA
2 mg. daily.

RECOMMENDED INTAKE
25 to 50 mg. daily.
Include in a daily multiple-vitamin/mineral supplement.
Vitamin B6 may be taken as an individual supplement.

DIETARY SOURCES
Sunflower seeds, brown rice, soybeans,
fish, hazelnuts, bananas,
whole grains.

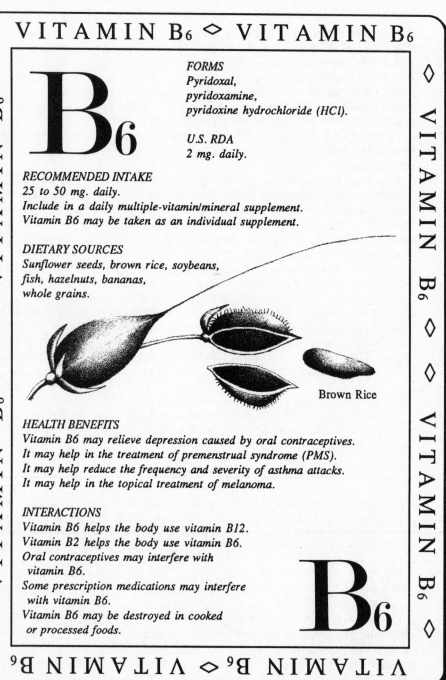

Brown Rice

HEALTH BENEFITS
Vitamin B6 may relieve depression caused by oral contraceptives.
It may help in the treatment of premenstrual syndrome (PMS).
It may help reduce the frequency and severity of asthma attacks.
It may help in the topical treatment of melanoma.

INTERACTIONS
Vitamin B6 helps the body use vitamin B12.
Vitamin B2 helps the body use vitamin B6.
Oral contraceptives may interfere with
 vitamin B6.
Some prescription medications may interfere
 with vitamin B6.
Vitamin B6 may be destroyed in cooked
 or processed foods.

B₆

VITAMIN B6 — PYRIDOXINE

Vitamin B6 is the generic term used for a group of three closely related compounds found in nature — pyridoxine, pyridoxal, and pyridoxamine. Pyridoxine is the form of vitamin B6 found in vegetables, while pyridoxal and pyridoxamine are the forms found in animal products. All three forms are equally active in the body, although it is pyridoxine that is usually designated as vitamin B6. Vitamin B6 is water soluble and stable when frozen or dehydrated. It breaks down when exposed to sunlight, and cooking destroys about one-fourth of its vitamin activity.

Vitamin B6 is found throughout the tissues of the body and is involved in triggering more than sixty enzymatic functions. Red blood cell production and cell multiplication are dependent on vitamin B6, which also acts as a coenzyme to form substances that regulate and stimulate brain and central nervous system responses. Vitamin B6 helps transport essential amino acids, broken down in the digestive system, to cells throughout the body and across cell membranes. It plays a significant role in metabolizing tissue proteins and synthesizing nucleic acids such as RNA and DNA, making it perhaps the most important of the B vitamins for a healthy body. New research indicates that vitamin B6 can decrease the frequency and severity of asthma attacks, and vitamin B6 is turning out to be important for a healthy immune system: Recent studies in which vitamin B6 deficiencies were induced in volunteers demonstrated that such deficiencies seriously compromised and weakened the immune system.

Bacteria in the human intestines are able to make some usable vitamin B6, but the vitamin is found in so many foods that a severe deficiency in it is fairly rare. Marginal deficiencies, however, with symptoms of oily skin, scaling lips, cracks at the corners of the mouth, and nervous irritability, are not uncommon. They can occur in alcoholics, people deficient in magnesium, and those with diets high in refined wheat products.

Estrogen and some of the other sex hormones interfere with vitamin B6 absorption, so women who are pregnant, using birth-control pills, undergoing estrogen-replacement therapy, or suffering from premenstrual syndrome (PMS), frequently benefit from up to 50 mg. of supplemental vitamin B6. Daily doses of more than 100 mg. of vitamin B6, however, should be taken with the supervision of a nutrition specialist. Until recently, megadoses of vitamin B6 were thought to be safe, and many women took as much as 2,000 mg. or more daily for relief of PMS. A 1983 medical report indicated, however, that these doses, over a period of only a few weeks, could cause serious neurological problems. Since then, doses of 500 mg. have been observed to produce similar symptoms.

The U.S. RDA for vitamin B6 is 2 mg. The actual amount a body needs to avoid deficiency depends on how much protein is being consumed. The body requires a ratio of at least 2 mg. of vitamin B6 for every 100 g. of dietary protein, with a minimum intake of 2 mg. Studies indicate that a daily supplement of 25 to 50 mg., in a multiple-vitamin/mineral formula, is a good way to take advantage of health benefits from vitamin B6.

41

B₁₂

FORMS
*Cobalamin,
cyanocobalamin.*

U.S. RDA
6 mcg. daily.

RECOMMENDED INTAKE
*6 to 30 mcg. daily. Include in a daily multiple-vitamin/mineral
supplement that also contains folic acid.*

DIETARY SOURCES
*Fish, shellfish, organ meats, cheese,
eggs, legumes.*

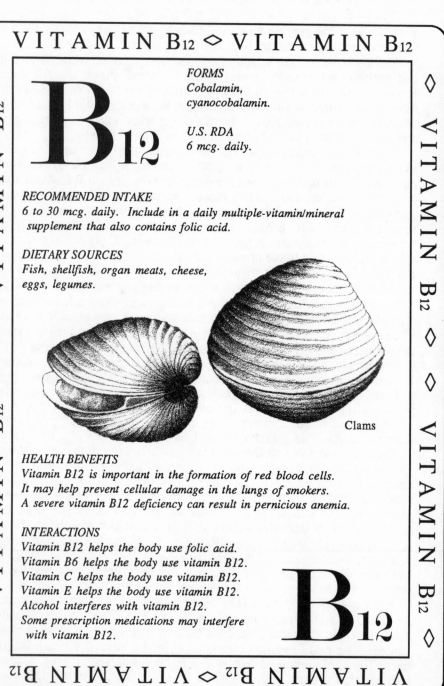

Clams

HEALTH BENEFITS
*Vitamin B12 is important in the formation of red blood cells.
It may help prevent cellular damage in the lungs of smokers.
A severe vitamin B12 deficiency can result in pernicious anemia.*

INTERACTIONS
*Vitamin B12 helps the body use folic acid.
Vitamin B6 helps the body use vitamin B12.
Vitamin C helps the body use vitamin B12.
Vitamin E helps the body use vitamin B12.
Alcohol interferes with vitamin B12.
Some prescription medications may interfere
with vitamin B12.*

B₁₂

VITAMIN B12 — COBALAMIN

Vitamin B12, sometimes referred to as cobalamin because of the single cobalt atom at its core, is found in foods as a protein complex. It is unique among the B vitamins for two reasons: First, with the exception of certain algae, vitamin B12 is not produced by plants but by bacteria that reside in the gastrointestinal tracts of animals — a minute amount of vitamin B12 is even produced by bacteria in the human intestine; second, although vitamin B12 is a water-soluble vitamin, it is stored primarily in the liver for long periods of time, just as fat-soluble vitamins are.

Vitamin B12 helps enzymes recycle folic acid. Together, vitamin B12 and folic acid participate in the synthesis of RNA and DNA, as well as in the reactions needed for cell division. Without them, body tissue is unable to grow normally. New studies indicate that a vitamin B12-folic acid combination, in high dosages, can help reverse cellular damage in the lungs of smokers. The vitamin B12-folic acid combination is particularly important in bone-marrow tissue for hemopoiesis — the manufacture of blood — and the maturation of red blood cells.

Vitamin B12 plays an active and unusual part in the metabolism of certain fats. The body normally breaks down fats into units with pairs of carbon atoms for energy production, but not all fats have an even number of carbon atoms. When fats with an odd number of carbon atoms are present, it is vitamin B12 that helps break them down further. In addition, vitamin B12 participates in nerve-tissue metabolism. It helps form myelin, a substance that sheathes and protects nerve fibers from damage.

Severe deficiency of vitamin B12 is extremely rare. Usually, if all vitamin B12 intake is stopped, symptoms of deficiency will not appear for three to five years, since the average human liver stores about one thousand days' worth of vitamin B12. Pernicious anemia, the vitamin B12 deficiency disease, is found primarily in people who have problems absorbing vitamin B12 into their bodies. Its symptoms include tingling sensations and numbness in the hands and feet, memory loss, a gradual loss of reflexes, sudden mood swings, and problems with vision.

Although even marginal vitamin B12 deficiencies are unusual, people who might benefit from supplemental vitamin B12 are those over fifty, those with poor diets, those who have been severely ill and need it for tissue repair and growth, women who are pregnant or breast-feeding, and smokers. Those who may be at some risk for this deficiency include vegans — strict vegetarians who do not eat eggs, milk, or other animal products.

The U.S. RDA for vitamin B12 is 6 mcg. Those who need additional amounts of this nutrient should try to get it from a multiple-vitamin/ mineral supplement rather than from an individual vitamin B12 supplement. This assures a proper balance between levels of vitamin B12 and its partner, folic acid. Vitamin B12 has no known toxic effects, even at daily doses above 100 mcg. Research indicates that a daily intake of vitamin B12 in a range of 6 to 30 mcg. can be beneficial.

FOLIC ACID

Fa

FORMS
Folic acid, folate, folacin.

U.S. RDA
400 mcg. daily.

RECOMMENDED INTAKE
400 mcg. daily. Include in a daily multiple-vitamin/mineral supplement that also contains vitamin B12.

DIETARY SOURCES
Soybeans, endive, garbanzo beans, lentils, whole wheat, uncooked vegetable greens.

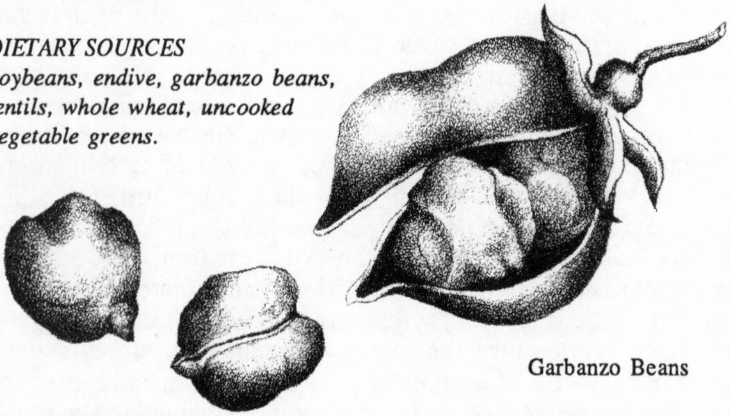

Garbanzo Beans

HEALTH BENEFITS
Folic acid is important for the proper function of the immune system. It may speed healing processes in injuries or illness.

INTERACTIONS
A high folic acid intake can interfere with the effects of some prescription medications.
Zinc helps the body use folic acid.
Aspirin, alcohol, and oral contraceptives may interfere with folic acid.
Some prescription medications may interfere with folic acid.
Folic acid may be destroyed in cooked or processed foods.

Fa

FOLIC ACID FOLIC ACID FOLIC ACID FOLIC ACID FOLIC ACID

FOLIC ACID

Folic acid, a member of the B-complex family of vitamins, derives its name from the Latin word for leaf, *folium*, because it was first extracted from dark green, leafy vegetables. Folic acid is actually the generic term used for all compounds that have folic acid activity. Two of the commonly used names for folic acid are folacin and folate, and the folic acid content of foods or supplements is defined by folacin equivalents. Folic acid is one of the least stable vitamins, and up to ninety percent of it can be destroyed by cooking or processing the foods that contain it.

Folic acid is made up of three acids, one of them being PABA, para-aminobenzoic acid. PABA itself, however, is not a nutrient for humans: Its only function is as a part of folic acid, and only bacteria and plants are capable of using it directly or synthesizing it into folic acid. Folic acid participates with vitamin B12 as a coenzyme for several vital processes. It is needed for cell growth and division, proper red blood cell development, and the formation of RNA and DNA, the genetic materials that determine every cell structure and function in the body. It is also important for the proper function of the immune system, since lymphocytes do not respond as quickly or as well as they should to infectious invaders when a folic acid deficiency is present.

Folic acid is particularly critical to bone-marrow tissue and the creation of heme, the iron-containing portion of red blood cells. A severe folic acid deficiency results in megaloblastic anemia, named for the technical term that indicates deformed red blood cells. It is the most common form of anemia in pregnant and breast-feeding women, since additional amounts of folic acid are needed for infant tissue development and growth. Symptoms of megaloblastic anemia include irritability, lack of energy, sleeping difficulties, and the loss of facial color. Many of these symptoms also appear when a marginal folic acid deficiency is present. Alcoholism, with its poor dietary habits, is considered the most common cause of folic acid deficiency. People who are injured, seriously ill, or undergoing surgery need extra amounts of folic acid, since folic acid is so integrally involved in tissue formation. Those on weight-loss diets are at risk for folic acid deficiency, and people suffering intestinal or stomach illnesses, infants fed on goat's milk, cigarette smokers, and women taking oral contraceptives may also benefit from supplemental folic acid.

The U.S. RDA for folic acid is 400 mcg., and this is the amount that should be included in a multiple-vitamin/mineral formula. Pregnant or breast-feeding women should double this amount, as they have increased folic acid needs. Although folic acid is considered nontoxic, doses of 1,000 mcg. (1 mg.) or more should not be taken without the supervision of a nutrition specialist, as they can mask symptoms of vitamin B12 deficiency and other problems. Also, people taking Dilantin should not exceed the U.S. RDA without consulting their physicians, as folic acid can interfere with the medication's effects.

B t

FORMS
Biotin.
Sometimes called vitamin H.

U.S. RDA
300 mcg. daily.

RECOMMENDED INTAKE
100 to 300 mcg. daily.
Include in a daily multiple-vitamin/mineral supplement.

DIETARY SOURCES
Soybeans, sunflower seeds, rice, legumes,
nuts, fish, whole grains.

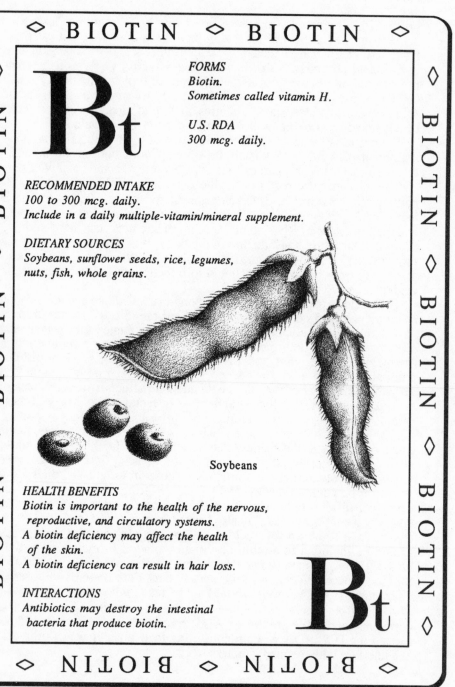

Soybeans

HEALTH BENEFITS
Biotin is important to the health of the nervous,
  reproductive, and circulatory systems.
A biotin deficiency may affect the health
  of the skin.
A biotin deficiency can result in hair loss.

INTERACTIONS
Antibiotics may destroy the intestinal
  bacteria that produce biotin.

B t

BIOTIN

Biotin was discovered in 1935 by a Dutch biochemist who named it vitamin H. While still occasionally called vitamin H, this colorless, crystalline compound is now referred to as biotin and considered a member of the B-complex. Priced at over four thousand dollars a pound, biotin is probably the most expensive vitamin in the world — one reason it is not included in many multiple-vitamin/mineral formulas.

Biotin is water soluble and is found in minute traces in all living things. It is one of the few vitamins that the human body can synthesize, as it is manufactured by microorganisms that reside in the intestine. Biotin acts as a coenzyme for such life-sustaining processes as the metabolism of carbohydrates, fatty acids, and proteins. It is important for maintaining the health of muscle tissue, hair, and skin, as well as that of the nervous, circulatory, and reproductive systems.

Biotin is so commonly available that a severe deficiency is extremely rare in adults. It can occur in patients on long-term intravenous-feeding programs where the IV solution does not contain biotin. However, biotin deficiency is usually caused by problems of absorption that may occur when a large section of the intestine is removed or when a diet extremely high in raw egg white is consumed. Raw egg white contains avidin, a carbohydrate-containing protein that binds biotin in the intestine to form a molecule which is too large to be absorbed into the body.

Symptoms of biotin deficiency include nausea, muscle pains, rashes, high cholesterol levels, depression, and a decrease in antibody production. Infants who receive their nourishment exclusively from breast-feeding will sometimes develop a biotin deficiency. It usually appears as a rash and is due to a combination of the low levels of biotin available in the mother's milk and undeveloped bacterial colonies in the infant's intestines. While there is no direct clinical proof at this time, circumstantial evidence has linked biotin deficiency to Sudden Infant Death Syndrome (SIDS), also known as crib death: Autopsies have revealed that SIDS victims had markedly lower biotin levels in their livers than infants who died of other causes.

The U.S. RDA for biotin is 300 mcg., available from such sources as soybeans, split peas, liver, rice, and sunflower seeds. Biotin is considered nontoxic, and there are no known therapeutic uses for biotin supplements at this time except to counter deficiency. People with infections that require antibiotics for treatment will probably benefit from biotin supplements, since the antibiotics destroy many of the friendly bacteria in the intestine that manufacture and process biotin. Women who are pregnant or breast-feeding may also benefit, as their blood biotin levels are often lower than normal. Biotin supplements may also be a good idea for dieters, who frequently upset their bacterial balances. A multiple-vitamin/mineral supplement that provides biotin in the 100 to 300 mcg. range will insure that the body's needs are met.

C

FORMS
*Ascorbic acid, sodium ascorbate,
calcium ascorbate.*

U.S. RDA
60 mg. daily.

RECOMMENDED INTAKE
*250 to 1,000 mg. daily. Include in a daily multiple-vitamin/mineral
supplement. Vitamin C may be taken as an individual supplement.*

DIETARY SOURCES
*Broccoli, peppers, spinach,
citrus fruits, berries, cabbage,
potatoes, tomatoes.*

Currants

HEALTH BENEFITS
*Vitamin C may help protect cells against environmental toxins.
It may help in the prevention of certain cancers.
It may accelerate the healing of wounds and burns.
It may help boost the immune system.
It may help in male infertility.*

INTERACTIONS
*Vitamin C helps the body use calcium and iron
from vegetable sources.
Excessive vitamin C (greater than 1,500 mg.)
can interfere with copper absorption.
Alcohol interferes with vitamin C.
Aspirin may interfere with vitamin C.
Vitamin C may be destroyed in cooked
or processed foods.*

C

VITAMIN C

Vitamin C was first isolated from citrus fruits, but, contrary to popular belief, citrus fruits are not the richest sources of vitamin C — broccoli, brussels sprouts, and spinach all have higher concentrations. All plants and almost all animals can convert vitamin C from glucose, its natural precursor. Humans, along with guinea pigs, monkeys, a bird called the red-whiskered bulbul, and a rare Indian fruit bat, are the few living things that cannot perform this conversion and must have vitamin C supplied from external sources.

Vitamin C is essential for making collagen, the "cement" in connective tissues such as tendons and cartilage. Vitamin C helps build and maintain bones, teeth, and vascular tissues. It also helps the body use folic acid from the liver, makes iron available for the formation and growth of red blood cells, and stimulates the adrenal glands to form hormones such as cortisone, a natural anti-inflammatory substance, and epinephrine, a nerve stimulant commonly known by its trade name Adrenalin.

Vitamin C inhibits the conversion of nitrates, frequently used as food preservatives, into carcinogenic nitrosamines and acts as an antioxidant to remove highly reactive molecules that can damage cells. Recent investigations indicate that this antioxidant activity makes vitamin C up to thirty times more prevalent in the eye than in the blood. It is a major factor in preventing the development of cataracts — cloudy areas in the eye's lens that are the result of eye proteins being oxidized. Large doses of vitamin C have also been shown to boost the production and activity of interferon, a substance that fights viruses. While studies have shown that 250 to 1,000 mg. daily may not prevent a cold, they indicate that these doses can minimize a cold's severity and shorten its duration by almost one-third.

Severe vitamin C deficiency results in a deadly disease called scurvy, while marginal vitamin C deficiency, fairly common, greatly increases the risk for developing certain types of cancer, according to recent evidence. About one-third of the women in the United States have a daily vitamin C intake of under 70 mg., yet studies have found that women whose daily vitamin C intake is under 90 mg. are more than twice as likely to develop cervical dysplasia, or precancerous cells. Those with an intake of under 30 mg. are seven times more likely to develop this condition. Alcoholics, people with infections, or those recovering from wounds, burns, or surgery, also have an increased need for vitamin C, as do any women who are pregnant, breast-feeding, or taking oral contraceptives. Cigarette smokers, smog breathers, and those in physically or emotionally stressful situations will also benefit from supplemental vitamin C.

The U.S. RDA for vitamin C is 60 mg., an amount that is subject to considerable dispute, particularly in light of the correlation between low vitamin C intake and the increased risk for some cancers. Most nutritional researchers find that a daily intake in the range of 250 to 1,000 mg. is best for promoting and maintaining a healthy body. Vitamin C is water soluble and considered generally nontoxic. However, many researchers caution against the long-term intake of 4,000 mg. or more, since some adverse effects have been reported.

D

FORMS
Cholecalciferol,
calciferol,
ergocalciferol.

U.S. RDA
400 IU daily.

RECOMMENDED INTAKE
400 IU daily.
Include in a daily multiple-vitamin/mineral supplement.

DIETARY SOURCES
Fortified dairy products (supplemental vitamin D added),
sardines, salmon, tuna, mushrooms,
sunflower seeds.

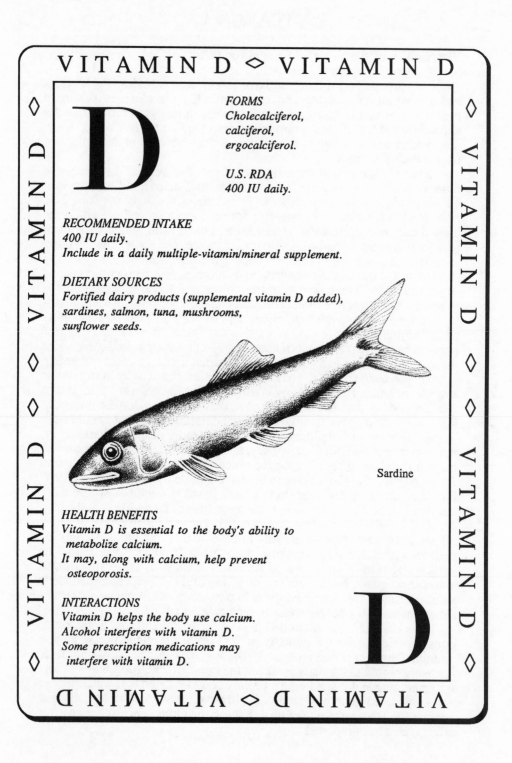

Sardine

HEALTH BENEFITS
Vitamin D is essential to the body's ability to
  metabolize calcium.
It may, along with calcium, help prevent
  osteoporosis.

INTERACTIONS
Vitamin D helps the body use calcium.
Alcohol interferes with vitamin D.
Some prescription medications may
  interfere with vitamin D.

D

VITAMIN D

Vitamin D is one of the vitamins that can actually be manufactured by the human body with a little help from the sun. Ultraviolet rays in sunlight convert a fatty substance under the skin, which is a form of cholesterol, into a form of vitamin D called cholecalciferol. This is why vitamin D is sometimes called the "sunshine vitamin." Cholecalciferol is also found in fish liver oils and egg yolks. The sun's ultraviolet rays also convert another form of vitamin D, ergocalciferol, from a fatty substance called ergosterol found in plants. This plant-derived form of vitamin D is the one commonly used to fortify foods such as milk and margarine. Both forms are equally potent and are converted by the liver and kidneys into the active form of vitamin D, calcitriol, which the body can use.

Vitamin D is essential to the health of the bones and teeth, as well as to other processes that depend on calcium, including muscle control, heart functions, blood clotting, white blood cell formation, calm nerves, and the maturation of collagen, the "glue" in connective tissues. Vitamin D is also important for the body's absorption of phosphorus and calcium from the intestine and the prevention of their loss from the body in urine. The effectiveness of both calcium and phosphorus is dependent on a carefully maintained balance of their levels in the blood: When blood levels of calcium fall, phosphorus levels rise, triggering the body to release calcium from the bones, where about ninety-nine percent of it is stored. This can produce two major problems: tetany, a condition of spontaneous and uncontrollable spasms in the wrists and ankles; and brittle, easily broken bones, which result from not having enough calcium in them.

Vitamin D deficiency is most likely to occur in people with problems absorbing fat; in pregnant or breast-feeding women, who have increased calcium needs; in individuals who stay out of the sunlight either to avoid dangerous ultraviolet radiation or because they are office- or housebound; and in alcoholics. A severe vitamin D deficiency in children can result in rickets, characterized by weak muscles, bent and bowed legs, and late or inadequate tooth development. In adults, a severe vitamin D deficiency triggers osteomalacia (adult rickets), the decalcification of bones through-out the body, which leaves them abnormally soft, brittle, and porous. Osteomalacia should not be confused with osteoporosis, a common bone condition among older women where calcium is lost in specific areas of the skeleton, usually the spinal vertebrae. Women can help prevent osteo-porosis by taking daily calcium and vitamin D supplements during their twenties, thrities, and forties.

The U.S. RDA for vitamin D is 400 IU. At this time, no maximum safe dose for vitamin D has been determined, although daily doses of 2,000 IU or more may lead to some abnormal nutrient balances. Since vitamin D can be very toxic and accumulates in the body, exceeding the U.S. RDA is probably not a good idea. Vitamin D toxicity can result in weakness, excessive thirst and urination, high blood pressure, hardening of the arteries, liver damage, and kidney failure.

VITAMIN E ◇ VITAMIN E

E

FORMS
Tocopherol, d-alpha-tocopherol acetate, d-alpha-tocopherol succinate, dl-alpha-tocopherol acetate, dl-alpha-tocopherol succinate.

U.S. RDA
30 IU daily.

RECOMMENDED INTAKE
200 to 400 IU daily.
Include in a daily multiple-vitamin/mineral supplement.
May be taken as an individual supplement.

DIETARY SOURCES
Whole grains, wheat germ, green leafy vegetables, vegetable oils, sunflower seeds, nuts.

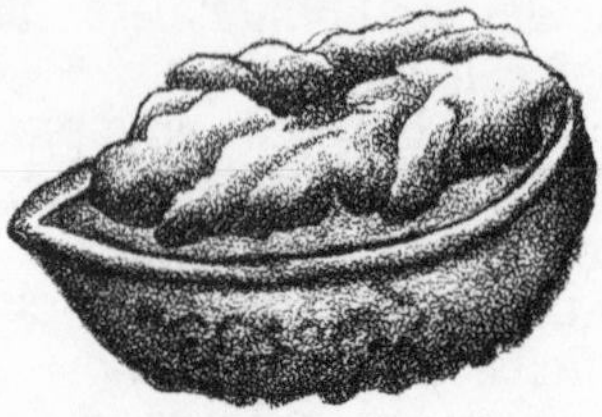

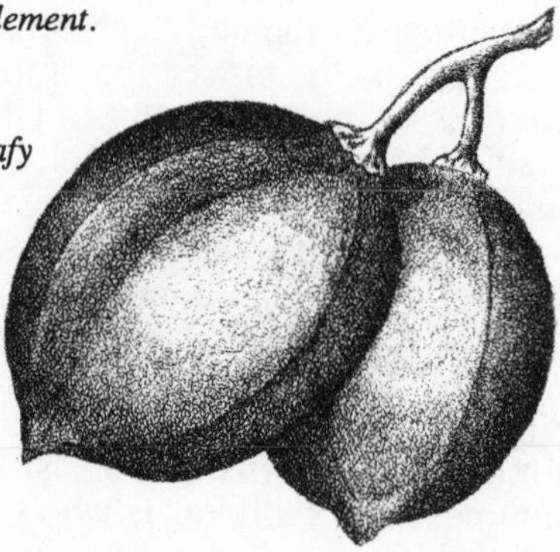

Walnuts

HEALTH BENEFITS
Vitamin E may help protect cells against environmental toxins.
It may help relieve nocturnal leg or foot cramps.
It may help boost the immune system.

INTERACTIONS
Vitamin E helps the body use vitamin A.
Vitamin E interferes with the absorption of inorganic iron supplements.
Oral contraceptives may interfere with vitamin E.
Vitamin E may be destroyed in cooked or processed foods.

E

VITAMIN E ◇ VITAMIN E ◇ VITAMIN E ◇ VITAMIN E ◇ VITAMIN E ◇ VITAMIN E ◇

VITAMIN E

Vitamin E is the term used to refer to any of the forms of a substance called tocopherol, including alpha-, beta-, gamma-, and delta-tocopherol. Of the four, alpha-tocopherol is the most commonly used form of vitamin E, as it is the most active. Vitamin E was named tocopherol — from the Greek words *tokos*, "childbirth," and *pherein*, "to bear" — because studies found that it was an important factor for fertility and reproduction in rats. Ironically, it has just the opposite effect on human reproduction, reducing rather than increasing gonad activity, and claims that vitamin E enhances sexual prowess and human fertility have been found to be false. Although vitamin E was first isolated in 1936, its functions have been such a mystery that it was not included on the U.S. RDA list by the Food and Drug Administration (FDA) until 1968.

Vitamin E, unlike the other fat-soluble vitamins, is not stored in specific parts of the body such as the liver or kidneys but is found in all the body tissues. Cells with sufficient amounts of vitamin E are the most efficient producers of energy for the body's use. Vitamin E blocks the conversion of nitrates and nitrites, sometimes used as food preservatives, into nitrosamines, substances that have been linked with some forms of cancer, particularly stomach cancer. The most potent of the fat-soluble antioxidants, vitamin E acts to maintain the stability of cell membranes and protects them from the destructive effects of organic peroxides, inactive solids formed when oxygen reacts with certain kinds of fatty acids. This means that vitamin E may help protect cells, such as those lining the lungs, from the toxic effects of such hazards as air pollution, cigarette smoke, and lead poisoning. Recent studies have also found that supplemental vitamin E seems to decrease the severity and incidence of breast lumps (fibrocystic condition) in women, to shorten the healing time of wounds, and to reduce the severity of a condition called intermittent claudication, pains in the calf that are the result of clogged leg arteries.

While severe vitamin E deficiency is fairly rare in humans, newborns (particularly premature babies), people with nutrient-absorption problems or poor diets, those recovering from injury or surgery, and pregnant or breast-feeding women will have increased vitamin E needs and will probably benefit from a supplemental intake. The U.S. RDA for vitamin E is 30 IU, but research indicates that a daily supplemental intake in the range of 200 to 400 IU may provide additional health benefits. Vitamin E is considered nontoxic at doses up to 3,000 IU, but a long-term daily intake exceeding 600 IU is not recommended without the supervision of a nutrition specialist. Symptoms of vitamin E toxicity, usually the result of long-term, high-dose intake, include blurred vision, nausea, headache, fatigue, and slower blood clotting. People who are taking anticoagulant medications, who have high blood pressure, or who have had rheumatic heart disease should consult their physicians before taking supplemental vitamin E in doses above the U.S. RDA.

V_k

FORMS
*Phylloquinone (plant source),
phytonadione (plant source),
menaquinone (animal source).*

U.S. RDA
None.

RECOMMENDED INTAKE
*0 to 100 mcg. daily. Supplemental vitamin K may be included in some
multiple-vitamin/mineral formulas.*

DIETARY SOURCES
*Brussels sprouts, turnip greens,
egg yolks, oats, spinach, cabbage,
soybeans.*

Brussels Sprouts

HEALTH BENEFITS
*Vitamin K is essential for normal blood-clotting functions.
It may play an important role in fetal bone development.*

INTERACTIONS
*Vitamin K can interfere with the effects
of anticoagulant drugs.
Some antibiotic therapies may destroy the
intestinal bacteria that produce vitamin K.
Very high intake of vitamin E interferes
with coagulant functions of vitamin K.
Vitamin K may be destroyed in cooked
or processed foods.*

V_k

VITAMIN K

Vitamin K was discovered by a Danish biochemist named Henrik Dam. He noticed that chicks fed a completely fat-free diet tended to hemorrhage easily and found that they were missing a factor responsible for blood clotting. Dam was able to determine that the factor was a fat-soluble substance he named *koagulationsvitamin*; or vitamin K. He later went on to isolate it from alfalfa and was awarded a Nobel prize for his work. The form of vitamin K that Dam isolated, the major one found in plants, is called phylloquinone and is usually referred to as vitamin K1. Another natural form of vitamin K, called menaquinone, or vitamin K2, is manufactured in the human intestine by the bacteria that reside there. A third form of vitamin K, menadione, or vitamin K3, is synthetic and for use only in medical situations. All three forms have similar biologic activity in the body.

While vitamin K may be involved in fetal bone development, its most important function in the human body is as a catalyst for forming certain proteins in the liver that act as blood-clotting factors. The blood-clotting process involves at least eleven known factors, and vitamin K is vital for producing at least four of these, the best known being prothrombin, from the Greek words *pro*, "before," and *thrombos*, "a clot."

Vitamin K is stored in the liver and released very slowly for use. Since the body needs only tiny amounts of it, amounts that are easily derived from a combination of intestinal bacteria and dietary sources, deficiency in vitamin K is almost unknown in humans. The exceptions are people who are dependent on intravenous feeding or those who have chronic digestive problems that interfere with vitamin K absorption. Newborns are also susceptible to vitamin K deficiencies, which can produce hemorrhages and other blood-clotting problems because their intestinal tracts are sterile at birth — they need four or five days to acquire the bacteria necessary to produce vitamin K. To prevent such problems from arising, almost all newborns in the United States receive a vitamin K shot at birth, which protects them until they can produce their own vitamin K supply. Some of the signs of vitamin K deficiency are blood in the urine, small bruises scattered around the body, and spontaneous nosebleeds.

Since vitamin K deficiency is so rare, many multiple-vitamin/mineral formulas do not include vitamin K, and there is no established U.S. RDA for it. Instead, an "estimated safe and adequate amount" for adults falls in the range of 70 to 140 mcg., a range that is normally met by intestinal bacteria production and diets that include leafy green vegetables, cheeses, or egg yolks. The multiple vitamins that do include vitamin K do so in low dosages, and people taking antibiotics may benefit from a small supplemental intake, as antibiotics can kill the intestinal bacteria that manufacture vitamin K. Generally, it is unnecessary to take therapeutic doses of supplemental vitamin K unless prescribed by a physician.

CHAPTER TWO

THE MINERALS

Calcium
Chromium
Copper
Fluorine
Iodine
Iron
Magnesium
Manganese
Molybdenum
Phosphorus
Potassium
Selenium
Sodium
Zinc

Ca

FORMS
Calcium carbonate, calcium caseinate,
calcium citrate, calcium gluconate,
calcium lactate, calcium phosphate,
dibasic calcium phosphate,
tribasic calcium phosphate.

U.S. RDA
1,000 mg. daily.

RECOMMENDED INTAKE
1,000 to 1,500 mg. daily.
Calcium may be taken as an
 individual supplement.

DIETARY SOURCES
Milk products, sardines,
green leafy vegetables,
sesame seeds,
seaweed.

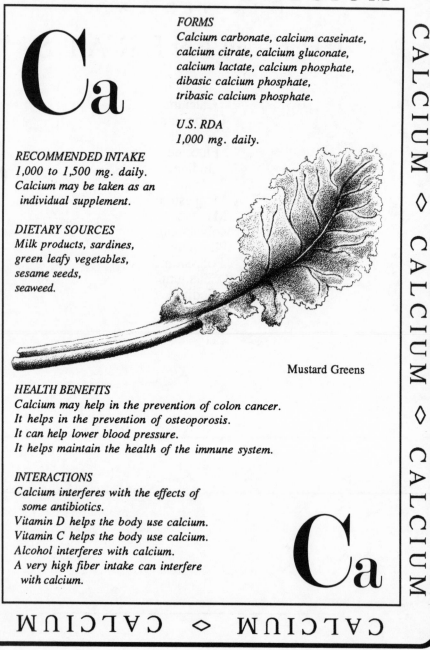

Mustard Greens

HEALTH BENEFITS
Calcium may help in the prevention of colon cancer.
It helps in the prevention of osteoporosis.
It can help lower blood pressure.
It helps maintain the health of the immune system.

INTERACTIONS
Calcium interferes with the effects of
 some antibiotics.
Vitamin D helps the body use calcium.
Vitamin C helps the body use calcium.
Alcohol interferes with calcium.
A very high fiber intake can interfere
 with calcium.

Ca

CALCIUM

Calcium is a whitish substance that is the main ingredient in materials as diverse as chalk, pearls, ivory, and bones. It is the fifth most common element in the earth's crust and the leading mineral in the body. About ninety-nine percent of the body's calcium is found in the bones and teeth; the remainder is in blood plasma and other body fluids.

Calcium is essential for muscle functions and the transmission of nerve impulses, triggering the flow of signals from nerve to nerve and between nerve and muscle. Bones and teeth get their strength and rigidity from calcium, blood needs calcium to clot, and, since calcium controls much of what passes in and out of the cells, it is needed for the health and permeability of cell membranes. Calcium affects the body's immune system, the heartbeat, the maturation of collagen, and the release of many hormones, including some that affect blood pressure. In fact, recent studies show that a daily supplemental calcium intake of 1,000 mg. (1 g.) can reduce blood pressure levels within just a few weeks. Recent research also shows that calcium can reverse detrimental changes in the cells that line the colon, which means that calcium may help prevent one of the leading cancer killers in the United States, colon cancer.

Severe calcium deficiency occurs in people with thyroid and para-thyroid gland problems or with a severe vitamin D deficiency. These conditions upset the delicate calcium-phosphorus balance in the body. When blood levels of calcium fall, phosphorus levels rise, triggering the body to release calcium from the bones in an attempt to rebalance. The bones become weak and brittle, and the body could suffer uncontrollable muscle spasms or convulsive seizures.

Marginal calcium deficiency is surprisingly common and includes people on very high-fiber or high-protein diets; alcoholics; and pregnant, breast-feeding, or postmenopausal women. Those who consume antacids with aluminum, steroids such as cortisone, and tetracycline on a long-term basis are particularly at risk. It is estimated that well over half of all adults, particularly young women, have a calcium intake that is consistently too low. This is an alarming situation: While no one knows exactly what percentage of osteoporosis may be nutritionally related, many of the studies underway at this time indicate that an adequate calcium intake, particularly in the first thirty to forty years of life, may help prevent it. Osteoporosis is a debilitating condition in which bones, particularly of the spine, lose so much of their calcium that they become brittle enough to crack at the slightest pressure, even from their own weight. Over twenty million people in the United States, mostly women over the age of forty-five, are affected by osteoporosis, and complications from it will kill more older women than will heart attacks, strokes, or breast cancer.

The U.S. RDA for calcium is 1,000 mg. Those whose diets do not include a very high intake of dairy products will find that daily supplemental doses of 1,000 to 1,500 mg. can provide many important health benefits. Although most sources of calcium are considered nontoxic, dolomite and bone meal should be avoided, as they have been known to contain toxic elements such as lead.

Cr

FORMS
GTF chromium from yeast,
chromium acetate,
chromium chloride,
chromium trichloride.

U.S. RDA
None.

RECOMMENDED INTAKE
100 to 200 mcg. daily.
Include in a daily multiple-vitamin/mineral supplement.
Chromium may be taken as an individual supplement.

DIETARY SOURCES
Oysters, eggs, chicken, mushrooms,
green vegetables, brewer's yeast,
dried beans and peas, cheese,
whole grains.

Mushrooms

HEALTH BENEFITS
Chromium increases the body's sensitivity to insulin.
It may help control maturity-onset diabetes.
It helps lower LDL cholesterol levels
    and raise HDL levels, which can help
    to prevent heart disease.

INTERACTIONS
None known.

Cr

CHROMIUM

The trace element chromium was considered a toxic metal for humans until the early 1950s, when a series of experiments was conducted to examine glucose intolerance in rats. Glucose intolerance, typical in diabetes, is the body's inability or impaired ability to use glucose, the sugar that is the all-purpose fuel for the cells. The experiments determined that feeding the rats brewer's yeast, which contains chromium, corrected glucose intolerance. Chromium was found to be the key element in a molecule called the glucose tolerance factor (GTF), a molecule that enhances insulin activity. This data on rats turned out to be valid for humans as well, and chromium was finally recognized as an essential nutrient.

As people grow older, their ability to effectively process glucose declines, although their insulin production does not, and many of them develop a condition known as maturity-onset diabetes. Because of its role in the GTF, chromium is being investigated as a factor in controlling the glucose intolerance associated with this condition. Studies have not presented any direct evidence that chromium will prevent diabetes, but it can increase glucose tolerance, perhaps by restoring cellular sensitivity to insulin. Chromium makes an important contribution to cardiovascular health as well. It lowers overall blood cholesterol levels by lowering low density lipoprotein (LDL) levels. It also increases high density lipo-protein (HDL) levels, which are believed to protect the arteries from becoming clogged.

Most of the chromium in the human body is found in the skin, with additional stores in the adrenal glands and the brain, as well as in the muscles and fat. Chromium levels in body tissues are highest at birth, decreasing slowly as the body ages, so that the elderly are at risk for deficiency. Evidence also indicates that a marginal chromium deficiency is extremely common in the United States and other countries where refined flour and sugar play a large part in the diet. People who regularly engage in strenuous exercise, such as running, are at risk of chromium deficiency, and pregnant women are especially susceptible. Women who have borne several children are predisposed to a higher risk of maturity-onset diabetes, possibly the result of a chromium deficiency induced by repeated pregnancies.

It is surprising that, up to now, so little attention has been focused on maintaining adequate chromium levels in the body. This is changing, however, and many experts foresee chromium supplements playing a larger and larger role in preventive medicine. There is no U.S. RDA for chromium, but the estimated adequate daily intake range is 50 to 200 mcg. Chromium is considered safe in doses up to 1,000 mcg. (1 mg.), but long-term daily doses greater than 500 mcg. are not recommended without the supervision of a nutrition specialist. Chromium is absorbed in the intestine along with zinc, so the best way to take supplemental chromium is in a multiple-vitamin/mineral supplement.

Cu

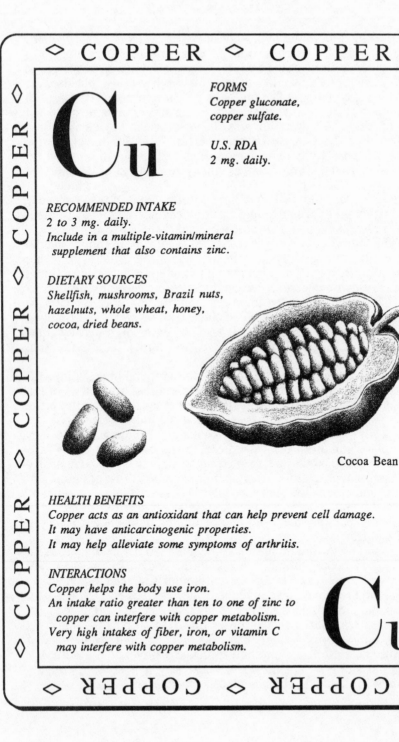

FORMS
*Copper gluconate,
copper sulfate.*

U.S. RDA
2 mg. daily.

RECOMMENDED INTAKE
*2 to 3 mg. daily.
Include in a multiple-vitamin/mineral
  supplement that also contains zinc.*

DIETARY SOURCES
*Shellfish, mushrooms, Brazil nuts,
hazelnuts, whole wheat, honey,
cocoa, dried beans.*

Cocoa Bean

HEALTH BENEFITS
*Copper acts as an antioxidant that can help prevent cell damage.
It may have anticarcinogenic properties.
It may help alleviate some symptoms of arthritis.*

INTERACTIONS
*Copper helps the body use iron.
An intake ratio greater than ten to one of zinc to
  copper can interfere with copper metabolism.
Very high intakes of fiber, iron, or vitamin C
  may interfere with copper metabolism.*

Cu

COPPER

Copper is a trace element that is found in almost every cell of the body. It is a key element in the production of melanin, the pigment that gives distinctive color to the skin, hair, and eyes. Along with vitamins C and E and the mineral selenium, copper is an important antioxidant that acts to remove free radicals — highly reactive molecules that can damage the cells when they oxidize — from the body. Recent studies indicate that copper acts as an anti-inflammatory agent, and, since it can be absorbed through the skin, there seems to be some validity to the folk cure of wearing a copper bracelet for relief from the symptoms of arthritis.

Copper is active in the formation of proteins that strengthen and maintain the elasticity of blood vessels such as the coronary arteries. It also helps forge the protective myelin sheath found around nerve fibers, necessary for clear thinking and calm nerves. Copper is a component in many cellular enzymes and is an integral part of the system in cells that produces chemical energy. It helps release and transport iron from the intestines and helps recycle the iron from dead red blood cells. These are essential steps in the formation and function of hemoglobin, the oxygen-carrying part of blood.

Copper deficiency, once considered rare, is increasing and has been linked to high cholesterol levels and heart problems. Anyone who lives in an area with naturally soft water, and drinks at least two quarts of it a day, gets plenty of dietary copper, but the U.S. Department of Agriculture (USDA) estimates that the average American diet contains about half the adequate amount of copper, due in part to changes in the modern diet. Processed foods, especially those made from white flour and white sugar, are very poor in copper. Furthermore, a decline in the use of copper pipes for plumbing removes a reliable source of copper from the diet.

Copper deficiency most commonly appears as anemia, since the presence of copper is necessary for the body to utilize iron. Severe copper deficiency is rare and most likely to occur in patients dependent on long-term intravenous feeding for their nourishment, where the IV solution does not contain copper. Vegans, however, can be susceptible to marginal copper deficiencies because a large intake of dietary fiber can interfere with the body's absorption of copper. Interference in copper absorption can also occur when large doses of vitamin C are taken or when prolonged intake levels of zinc exceed an approximate ten-to-one ratio of zinc to copper.

The U.S. RDA for copper is 2 mg. per day for adults, which can be met adequately with a serving of shellfish or a few mushrooms. A multiple-vitamin/mineral formula that contains 2 to 3 mg. of copper will insure the health benefits from a daily intake of copper. At this time, there appear to be no additional benefits from amounts above 5 mg. per day, and a long-term intake of 10 mg. or more can be toxic, producing nausea, stomach pains, and muscle aches. Fortunately, the body is often able to protect itself from too much or too little copper. When the intake is excessive, the body excretes more copper; when it is insufficient, the body absorbs more copper from food.

F

FORMS
Fluoride,
calcium fluoride.

U.S. RDA
None.

RECOMMENDED INTAKE
2 to 4 mg. daily.
Supplemental intake is not necessary if water source
is fluoridated or if dietary sources are adequate.

DIETARY SOURCES
Sardines, salmon, apples,
tea, gelatin, eggs.

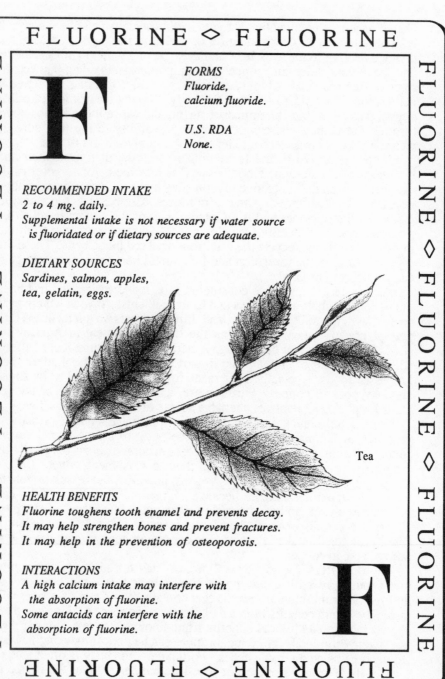

Tea

HEALTH BENEFITS
Fluorine toughens tooth enamel and prevents decay.
It may help strengthen bones and prevent fractures.
It may help in the prevention of osteoporosis.

INTERACTIONS
A high calcium intake may interfere with
the absorption of fluorine.
Some antacids can interfere with the
absorption of fluorine.

F

FLUORINE

Fluorine, from the Latin *fluere*, "to flow," is a poisonous, pale yellow gas that is the most naturally reactive of all the elements in nature. Consequently, fluorine bonds easily to other elements and is usually found as the compound referred to as fluoride. Fluorine is an essential trace element that is found primarily in the teeth and bones.

The fluoridation of drinking water, a major topic of debate in the fifties and early sixties, has been the single largest contributor to the decrease in tooth decay, particularly in children. Over half the water supply of the United States is fluoridated, and fluoride in the amount of 1 ppm (part per million) in water has been shown to decrease children's dental caries by almost two-thirds. Fluorine, as fluoride, is absorbed directly by teeth, increasing their strength and rigidity and inhibiting caries. The teeth are composed of calcium crystals, called hydroxyapatite crystals, that are constantly forming and breaking down. When fluoride is present, some of the calcium crystals in the teeth are replaced by fluorine-rich crystals known as fluoroapatite crystals. These crystals are stronger than the calcium ones and more resistant to destructive acids. Fluoride can also draw calcium phosphate out of saliva and may use it to help renew or repair tooth structure once decay has begun.

As of this writing, experiments have begun to determine whether teeth-repairing functions can be triggered directly in humans, as they have been in animals. Dental chemists have developed a compound that causes the calcium crystals in teeth to convert into an unstable substance. This unstable substance will then bond with any fluoride in the mouth to form the tougher, more decay-resistant fluoroapatite crystals, helping remineralize the teeth into stronger units. The compound itself contains no fluorine — it just makes the teeth more receptive to any fluoride that is available — and can be included in toothpastes, in mouth rinses, and even in chewing gum.

Other roles of fluorine in human nutrition are still being explored. It seems to protect against the overall effects of magnesium deficiency and is being studied as a possible agent in preventing osteoporosis, a debilitating condition wherein bones lose their mineral content, particularly calcium, and become weak and brittle. Recent studies in Finland have shown that in towns with fluoridated water, older citizens, especially post-menopausal women, had substantially fewer fractures that were attributable to osteoporosis.

There is no U.S. RDA for fluorine or fluoride, and it is rarely included in multiple-vitamin/mineral supplements. A range of 1.5 to 4 mg. has been estimated to be both safe and adequate. Good dietary sources of fluoride are apples, sardines, and other fish and fish products, as well as fluoridated water. Fluorine deficiency in humans is unknown. Toxicity is rare, usually caused by consuming deep-well water that passes through heavily fluoridated rock.

I

FORMS
*Potassium iodide,
kelp (seaweed).*

U.S. RDA
150 mcg. daily.

RECOMMENDED INTAKE
*150 mcg. daily.
Include in a multiple-vitamin/mineral supplement.*

DIETARY SOURCES
*Seaweed, fish, shellfish, sunflower seeds,
iodized salt, dairy products,
turnip greens.*

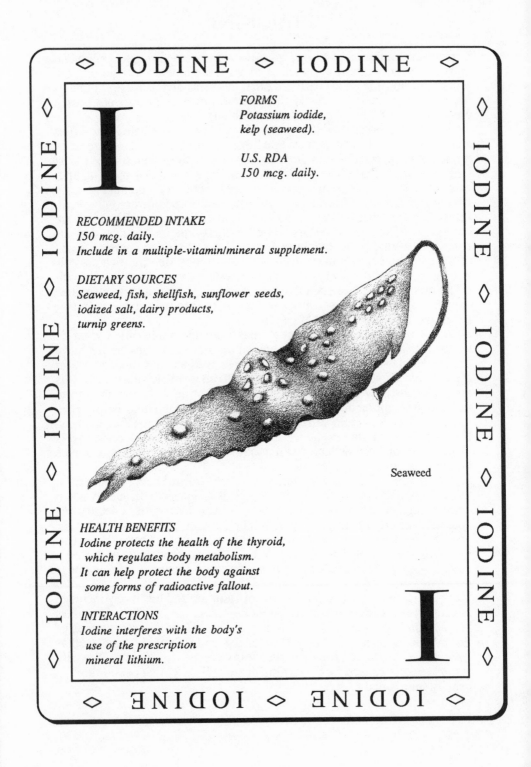

Seaweed

HEALTH BENEFITS
*Iodine protects the health of the thyroid,
which regulates body metabolism.
It can help protect the body against
some forms of radioactive fallout.*

INTERACTIONS
*Iodine interferes with the body's
use of the prescription
mineral lithium.*

I

IODINE

The trace element iodine probably has the longest history of study of any of the essential minerals, with the possible exception of iron. In fact, sixty years ago, iodine and iron were the only minerals believed to be essential. Iodine solutions are commonly used in hospitals to sterilize the skin prior to surgery. One of iodine's most familiar uses is as a bright orange tincture that, when painted on wounds, helps prevent infection.

The average adult has 20 to 50 mg. of iodine in the body at all times. Some of the iodine is dispersed in the muscles, skin, skeleton, and nervous system, but over eighty percent of it is found in the thyroid, the yellowish red, bow-tie-shaped gland at the base of the neck. At this time, the only known function of iodine in the body is to form thyroid hormones such as thyroxine. Thyroxine is a metabolic regulator that exerts a tremendous overall influence on the body's metabolism, including speeding up many of the enzymatic reactions that process glucose, the body's all-purpose fuel.

When too much thyroxine is secreted, a condition called hyperthyroidism develops — the body's organs start to function like a motor given too much fuel. The symptoms of hyperthyroidism include nervousness, weight loss, bulging eyes, and rapid pulse; and, if the pace is not slowed, heart failure. When too little thyroxine is present, usually in people with iodine deficiencies, hypothyroidism develops. Some of its symptoms include physical and mental sluggishness, weight gain with puffiness in the face and hands, hair loss, thickened skin, decreased body temperature, and goiter — an enlarged, bulging thyroid gland. At the turn of the century, goiter was one of the common deficiency diseases, especially in areas that were distant from the ocean — the largest source of iodine on earth. As a public-health measure in the 1920s, the United States and many other countries added iodine to salt, and by the 1950s goiter appeared only rarely in these nations.

Iodine came into the news again in 1986 during the Chernobyl nuclear power plant accident in the Ukraine, where a vast cloud of radioactive gas (including radioactive forms of iodine) was released into the atmosphere. Throughout Europe, citizens were given iodine supplements to saturate their blood and thyroid glands so that they would not absorb radioactive iodine from the air or from foods grown in contaminated areas. In response to this accident, the Food and Drug Administration (FDA) has now approved a nonprescription drug, Iosat, that can help block the body's absorption of some types of radioactive fallout.

The U.S. RDA for iodine is 150 mcg., although a 1983 study released by the FDA indicates that the iodine content of the average American diet, even without iodized salt, may surpass that. Nevertheless, iodine deficiency is still a world health problem affecting an estimated 200 million people. Iodine is an important mineral, and it is prudent to be certain that the U.S. RDA is met each day, either through a multiple-vitamin/mineral supplement or through the diet. Dosages under 3,000 mcg. daily are believed to be nontoxic, but daily supplementation in excess of 150 mcg. should be supervised by a nutrition specialist.

Fe

FORMS
Ferrous fumarate,
ferrous gluconate,
ferrous sulfate.

U.S. RDA
18 mg. daily.

RECOMMENDED INTAKE
18 to 30 mg. daily. Include in a multiple-
  vitamin/mineral supplement
  that also contains vitamin C.

DIETARY SOURCES
Seaweed, pumpkin seeds,
lentils, organ meats,
chicken,
fish.

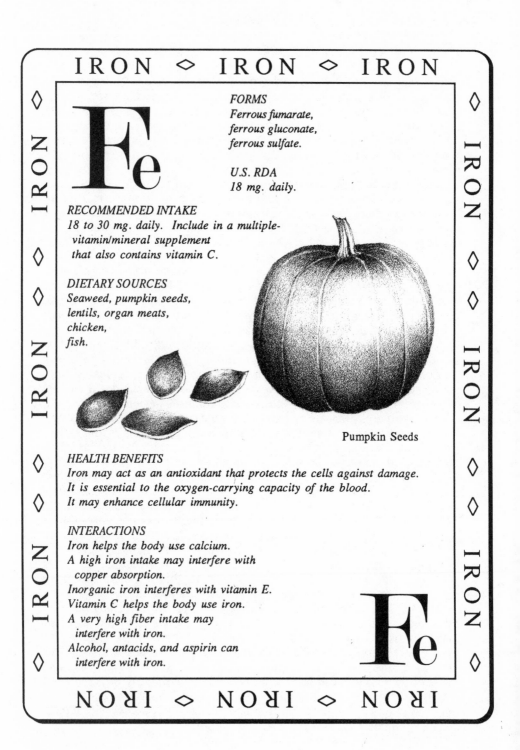

Pumpkin Seeds

HEALTH BENEFITS
Iron may act as an antioxidant that protects the cells against damage.
It is essential to the oxygen-carrying capacity of the blood.
It may enhance cellular immunity.

INTERACTIONS
Iron helps the body use calcium.
A high iron intake may interfere with
  copper absorption.
Inorganic iron interferes with vitamin E.
Vitamin C helps the body use iron.
A very high fiber intake may
  interfere with iron.
Alcohol, antacids, and aspirin can
  interfere with iron.

Fe

IRON

Iron is probably the most important of the trace elements. It is needed to create healthy red blood cells, maintain the immune system, regulate and produce many of the brain's neurotransmitters, and to make collagen — an important component of connective tissues. Iron is absolutely vital to the body for respiration, the process that generates the energy that sustains all living functions. The performance of the heart muscle requires iron, and a deficiency in it, especially in people with coronary disease, can cause other cardiovascular problems. Also, recent studies suggest that some forms of iron may have antioxidant properties and could be anticarcinogenic.

Most of the body's iron, about seventy percent, is found in hemoglobin, the protein in red blood cells that transports oxygen from the lungs to the cells of the body; another five percent is in myoglobin, the protein that transfers oxygen to the muscles, which is necessary for their work. Of the remaining iron, a small amount, dispersed throughout the cells, is used for an assortment of enzymatic functions that trigger energy production; the rest is stored in the liver, spleen, and bone marrow.

Dietary iron comes in two forms: nonheme iron, found in plants, animals, and fish; and heme iron, found only in fish and animal tissues. Nonheme iron, referred to as inorganic iron, is difficult for the body to absorb — only two to ten percent of it is available for the body's use. Heme, or organic, iron is a little more bioavailable; the body can use about thirty percent of it. Since so little dietary iron is usable, iron deficiency is one of the most prevalent worldwide nutritional problems, and the U.S. Department of Agriculture (USDA) lists it as the most common mineral deficiency in America.

In its most extreme form, iron deficiency results in anemia, a condition in which red blood cells are abnormally small and pale in color, with symptoms that include exhaustion, susceptibility to infection, and heart palpitations. Marginal iron deficiency, even when anemia is not present, can trigger fatigue, learning and behavioral disorders, skin pallor, muscle weakness, and decreased alertness. Those most at risk for iron deficiency are women who are menstruating or pregnant, infants, adolescents, vegans, the elderly, anyone who has suffered blood loss through injury or surgery, and anyone on a low-calorie diet.

The U.S. RDA for iron is 18 mg. Since the average American diet provides only about 13 mg. of iron, it is clear why iron deficiency is so prevalent and why supplemental iron is important. For optimum health, supplemental iron intake should be in the range of 18 to 30 mg. daily. Iron toxicity, or iron overload, is very rare, but can occur when prolonged supplemental iron intake exceeds 100 mg. daily. In addition, about three of every thousand people have a genetic disorder that predisposes them to hemochromatosis, iron overload that happens because the body is unable to stop absorbing iron once its needs are met. The iron builds up to levels that can trigger cirrhosis of the liver, diabetes, and heart problems — levels that can even be high enough to set off airport metal detectors.

Mg

FORMS
Magnesium carbonate,
magnesium gluconate,
magnesium hydroxide,
magnesium oxide.

U.S. RDA
400 mg. daily.

RECOMMENDED INTAKE
400 to 600 mg. daily.
Magnesium may be taken as an individual supplement.

DIETARY SOURCES
Molasses, pistachio nuts,
sunflower seeds, almonds,
green vegetables,
seafood,
beans.

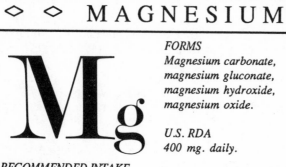

Pistachio Nuts

HEALTH BENEFITS
Magnesium helps in the prevention of kidney stones.
It may help in the treatment of premenstrual syndrome (PMS).
It may help protect against some
  cardiovascular problems.
It may help alleviate depression
  in the elderly.

INTERACTIONS
Magnesium helps the body use calcium.
Alcohol depletes the body's
  supply of magnesium.

Mg

MAGNESIUM

Magnesium, an element found in all the cells, is an essential mineral in every biological process in the body. It is needed for transmitting nerve impulses, forming nucleic acids and proteins, and keeping blood vessels well toned and the heart beating rhythmically. Magnesium helps maintain cell membranes, forms bones and teeth, and is vital for converting glycogen — sugar that has been stored in the liver and muscles — into glucose for use as the body's fuel. Recent research suggests that magnesium may help prevent some types of migraine headaches and block the formation of some types of kidney stones. It may also decrease the incidence and severity of angina, chest pain caused by the blockage of a coronary artery by plaque; and it may protect against ischemic heart disease, a condition that occurs when the heart muscle does not get the oxygen it needs because of a spasm or narrowed, clogged arteries.

Most of the body's supply of magnesium is stored, like calcium, in the skeleton and teeth, and calcium-magnesium interactions are extremely important in the body. For example, when calcium passes into muscle cells, it triggers a set of reactions that cause the muscle to contract. The muscle relaxes when the calcium is replaced by magnesium. Recent evidence indicates that an imbalance between calcium and magnesium in the body, where there is not enough magnesium, may increase the risk of developing cardiovascular disease and may play a role in high blood pressure. This type of imbalance is present in a large segment of the American population. Those least likely to have such an imbalance are adult females, but, unfortunately, this is due not to adequate calcium-magnesium levels but instead to a calcium deficiency in so many women.

Although the body conserves magnesium levels efficiently, most Americans do not receive enough magnesium from dietary sources. While severe magnesium deficiency, with symptoms of convulsions and delirium, is fairly rare, marginal deficiency is quite common. This marginal deficiency can increase the risk of developing disruptions in the normal heart rhythm and may be one of the factors triggering the discomforts of premenstrual syndrome (PMS). New research also indicates that low magnesium levels may be the cause of eclampsia — convulsions in pregnancy. Those most at risk for magnesium deficiency are alcoholics, diabetics, the elderly, those on low-calorie diets, those who engage in regular, strenuous exercise, and pregnant women.

The U.S. RDA for magnesium is 400 mg. Since the typical diet contains only 180 to 300 mg., a supplemental intake in the 400 to 600 mg. range will insure adequate levels of magnesium. People with heart or kidney problems should consult a nutrition specialist before taking any supplemental magnesium. Toxicity is rare. It usually affects only those individuals with kidney problems and those who use magnesium-based laxatives excessively.

Mn

FORMS
*Manganese gluconate,
manganese sulfate.*

U.S. RDA
None.

RECOMMENDED INTAKE
*5 to 10 mg. daily.
Include in a daily multiple-vitamin/mineral supplement.*

DIETARY SOURCES
*Seaweed, avocados, coconuts, pecans, chestnuts,
hazelnuts, whole grains, sunflower seeds,
coffee beans, bananas,
grapefruit,
seafood.*

Pecan

HEALTH BENEFITS
*Manganese is a key component in enzymes
that help release energy to the body.
It may act as an antioxidant
that helps prevent
brain-cell damage.*

INTERACTIONS
None known.

Mn

MANGANESE

Manganese is a gray white element that is added to steel to increase its hardness and strength. It is also essential for human growth and bone formation and is a necessary part of many enzymes that help generate energy for the body's use. Manganese participates in muscle co-ordination, the metabolism of fats and carbohydrates, and production of prothrombin — an important factor in the mechanism of blood clotting. It may also be a factor in human reproduction and may be useful in the treatment of osteoporosis and osteoarthritis, a degenerative joint disease in which the cartilage cushioning a joint thins and eventually wears out. Since there are high manganese levels in the part of brain that controls the production and regulation of neurotransmitters, particularly dopamine, it is thought that manganese may help protect against some degenerative neurological diseases.

Many of the functions of manganese in the human body still elude researchers. It can exist as a pro-oxidant, an element that forms highly reactive molecules that can damage cells, and yet its chief role seems to be as an antioxidant. Manganese has been held forth as a deterrent to aging because it is part of superoxide dismutase (SOD), an antioxidant that uses up excess oxygen molecules which would otherwise damage cells and speed up their aging. No studies to date have supported this role, although it is interesting to note that most tumors that have been studied show lower-than-normal levels of SOD, leading to the possibility that inadequate manganese levels might be involved in the deterioration of body tissue.

It is difficult to determine the effects of low manganese levels, since deficiency in manganese seems to be rare in nature and hard to trigger in animals under experimental conditions. At this time, there has been only one reported human case of severe manganese deficiency, in a hospital patient who had been on a manganese-deficient diet for several months. The patient developed a decreased serum cholesterol level, broke out in a rash, suffered a loss in weight, and had his black hair and beard change to a rusty color.

There is no established U.S. RDA for manganese, but a range of 2.5 to 5 mg. is estimated to be both safe and adequate for preventing a severe manganese deficiency. Good dietary sources of manganese include avo-cados, seaweed, and nuts. A daily intake of supplemental manganese in the range of 5 to 10 mg. will insure that the body's manganese needs are met. It is considered nontoxic, and the incidence of manganese toxicity from oral supplements or dietary sources is quite rare. Manganese is added to many gasolines to replace lead as an "antiknock" substance, but the effects on humans of increased levels of airborne manganese and its compounds have not yet been determined. However, miners and ore refiners who are exposed to manganese dust in the course of their work may develop a disorder with symptoms similar to those of Parkinson's disease — a disease in which the nerve cells of the brain degenerate.

M_o

FORMS
Sodium molybdate.

U.S. RDA
None.

RECOMMENDED INTAKE
100 to 200 mcg. daily.
Include in a multiple-vitamin/mineral supplement
that also contains copper.

DIETARY SOURCES
Beef, chicken, whole wheat,
dried beans and peas,
oats.

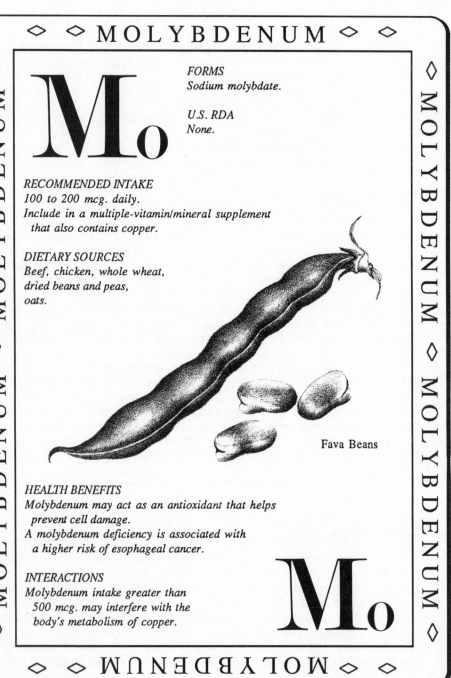

Fava Beans

HEALTH BENEFITS
Molybdenum may act as an antioxidant that helps
prevent cell damage.
A molybdenum deficiency is associated with
a higher risk of esophageal cancer.

INTERACTIONS
Molybdenum intake greater than
500 mcg. may interfere with the
body's metabolism of copper.

M_o

MOLYBDENUM

Molybdenum, a gray mineral used in dyes, enamels, and fertilizers, has been shown to be an essential mineral for animals, but its nutritional activity in humans has only recently become the focus of major interest. Found in almost all the body's tissues, molybdenum helps trigger a number of metabolic reactions by being a catalyst for the activities of several important enzymes. These enzymes include aldehyde oxidase, which is necessary for processing fats; sulfite oxidase, which may neutralize sulfites (food preservatives that can be toxic to the nervous system); and xanthine oxidase, which produces the waste product uric acid and acts as an antioxidant that scavenges harmful forms of oxygen. Xanthine oxidase may also help release iron stored in the liver for the body's use.

As an activator of the enzyme xanthine oxidase, molybdenum may work to maintain uric acid levels in the body. Too much molybdenum can trigger too much xanthine oxidase activity. This, in turn, leads to too much uric acid production, more than the kidneys can process and excrete from the body. The excess uric acid stays in the blood, which deposits it in the joints. As the uric acid accumulates, it crystallizes, which inflames the joints and results in a painful condition known as gout. However, there are no conclusive studies at this time proving that a decrease in molybdenum intake correlates to a decrease in gout.

Molybdenum is also being investigated as an anticarcinogen. Recent research indicates that rats fed supplemental molybdenum were more resistant to chemical carcinogens, but there are no studies at this time showing that this same effect occurs in humans. Evidence for the positive effects of molybdenum in human nutrition is epidemiological, based on observations of a small region in China that has had high levels of esophageal cancer for nearly two thousand years. Medical investigators discovered that the residents of the region were deficient in vitamin C and that the soil their vegetables grew in was deficient in molybdenum. Molybdenum is required by bacteria in soil to convert nitrogen substances into amines that plants can use. Without molybdenum, the nitrogen substances are converted into cancer-causing nitrosamines. Vitamin C has been shown to protect humans from some of the toxic effects of nitrosamines, so the presence of high levels of nitrosamines, combined with the absence of vitamin C, may have triggered the high incidence of esophageal cancer. The situation in China is improving since the soil has been enriched with molybdenum and supplemental vitamin C has been introduced to the populace.

There is no U.S. RDA established for molybdenum, but a daily intake of 100 to 200 mcg. will insure that the body has adequate levels of it. Molybdenum is not considered toxic; however, people suffering from gout should consult a nutrition specialist before taking supplemental molybdenum. Amounts of supplemental molybdenum greater than 500 mcg. have been shown to interfere with copper levels in the body.

P

FORMS
*Dibasic calcium phosphate,
sodium phosphate.*

U.S. RDA
1,000 mg. daily.

RECOMMENDED INTAKE
*1,000 mg. daily from dietary sources.
Supplemental phosphorus may be
 included in some multiple-vitamin/mineral formulas.*

DIETARY SOURCES
*Milk, sunflower seeds, dried peas and beans,
soybeans, almonds, meat,
fish, whole grains,
peanuts.*

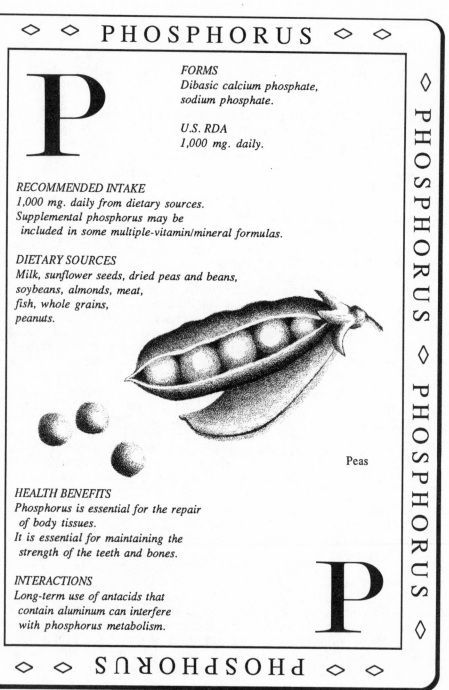

Peas

HEALTH BENEFITS
*Phosphorus is essential for the repair
 of body tissues.
It is essential for maintaining the
 strength of the teeth and bones.*

INTERACTIONS
*Long-term use of antacids that
 contain aluminum can interfere
 with phosphorus metabolism.*

P

PHOSPHORUS

PHOSPHORUS

Phosphorus is a poisonous, highly flammable element used in matches, fireworks, and fertilizers; and it is second only to calcium as the most abundant mineral in the body. A major essential mineral, phosphorus is found in every living cell and is involved in almost every human biochemical reaction, from building and repairing tissues to maintaining the important acid-alkaline balance of the blood. The energy that the body derives from food is either used immediately or stored — and both processes require phosphorus. Phosphorus combines with glucose and glycerol (from fat) in the intestine to aid in their absorption; it also bonds with fatty acids in the blood to form phospholipids, essential elements in cell structure.

Many of the functions of phosphorus are directly related to those of calcium: About eighty percent of the body's phosphorus is bound with calcium in the bones and teeth, giving them their rigidity and strength. Phosphorus-calcium levels in the blood are tightly controlled by hormones from the parathyroid glands. Like calcium, phosphorus is constantly being deposited into or removed from the skeleton: When blood levels of phosphorus fall, calcium levels will rise, so the parathyroid hormones trigger the body to release phosphorus from the bones. When blood levels of phosphorus become too high, the body will release calcium from the bones to rebalance. If too much of either mineral is released over a period of time, usually due to an inadequate intake of one of the minerals, the bones become weak and brittle and, in extreme cases, the body may suffer muscle spasms or convulsive seizures.

Phosphorus deficiency is fairly uncommon. This is probably due to the fact that phosphorus is present in almost all foods. When phosphorus deficiency does appear, it is often due to the overuse of antacids that contain aluminum, a mineral that interferes with phosphorus absorption in the body. Bone diseases that upset the phosphorus-calcium levels, and intestinal diseases that hinder phosphorus absorption, can also trigger a deficiency in phosphorus, with symptoms that include muscle weakness, a loss of appetite, and bones that break easily.

The U.S. RDA for phosphorus is 1,000 mg. (1 g.), and women who are pregnant or breast-feeding may want to increase their daily intake to 1,200 mg. The best dietary sources for phosphorus are fish, meat, milk, and milk products, as well as soybeans, pumpkin seeds, and dried peas and beans. There is a growing concern among some nutrition experts that many people in the United States and other Western nations might be receiving unusually high levels of phosphorus from processed foods and, especially, carbonated soft drinks. Since many of these people also have low levels of calcium in their bodies, as well as an insufficient calcium intake from dietary or supplemental sources, they risk upsetting their phosphorus-calcium balances. Toxicity from phosphorus is rare, though, and most frequently appears in people with kidney diseases that prevent adequate phosphorus excretion.

K

FORMS
*Potassium aspartate,
potassium citrate,
potassium chloride,
potassium gluconate.*

U.S. RDA
None.

RECOMMENDED INTAKE
*2,000 to 6,000 mg. daily from dietary sources.
Supplemental potassium may be included in some
 multiple-vitamin/mineral formulas.
Potassium may be taken as an individual supplement
 by those engaged in strenuous exercise.*

DIETARY SOURCES
*Raisins, whole potatoes, bananas,
legumes, tomatoes, oranges,
beef, broccoli, leafy green
vegetables.*

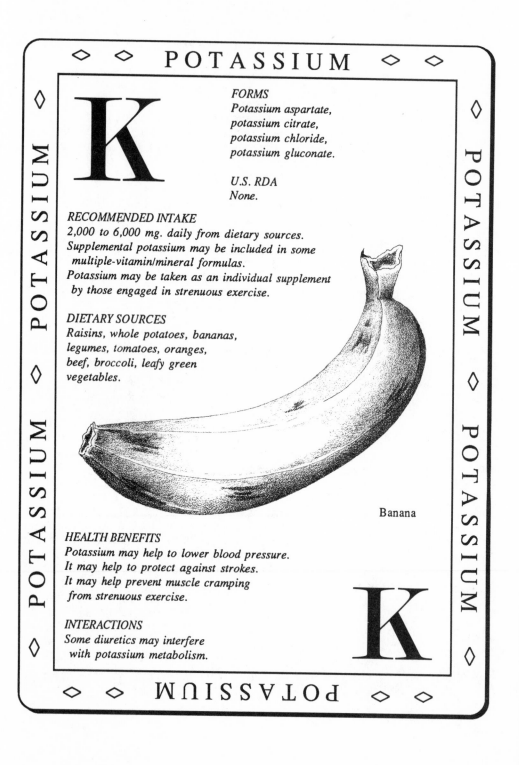

Banana

HEALTH BENEFITS
*Potassium may help to lower blood pressure.
It may help to protect against strokes.
It may help prevent muscle cramping
 from strenuous exercise.*

INTERACTIONS
*Some diuretics may interfere
 with potassium metabolism.*

K

POTASSIUM

Potassium, used to make fertilizers and soaps, is a highly reactive, even explosive, silver white mineral. Most of the body's potassium is found inside the cells, where it does not act the way most minerals do: Its primary function is not as a catalyst in metabolic processes, but as an electrolyte. Along with two other important electrolytes, sodium and chloride, potassium helps maintain the balance of water inside and outside the cells and regulates what passes in and goes out of them. Potassium influences the body's acid-alkaline balance. It is needed for converting glucose in the blood into glycogen that can be stored in tissues for later use. Sodium and calcium team up with potassium to regulate nerve-muscle interactions, transmitting signals in the nervous system and causing muscles to contract.

People with high blood pressure often have low potassium levels. This situation can be aggravated by diuretics, which cause potassium excretion from the body. Recent studies indicate that an increased intake of potassium may help to control hypertension and decrease damage to the kidneys caused by this condition. Potassium also seems to help the arteries to the brain contend with higher-than-normal blood pressure, and there is evidence that potassium may protect against strokes, even in people with high blood pressure. In addition, a 1987 study indicates that extra dietary potassium can reduce the incidence of death from stroke by up to forty percent.

Potassium helps determine how fast the heart beats and how strongly it contracts. It is so important to the heart that even a small variation in the amount present in the blood will produce changes in an electrocardiogram (ECG). When too much potassium is present, usually due to kidney failure or shock, a potentially life-threatening condition called hyper-kalemia occurs — the heart muscle relaxes too much and the heart beats too slowly to maintain its circulatory functions. When not enough potassium is available, due to diuretics or protracted vomiting or diarrhea, hypokalemia occurs, with symptoms that include muscle spasms and cramps, lethargy, and an abnormal, galloping heartbeat.

There is no established U.S. RDA for potassium, but a daily intake of potassium in the range of 1,875 to 5,625 mg. is considered safe and adequate for meeting the body's needs. The average diet provides about 2,000 to 4,000 mg. of potassium when it includes foods such as bananas, oranges, raisins, potatoes (with their skins), and leafy green vegetables. As a result, supplemental potassium is usually unnecessary. However, individuals who regularly engage in strenuous exercise may need to take supplemental potassium, since potassium is lost from the body through sweat. Also, those taking diuretics may need such supplementation and should discuss this possibility with their physicians. When supplemental potassium must be taken, it is best to incorporate it into a multiple-vitamin/mineral supplement rather than to take it on a stand-alone basis. Individuals with any type of heart problem should consult their physicians before taking supplemental potassium.

Se

FORMS
Sodium selenite (inorganic),
selenium from yeast (organic).

U.S. RDA
None.

RECOMMENDED INTAKE
100 to 200 mcg. daily of organic selenium. Include in a daily multiple-
vitamin/mineral supplement that also contains vitamin E.
Selenium may be taken as an
individual supplement.

DIETARY SOURCES
Seafood, broccoli, cabbage,
whole grains, mushrooms.

Broccoli

HEALTH BENEFITS
Selenium has a preventive effect on cancers of the breast,
colon, pancreas, ovary, and prostate.
It acts as an antioxidant to protect cell membranes from oxidation damage.
It helps reduce the potential toxicity of certain heavy metals.
It may help lower the risk of developing heart disease.
It may help stimulate the immune system.
It may have a beneficial effect on arthritis.

INTERACTIONS
Vitamin E works together with selenium
in its antioxidant activities.
Vitamin C interferes with the metabolism
of inorganic selenium.

Se

SELENIUM

Selenium is a gray element related to sulfur that is used in the manufacture of red glass and computer microchips. It is an unusual element: Its ability to conduct electricity varies in accordance with the intensity of available light, making it an ideal material for photoelectric cells such as those that turn lights on and off automatically at dusk and dawn. Selenium was established as essential to humans in 1957, although its mechanisms are just now coming under scrutiny. Along with vitamin C and beta-carotene, selenium has gained a prominent place in biological research, particularly in the area of preventive medicine.

Veterinarians were the first to recognize selenium's beneficial effects. In animal studies, supplemental selenium lowered the risks of cardio-vascular diseases, inhibited many types of tumor development, increased resistance to heavy-metal poisoning, and countered the growth of certain cancers — particularly breast and colon cancers. As a result, animal feed is now regularly supplemented with selenium. Selenium's effects on humans are now being investigated, and epidemiological evidence in-dicates that they may closely parallel those found in animal studies. Finland, parts of China, and areas of the southeastern United States, such as Ohio, Georgia, and the Carolinas, which have low levels of selenium in their soils, have some of the highest rates of stroke, heart disease, and other cardiovascular problems, as well as unusually high incidences of certain forms of cancer and leukemia. Japan and South Dakota, which have high levels of dietary selenium, have correspondingly lower rates of breast cancer and other cancers.

Selenium has been shown in animal studies to stimulate the immune system and affect cell development and division. It is an integral part of glutathione peroxidase, one of the most important antioxidant enzymes, present in the fluids surrounding all the body's cells except fat cells. The selenium in glutathione peroxidase is believed to work with vitamin E, found inside the cells, to protect the cells and their membranes from dam-age caused by oxidation. Since oxidation is a common factor in the var-ious diseases of aging, such as arteriosclerosis and arthritis, selenium is being carefully examined as a possible anti-aging substance.

There is no established U.S. RDA for selenium. The estimated safe and adequate range for daily intake is 50 to 200 mcg. Good dietary sources of selenium include meats, fish, cabbage, mushrooms, onions, and whole grains. Studies indicate that a daily intake of 100 to 200 mcg. of organic selenium derived from yeast, incorporated into a multiple-vitamin/mineral formula that also contains 100 to 400 IU of vitamin E, is the best way to take advantage of the health benefits of selenium. Daily amounts above 400 mcg. should be taken only with the supervision of a nutrition specialist. Inorganic selenium, found as sodium selenite, should be avoided: Vitamin C interferes with its absorption in the body, and it can be highly toxic at doses above 1,000 mcg. (1 mg.).

Na

FORMS
Sodium chloride,
table salt.

U.S. RDA
None.

RECOMMENDED INTAKE
Decrease intake to no more than one teaspoon of salt daily
* (under 3 g. per day).*

DIETARY SOURCES
Beef, chicken, milk, cabbage, beets, raisins,
lima beans, tomatoes, potatoes, celery,
parsley, green beans,
mineral water.

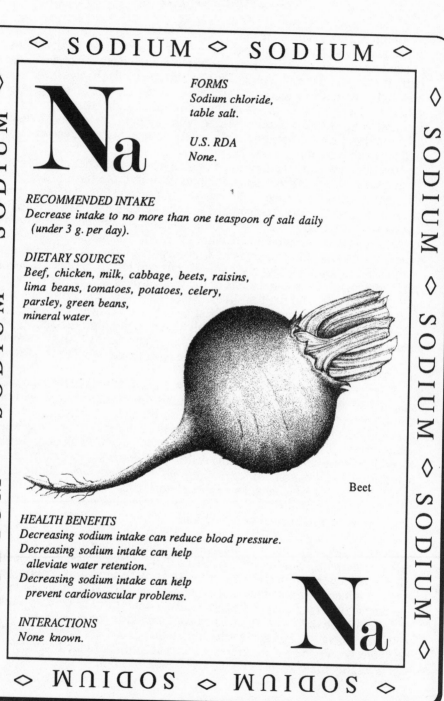

Beet

HEALTH BENEFITS
Decreasing sodium intake can reduce blood pressure.
Decreasing sodium intake can help
* alleviate water retention.*
Decreasing sodium intake can help
* prevent cardiovascular problems.*

INTERACTIONS
None known.

Na

SODIUM

Sodium is a soft, silvery, highly reactive mineral that, combined with chloride, gives food its salty taste. About one-third of the body's sodium is in the skeleton, bound to other elements; the rest is found mostly in the fluids that surround each of the body's cells. Sodium influences the body's acid-alkaline balance and blood pH. Its primary function is not as a catalyst in metabolic processes, but, like potassium, it acts as an electrolyte. As such, sodium helps maintain the balance of water between the inside and the outside of cells, as well as regulate what passes through their membranes. In conjunction with calcium and potassium, sodium transmits signals in the nervous system. It also regulates the interactions between nerves and muscles, and triggers the muscles to contract. Sodium levels in the body are controlled by a powerful hormone called aldosterone, which sends messages to the kidneys to recycle sodium back into the body or excrete it. This, in turn, determines water levels in the body, affecting such conditions as thirst, water retention, and blood pressure.

Essential hypertension, or high blood pressure, is a major public health problem. Its causes are still a mystery, but its results are fairly well established — hypertension increases the risk of developing cardio-vascular disease and increases the incidence of stroke. Sodium's effect on hypertension is a controversial subject. The primary dietary source of sodium is sodium chloride, common table salt: Forty percent of salt is sodium, with chloride (also an electrolyte) making up the balance. Many studies have linked excessive salt consumption with high blood pressure, and hypertensive patients who restrict their salt intake can often lower their blood pressure. At issue is whether it is the sodium or the chloride in salt that affects blood pressure, since both elements act as electrolytes. In both animal and human studies, the intake of sodium as sodium bicarbonate has not increased blood pressure, pointing to chloride as a possible culprit. On the other hand, when hypertensives are placed on a low-salt diet, potassium chloride is used as a salt substitute with good results, perhaps acquitting chloride and indicting sodium. In the end, it may be that it is the combination of sodium and chloride that is the endangering factor, affecting such things as the potassium balance in the body, how strongly the heart contracts, and how often it beats.

There is no U.S. RDA for sodium, but a daily intake in the range of 1,000 to 3,000 mg. is estimated to meet the body's needs. Most individuals will probably benefit from decreasing their overall sodium intake, since typical diets contain from 2,000 to 12,000 mg. of sodium, primarily from salt. The American Heart Association strongly recommends that total daily sodium intake not exceed 3,000 mg. (3 g.), about as much as is found in a teaspoon of salt. Despite folk wisdom, salt itself is not a physiological necessity but an acquired taste, and sodium itself is present in many other dietary forms. Sodium deficiency is rare, occurring primarily in athletes with strenuous workouts and occasionally in pregnant women on low-sodium diets.

Zn

FORMS
Zinc acetate, zinc citrate,
zinc gluconate, zinc sulfate.

U.S. RDA
15 mg. daily.

RECOMMENDED INTAKE
15 to 30 mg. daily. Include in a multiple-vitamin/mineral supplement
  that also contains copper. Zinc may be taken as an individual supplement.

DIETARY SOURCES
Fish, oysters, wheat germ, sesame seeds,
eggs, whole grains.

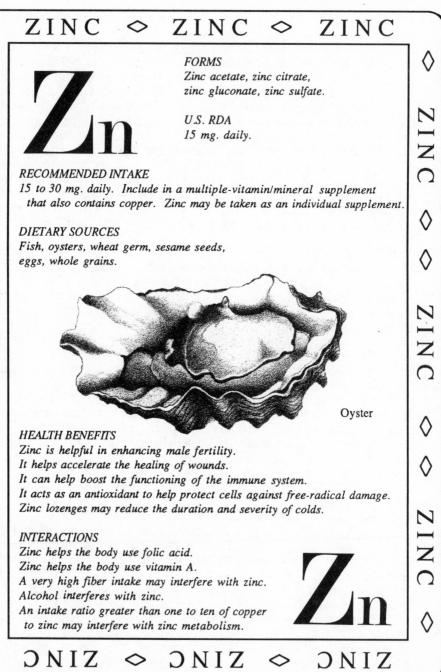

Oyster

HEALTH BENEFITS
Zinc is helpful in enhancing male fertility.
It helps accelerate the healing of wounds.
It can help boost the functioning of the immune system.
It acts as an antioxidant to help protect cells against free-radical damage.
Zinc lozenges may reduce the duration and severity of colds.

INTERACTIONS
Zinc helps the body use folic acid.
Zinc helps the body use vitamin A.
A very high fiber intake may interfere with zinc.
Alcohol interferes with zinc.
An intake ratio greater than one to ten of copper
  to zinc may interfere with zinc metabolism.

Zn

ZINC

Zinc is a bluish white element that is used in industry to galvanize iron, protecting it from oxidizing, or rusting. In the human body, zinc seems to act similarly, preventing oxidation damage in cells. Zinc is a part of the enzyme superoxide dismutase (SOD), an important antioxidant. Besides superoxide dismutase, over seventy other enzymes need zinc to perform their work, including those affecting protein digestion, carbohydrate metabolism, and the transfer of toxic carbon dioxide from the blood to the lungs for removal from the body. In addition, zinc acts to strengthen and maintain the body's immune system, particularly at a cellular level; and zinc lozenges, dissolved in the mouth, have been shown to shorten the duration of the common cold. Zinc is also believed to prevent or repair some of the cell damage that occurs as the body ages.

Zinc is crucial for the synthesis of DNA and RNA, the nucleic proteins that build, develop, reproduce, and repair all cells. This makes zinc an essential nutrient of major importance to human growth and development. This may also be why zinc dramatically affects the speed at which wounds or surgical incisions heal. Recent studies indicate that supplemental zinc intake can reduce healing time by almost half — even gastric ulcers show major signs of improvement in a shorter time. Several of the senses require zinc to perform properly: It affects the ability to taste and smell, and helps transport and activate vitamin A, important for night vision and the health of the immune system. Zinc is also necessary for sexual development and reproductive functions, particularly in males. It may help control testosterone metabolism and has been useful in overcoming some forms of male infertility and impotence.

While severe zinc deficiency is fairly uncommon, most American and Western European populations seem to have low zinc intakes and may be at risk for marginal zinc deficiency. Symptoms of deficiency include a loss of appetite, decreased sexual interest, and a weakening of taste and smell sensations. Zinc deficiency may also contribute to the progressive breakdown of the immune system as the body ages. Supplemental zinc has been shown in recent studies to improve immune responses, even in people over the age of seventy. Women who take oral contraceptives or are pregnant or breast-feeding are particularly at risk of zinc deficiencies, as are athletes who lose large amounts of zinc through sweating. Vegans, cigarette smokers, diabetics, frequent dieters, and people in stressful situations, suffering from infections, or taking steroids are also at risk.

The U.S. RDA for zinc is 15 mg. Like iron, zinc from dietary sources often combines with other elements to become a substance the body cannot absorb or use. Therefore, daily zinc supplements can be important. Research indicates that 15 to 30 mg. of zinc, incorporated into a multiple-vitamin/mineral supplement, insures that the body's zinc needs are adequately met. Zinc is believed to be nontoxic at doses below 150 mg. Zinc supplementation creates a demand in the body for copper. To help keep these minerals in balance, approximately 1 mg. of copper should be taken for every 10 mg. of zinc.

CHAPTER THREE

OTHER SUPPLEMENTS

EPA
Fiber
L-arginine with L-lysine
L-carnitine
L-cysteine
Water

Ep

FORMS
Eicosapentaenoic acid,
MaxEPA, Super EPA,
omega-3 fatty acids.

DIETARY SOURCES
Cold-water fish, salmon, cod, tuna,
catfish, mackerel, trout, shrimp.

RECOMMENDED INTAKE
1,000 to 2,000 mg. of marine-lipid concentrate as
MaxEPA or Super EPA daily for individuals
who are at risk of heart disease.

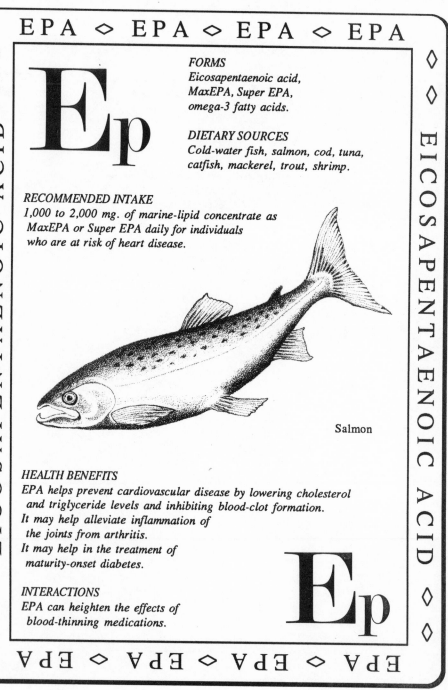

Salmon

HEALTH BENEFITS
EPA helps prevent cardiovascular disease by lowering cholesterol
and triglyceride levels and inhibiting blood-clot formation.
It may help alleviate inflammation of
the joints from arthritis.
It may help in the treatment of
maturity-onset diabetes.

INTERACTIONS
EPA can heighten the effects of
blood-thinning medications.

Ep

EICOSAPENTAENOIC ACID

EPA

Eicosapentaenoic acid, commonly known as EPA, is a fatty acid found in cold-water fish that eat EPA-producing plankton. In humans, it seems to affect the production and function of the prostaglandins, hormonelike substances that regulate many of the body's processes, including blood clotting. Just how it affects the prostaglandins is still not understood, but EPA has been shown to lower cholesterol levels, decrease blood triglyceride levels, and help inhibit the formation of blood clots that could block a plaque-lined, partially-clogged artery. As a result, EPA has been hailed as an important contributor to decreasing the risk and preventing the development of cardiovascular diseases. EPA is also under investigation for possible relief of migraines, as well as anti-inflammatory effects that may prove to be useful someday in the treatment of certain forms of arthritis. Furthermore, new findings indicate that EPA may be effective in treating maturity-onset diabetes by improving the cellular sensitivity to insulin.

EPA, also called an omega-3 fatty acid, first came to the attention of medical researchers when they found that the Eskimo and similar groups of people had low levels of cholesterol in their blood and a low incidence of cardiovascular disease despite low-carbohydrate, low-fiber diets that centered around high-cholesterol fatty fish and high-fat seal and whale meat. The mystery deepened after other researchers, trying to establish ties between dietary cholesterol intake and increased blood cholesterol levels, fed subjects large quantities of shrimp, a food very high in cholesterol. Instead of the expected rise in blood cholesterol levels, the researchers found that the levels were either unchanged or, surprisingly, even lower than they had been at the beginning of the study. This data, coupled with the results of several studies linking diets high in fish with dramatically lower incidences of heart disease, led to the isolation of EPA as one of the primary factors that made the difference.

EPA is not produced by the human body. As a dietary supplement, EPA is available in many health food stores and certain pharmacies. Two particularly good products are MaxEPA and Super EPA, marine-lipid concentrates that have been used in many of the EPA-cardiovascular research studies. These concentrates contain not only EPA but also other protective omega-3 fatty acids. MaxEPA and Super EPA are derived from fish flesh, not fish livers, so a daily intake of 1,000 mg. of either contains under 100 IU of vitamin A and under 10 IU of vitamin D, well below levels that could affect normal dosages of supplemental vitamins. Both are available as 500 or 1,000 mg. gelatin capsules and should be taken according to the instructions on the label. Those prone to bleeding problems or stroke should consult a nutrition specialist before beginning long-term supplemental EPA therapy.

Half of all Americans are believed to have high levels of cholesterol in their blood, primarily from dietary sources such as meats and other saturated fats, so making a switch to fish could be an important step in maintaining the health of the heart. Eating three to four servings of cold-water fish each week can help provide EPA's protective effects.

Fb

FORMS
Insoluble: wheat bran, miller's bran.
Soluble: oat bran, psyllium seeds.

DIETARY SOURCES
Insoluble: whole grains, brown rice,
bran cereals, berries, vegetables.
Soluble: oat bran cereal, dried beans
and peas, fruits.

RECOMMENDED INTAKE
25 to 50 g. of dietary fiber daily. For individuals with low dietary fiber
intake, 10 to 15 g. of supplemental fiber.
Those taking fiber supplements
should drink eight to ten
glasses of water
daily.

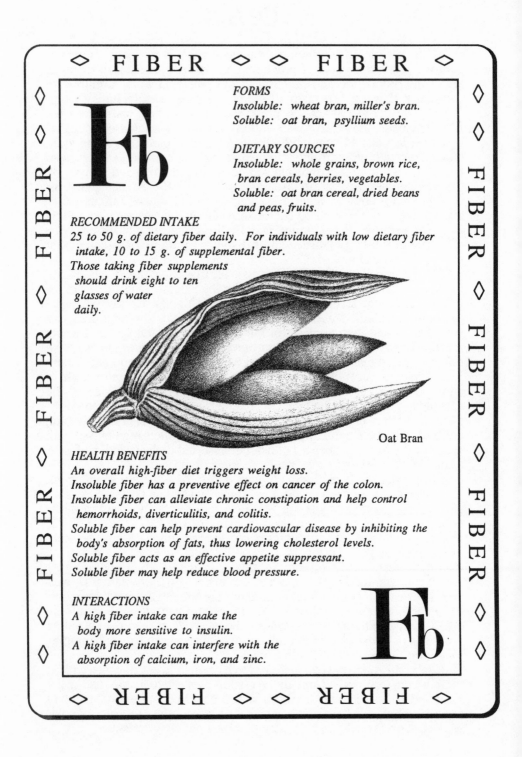

Oat Bran

HEALTH BENEFITS
An overall high-fiber diet triggers weight loss.
Insoluble fiber has a preventive effect on cancer of the colon.
Insoluble fiber can alleviate chronic constipation and help control
hemorrhoids, diverticulitis, and colitis.
Soluble fiber can help prevent cardiovascular disease by inhibiting the
body's absorption of fats, thus lowering cholesterol levels.
Soluble fiber acts as an effective appetite suppressant.
Soluble fiber may help reduce blood pressure.

INTERACTIONS
A high fiber intake can make the
body more sensitive to insulin.
A high fiber intake can interfere with the
absorption of calcium, iron, and zinc.

Fb

FIBER

Fiber is the name given to the parts of fruit, vegetables, grains, or other plant foods that cannot be digested by the human gastrointestinal system. There are two basic types of fiber — insoluble and soluble — and most fiber-containing foods offer a combination of the two. Insoluble fiber consists of two basic components: cellulose, the structural material of plant cell walls; and lignin, the woody parts of plants. Soluble fiber includes the gums extracted from tropical plants, pectins from fruits and vegetables, and algae derivatives. Fiber is neither a nutrient nor a dietary essential, and until the 1970s, food was processed to remove its fiber. Current research results indicate, however, that fiber plays a major role in maintaining the overall health and condition of the digestive system and may significantly affect the health of the rest of the body.

Insoluble fiber, which is found in the skins of fruits and vegetables, and in wheat bran, whole wheat, and almost all other cereal (except oat) products, tends to absorb and hold water like a sponge and act as a bulk laxative, speeding the passage of food through the intestine. As a result, insoluble fiber has become a standard substance for the prevention and treatment of chronic constipation and diverticulosis and may help prevent appendicitis in children. Evidence from recent epidemiological studies also suggests that insoluble fiber may contribute to the prevention of certain types of cancer, particularly of the colon, either by absorbing and diluting toxic, carcinogenic elements or by speeding their excretion from the body.

Soluble fiber — sources include oat bran, agar, fruit pulp, dried legumes, and psyllium seeds — is an excellent addition to many weight-control programs. When supplemental soluble fiber is taken on an empty stomach, it swells and triggers a sense of fullness. At the same time, it slows down the rate at which the stomach empties, delaying the feeling of hunger. Recent research indicates that soluble fiber reduces overall cholesterol levels in the blood. It also increases the amount of cardio-vascular-protective, high density lipoproteins (HDLs) as it decreases the dangerous, low density lipoproteins (LDLs). This occurs because soluble fiber coats the intestines and inhibits the absorption of fats. Soluble fiber also seems to reduce the need for insulin in some cases of diabetes and may help lower blood pressure in hypertensive patients.

The average diet has approximately 7 to 15 g. of fiber, an inadequate amount. This low intake has been associated with the increased incidence of digestive system problems, cancers of the colon and rectum, varicose veins, hemorrhoids, and certain cardiovascular problems. While there is no established U.S. RDA for fiber, estimates are that a daily intake of 25 to 50 g., which includes both soluble and insoluble fiber, will provide many beneficial effects. Fiber supplements for those with a low dietary fiber intake are available in capsule or powder form. Fiber intake above 25 g. may bind certain vital minerals, particularly calcium, iron, and zinc, reducing their absorption by the body. Deficiencies can be prevented by taking a daily multiple-vitamin/mineral supplement. Diabetics should consult a nutrition specialist before embarking on a high-fiber diet.

L l

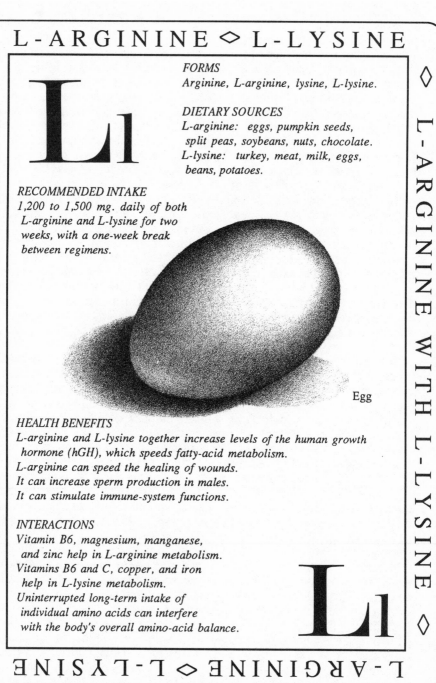

Egg

FORMS
Arginine, L-arginine, lysine, L-lysine.

DIETARY SOURCES
L-arginine: eggs, pumpkin seeds, split peas, soybeans, nuts, chocolate.
L-lysine: turkey, meat, milk, eggs, beans, potatoes.

RECOMMENDED INTAKE
1,200 to 1,500 mg. daily of both L-arginine and L-lysine for two weeks, with a one-week break between regimens.

HEALTH BENEFITS
L-arginine and L-lysine together increase levels of the human growth hormone (hGH), which speeds fatty-acid metabolism.
L-arginine can speed the healing of wounds.
It can increase sperm production in males.
It can stimulate immune-system functions.

INTERACTIONS
Vitamin B6, magnesium, manganese, and zinc help in L-arginine metabolism.
Vitamins B6 and C, copper, and iron help in L-lysine metabolism.
Uninterrupted long-term intake of individual amino acids can interfere with the body's overall amino-acid balance.

L l

L-ARGININE WITH L-LYSINE

L-arginine and L-lysine are two amino acids that work in combination to produce some dynamic results. Research studies on animals and preliminary findings on humans indicate that taking supplemental L-arginine with L-lysine, in equal amounts, increases the blood levels of hGH, the human growth hormone. Because of this function, these amino acids are being investigated for use in speeding the healing of wounds and stimulating immune-system functions. While L-arginine has been cited as the active factor for triggering the increase of hGH levels, very large doses of it are necessary to produce this effect. Taking L-arginine along with L-lysine, however, produces the same effect but requires substantially smaller amounts of each.

The human growth hormone helps maintain nitrogen balances in the body. It signals cells to conserve protein needed to rebuild damaged tissue and promote the growth of new tissue. It also accelerates the rate at which the body's fat tissues release their fatty acids into the bloodstream, meaning that it can speed up the body's fat-burning rate. Because of this, supplements such as L-arginine with L-lysine may help trim body fat and enhance weight-loss programs.

L-arginine's and L-lysine's respective roles in nurturing and inhibiting the herpes simplex virus have caused considerable controversy. The studies cited as proof of such activities, however, have been found to be very weak in both their data gathering and their data interpretation. Many of the subjects did not have their herpes infections, or remissions, confirmed by lab tissue cultures. In fact, more recent and more stringent studies, particularly on the suppression of the herpes virus by supplemental L-lysine, have not shown any effects on herpes at daily doses of 1,000 mg. of either amino acid.

L-arginine is a semiessential amino acid, and almost all adults can synthesize the amounts they need. L-lysine, on the other hand, is absolutely essential, not produced by the human body, and must be derived from dietary or other supplemental sources. L-arginine, combined with L-lysine, is available in capsule form at health food stores and some pharmacies. These amino acids should be taken together, in equal amounts, to be most effective. Dosages in the range of 1,200 to 1,500 mg. for each amino acid may be taken on a daily basis for up to two weeks. Generally, amino-acid supplements should only be taken for limited periods of time, as they can affect the body's overall amino-acid balances. Children and teenagers, whose bodies are still growing, and diabetics, who have glucose-tolerance problems, should not take supplemental amino acids, especially those that affect hGH levels, unless supervised by a physician. While toxicity levels for L-arginine and L-lysine have not been determined, extended daily doses above 3,000 mg. have been reported to cause nausea and diarrhea.

Lc

FORMS
*Carnitine, D-carnitine,
DL-carnitine, L-carnitine.*

DIETARY SOURCES
*Tempeh (fermented soybean),
beef, lamb, avocados.*

RECOMMENDED INTAKE
*500 to 1,000 mg. daily of carnitine in the L-carnitine form only.
Individuals taking L-carnitine for heart disease, weight loss,
 or aerobic endurance should also take a daily
 multiple-vitamin/mineral supplement.*

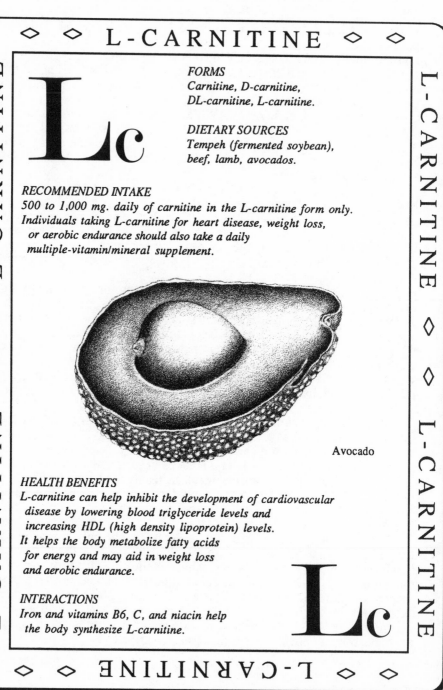

Avocado

HEALTH BENEFITS
*L-carnitine can help inhibit the development of cardiovascular
 disease by lowering blood triglyceride levels and
 increasing HDL (high density lipoprotein) levels.
 It helps the body metabolize fatty acids
 for energy and may aid in weight loss
 and aerobic endurance.*

INTERACTIONS
*Iron and vitamins B6, C, and niacin help
 the body synthesize L-carnitine.*

Lc

L-CARNITINE

L-carnitine is a substance that has been recognized only very recently as essential to human health. Vital to the production of energy for the heart and other muscles, L-carnitine transports fatty acids — fuel that is burned to provide muscles with energy for work — into the part of the cell that acts as a chemical laboratory for this burning process. Because of L-carnitine's function in the human metabolic system, it is becoming a promising nutrient in the treatment of cardiovascular disease. Recent studies have determined that when L-carnitine is taken by individuals with elevated blood fat levels, it reduces triglyceride levels while raising the high density lipoprotein (HDL) level. Triglycerides are among those blood fats that contribute to the continuing development of cardiovascular disease, while HDLs act to help protect the arteries from the dangerous buildup of plaque.

Since L-carnitine is instrumental to fatty-acid metabolism, it may be an important adjunct to weight-loss programs. The body's increased metabolism of fatty acids triggers reactions that provide energy to the brain, muscles, and other tissues, helping to quell the feelings of hunger and muscle weakness that often accompany reduced-calorie diets. L-carnitine has also been cited as an aid to muscle building. Research results so far, however, indicate that this seems to happen only when the body has already experienced muscular problems directly due to a deficiency in L-carnitine. L-carnitine may, however, be useful in prolonging aerobic endurance during exercise.

L-carnitine is manufactured by the body and is stored in the skeletal muscles. This store must be increased over a period of several weeks to achieve any beneficial effects from supplemental carnitine. Deficiencies in L-carnitine are not believed to be common. They can be due to genetic circumstances that prevent its absorption or synthesis, or they can result from long-term inadequate dietary intake of L-carnitine or of the nutrients needed to form it. People most likely to develop a deficiency in L-carnitine are patients with liver failure or undergoing frequent kidney dialysis. Newborn infants, vegans, and pregnant women or those who are breast-feeding are also vulnerable. Deficiency symptoms include irregular heartbeat, angina, general muscle weakness, and a feeling of confusion.

Carnitine actually exists in two natural forms — L-carnitine and D-carnitine — but D-carnitine is not biologically active in humans. A synthetic form, DL-carnitine, has been available for some time, but it is not as effective as the L-carnitine form and has been shown to produce certain neuromuscular disorders in people who have taken it for extended periods of time. The safe form, L-carnitine, is available in health food stores and pharmacies. Dosages in the range of 500 to 1,000 mg. seem to protect against deficiency and provide many health benefits. Although daily doses as high as 1,600 mg. taken for over a year have not produced symptoms of toxicity, individuals considering supplemental L-carnitine in very high dosages should first consult with a nutrition specialist.

Ly

FORMS
Cysteine,
L-cysteine.

DIETARY SOURCES
Cereal, egg yolks,
meat, milk.

RECOMMENDED INTAKE
1,000 mg. daily for one week with a one-week
  break between regimens.
Take daily during travel, visits to polluted environments,
  or exposure to industrial areas.
Take L-cysteine with vitamin C in a ratio
  of one part L-cysteine to
  three parts vitamin C.

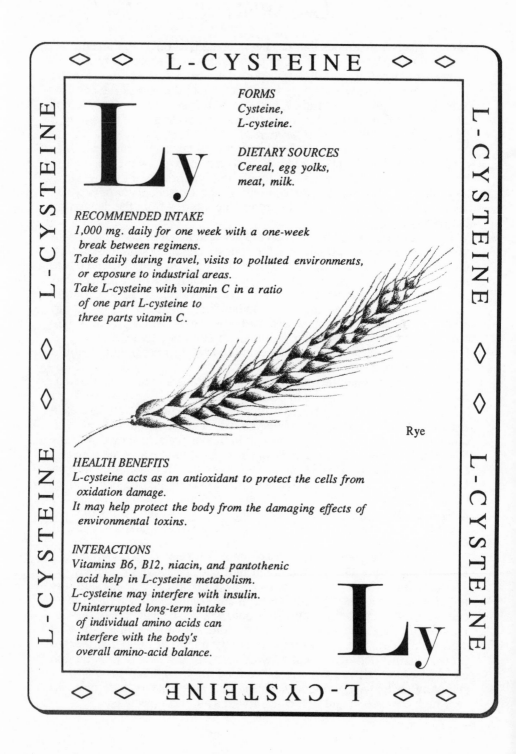

Rye

HEALTH BENEFITS
L-cysteine acts as an antioxidant to protect the cells from
  oxidation damage.
It may help protect the body from the damaging effects of
  environmental toxins.

INTERACTIONS
Vitamins B6, B12, niacin, and pantothenic
  acid help in L-cysteine metabolism.
L-cysteine may interfere with insulin.
Uninterrupted long-term intake
  of individual amino acids can
  interfere with the body's
  overall amino-acid balance.

Ly

L-CYSTEINE

L-cysteine is one of the amino acids considered nonessential for humans. This does not mean that humans can function without it, but that the human body is able to synthesize L-cysteine from other substances. Recently, supplemental L-cysteine has had many health benefits ascribed to it, and a number of these benefits appear to be supported by preliminary research. The two most important, reasonably substantiated claims are that L-cysteine acts as an antioxidant and that it is believed to protect the body from many of the effects of carcinogenic and toxic pollutants such as smog, cigarette smoke, and heavy metals.

The first claim, that L-cysteine acts as an antioxidant, is based on the fact that this amino acid contains sulfur. The particular form of sulfur in L-cysteine is believed to act as a scavenger for free radicals. It protects cells from them by disarming their dangerous oxidizing properties. As a result, L-cysteine is being investigated as both an anti-aging and an anticarcinogenic substance. Studies done on guinea pigs and mice found that injections of L-cysteine prolonged their lives. Animals fed diets deficient in both L-cysteine and methionine — the amino acid from which the body makes L-cysteine — generally had lower levels of specific enzymes believed to protect against certain carcinogens.

The second claim, that L-cysteine protects against toxic substances, is actually twofold. First, L-cysteine seems to offer dramatic protection from specific toxins called aldehydes, which are by-products of fats, air pollution, cigarettes, alcohol, and preservatives such as formaldehyde. Second, L-cysteine is one of the amino acids needed to form glutathione. Glutathione binds itself to many toxic metals and chemicals, rendering them harmless or, at least, reducing many of their harmful activities. As such, L-cysteine is being used experimentally to help fight many of the toxic effects of mercury and lead.

Deficiency in humans of L-cysteine is rare and usually due to a genetic malfunction or a deficiency in its precursor, methionine. At this time, the effect of such a deficiency on humans is not known; nor is there a profile that defines those people who might be deficient. Dietary sources of L-cysteine include grains, egg yolks, meat, and dairy products.

L-cysteine is available at most health food stores and at some pharmacies, usually in capsules of either 500 or 1,000 mg. Dosages in the range of 1,000 mg. appear to be effective in creating an antioxidant function. They may be taken on a daily basis for up to two weeks. Generally, amino-acid supplements should only be taken for limited periods of time, as they can affect the body's overall amino-acid balances. Those taking L-cysteine should also boost their vitamin C intake to three times the amount of L-cysteine. This will help prevent the conversion of L-cysteine into cystine, which has been implicated in the formation of certain types of kidney stones. L-cysteine users should take a multiple-vitamin/mineral supplement, as prolonged use could interfere with mineral absorption. Diabetics should consult with their physician before taking L-cysteine supplements.

H₂0

FORMS
*Bottled: distilled, mineral,
  purified, spring.
Ground: well, spring.
Reservoir: collected from streams.*

RECOMMENDED INTAKE
*Six to eight eight-ounce glasses daily of
  bottled water — distilled or purified.*

HEALTH BENEFITS
*A high water intake helps flush the body of toxins quickly,
  benefiting the liver, kidneys, and skin.
It can improve the appearance and
  condition of the skin.
It speeds digestion and elimination.
It helps increase physical stamina.*

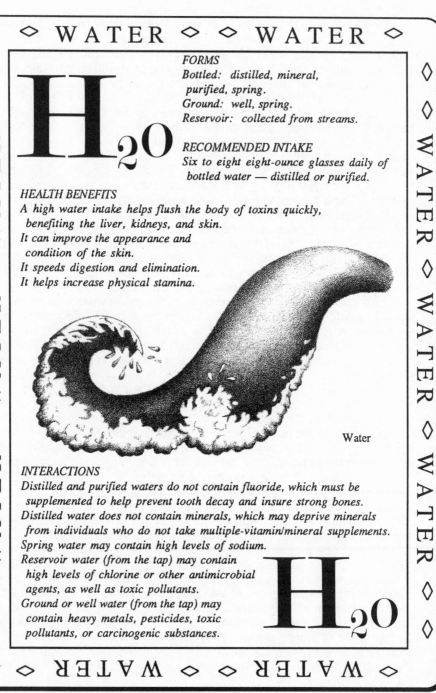

Water

INTERACTIONS
*Distilled and purified waters do not contain fluoride, which must be
  supplemented to help prevent tooth decay and insure strong bones.
Distilled water does not contain minerals, which may deprive minerals
  from individuals who do not take multiple-vitamin/mineral supplements.
Spring water may contain high levels of sodium.
Reservoir water (from the tap) may contain
  high levels of chlorine or other antimicrobial
  agents, as well as toxic pollutants.
Ground or well water (from the tap) may
  contain heavy metals, pesticides, toxic
  pollutants, or carcinogenic substances.*

H₂0

WATER

Water, after air, is the element most vital to human life; yet, it is perhaps the least discussed of the essential nutrients. The most abundant substance in the body, water accounts for over half the weight of the average adult and performs several basic functions. It provides an environment for cells to perform their metabolic functions, aiding them in their chemical reactions. It also gives body tissues their structure and form. Water acts as a carrier for nutrients, blood cells, respiratory gases, and wastes. Because of its remarkable ability to store and discharge heat, it helps maintain a stable body temperature despite widely varying climatic conditions. As the main component of blood plasma, muscles, and lymph, water lubricates the joints, cushions the body from impact, and maintains a balanced pressure in the eyes.

Overall water levels in the body are determined by thirst, which is triggered by control centers in the brain that monitor body fluid levels, and by hormones that control water retention and excretion processes, as well as the levels of minerals and electrolytes. Generally, there is about twice as much water inside the cells, where most metabolic processes take place, as there is surrounding them, a balance determined by the electrolytes sodium, potassium, and chloride. Changes in the relationship of the electrolytes, such as an increase in sodium from excessive salt intake or a loss of potassium from diarrhea, will change the fluid balance and can trigger conditions such as edema, muscle spasms, and cramps.

The average adult loses about five pints of water daily through urine, feces, perspiration, and breath, and must replenish this amount to avoid serious problems. Additional water is lost through sweat from physical exertion, dehydration due to alcohol or other drugs, vomiting or diarrhea from illness or stress, and external climatic conditions. Almost everyone has been deficient in water at some time, with symptoms that include acute thirst, muscle weakness, dizziness, and dry, flaky skin and scalp.

While food replaces a portion of the water lost, the best way to replenish it is to drink six to eight glasses of water every day. Confusion abounds as to what type of water is safest or best to drink. Tap water is usually from ground-water sources such as springs and wells, or from reservoirs that collect it from rain and streams. As such, tap water is subject to a number of contaminants, whether from natural sources, industrial wastes, pesticide runoff from agricultural areas, or additives such as chlorine used to fight microorganisms living in the water. While recent legislation has been passed to clean up and protect the nation's water supplies, the process is slow, so tap water or ground water should be avoided, generally. Bottled water is probably the safest for drinking, especially if its source is a spring that has been tested and certified for its purity. Purified (deionized) and distilled (evaporated and recondensed) water are relatively mineral-free, although their taste is somewhat flat. Bottled-water suppliers often add minerals back into these forms of water for flavor. The label on the bottle should provide information about how much of what was added. Many brands contain high levels of sodium, which may be undesirable.

CHAPTER FOUR

THE BOTANICALS

Angelica
Catnip
Cayenne
Comfrey
Garlic
Ginger
Ginseng
Goldenseal
Juniper Berries
Licorice
Olive Oil
Parsley
Peppermint
Valerian
White Willow
Yellow Dock
Yerba Mate

An

NAME
Angelica archangelica,
Angelica atropurpurea,
Angelica polymorpha,
Angelica sinensis,
dong quai, tang kuei.

PARTS USED
Root.

RECOMMENDED INTAKE
For treatment: Angelica may be used every day.

FUNCTIONS
Angelica is a smooth-muscle relaxant
and anti-inflammatory agent.
It can help regulate the
menstrual cycle.

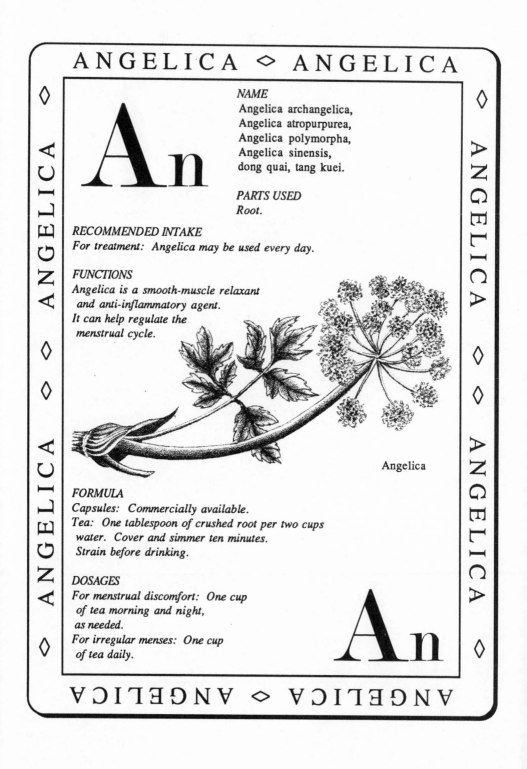

Angelica

FORMULA
Capsules: Commercially available.
Tea: One tablespoon of crushed root per two cups
water. Cover and simmer ten minutes.
Strain before drinking.

DOSAGES
For menstrual discomfort: One cup
of tea morning and night,
as needed.
For irregular menses: One cup
of tea daily.

An

ANGELICA

Angelica is an ancient herb surrounded by an aura of power, mystery, and controversy. European, or garden angelica, *Angelica archangelica*, is called herb of Trinity or herb of the Holy Ghost; also archangel and angelica. Many miraculous and supernatural properties are attributed to it. During the Middle Ages, it was believed to protect against contagious diseases, particularly the plague.

Today, the roots and fruits of angelica are used as flavorings in vermouth, certain gins, and liqueurs like Benedictine and Chartreuse, and as aromatics in perfumes and cosmetics. American angelica, *Angelica atropurpurea*, is often called dead nettle, purple angelica, or masterwort. While usually employed in the same manner as the European species, American angelica is less succulent and considered inferior in quality, strength, and flavor. Recently, another species of angelica has come into use in the United States from China under the names of *dong quai* or *tang kuei*. This species is *Angelica polymorpha*, often mislabeled as *Angelica sinensis*. It is considered an important medicinal plant for use by the Barefoot Doctors of China, the nationwide paramedic force that is the backbone of the Chinese public-health system.

European angelica is a purple, green, and white plant that is shaped like a giant celery. Its fleshy, fibrous root has brown bark and is white inside, yielding a thick, yellowish juice when cut. Its flowers are small, greenish white clusters that constantly attract insects. American angelica is similar in its celerylike shape, but is less colorful, with a purplish root and dark stem. The Chinese species of angelica, also purplish in color, looks more like parsley than celery, having thinner stems and more ragged leaves. Its root is brownish on the outside and spongy white inside. All three species are harvested in the late summer, and their roots are carefully washed, split, and dried for later use.

While the rest of the angelica plant is also used, the roots are the best parts for medicinal use. They contain oils that stimulate digestion, relieve intestinal gas, and destroy many kinds of bacteria. Herbalists, however, consider angelica first and foremost a woman's herb. It acts as a smooth-muscle relaxant and anti-inflammatory agent. Each of the three angelica species has been used for centuries to relieve menstrual cramps, to expel afterbirth, and, in extreme dosages, to induce abortion. Angelica tea is also used after an abortion or miscarriage to soothe and regulate the reproductive system. Because angelica can help regulate menses, it is believed to be one of the best fertility herbs for women with irregular periods.

All three species of angelica are available in health food stores, sometimes as whole dried plants, but usually as dried roots for tea or in capsule form. Capsules are the most convenient and commonly used form of angelica, but tea is equally effective. To make angelica tea, put one rounded tablespoon of the crushed dried root in a pot containing two cups of water. Cover the pot and simmer for ten minutes. Strain the tea before drinking it.

Ct

NAME
Nepeta cataria.

PARTS USED
Leaves.

RECOMMENDED INTAKE
For treatment: Catnip may be used every day.

FUNCTIONS
Catnip acts as a mild daytime sedative.
It relieves some of the symptoms of bronchitis and asthma.
It has antispasmodic properties that help relieve muscle cramps and spasms.
It can help relieve headaches.

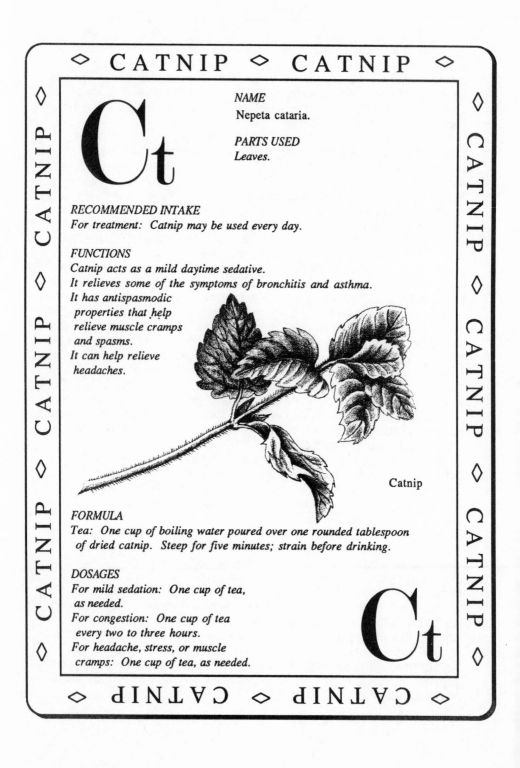

Catnip

FORMULA
Tea: One cup of boiling water poured over one rounded tablespoon of dried catnip. Steep for five minutes; strain before drinking.

DOSAGES
For mild sedation: One cup of tea, as needed.
For congestion: One cup of tea every two to three hours.
For headache, stress, or muscle cramps: One cup of tea, as needed.

Ct

CATNIP

Catnip is an herb that almost every cat loves to roll in and eat. It seems to get them high and turns them into silly, playful creatures. The effects are quite different in humans. With an abundance of health benefits ascribed to it, catnip is considered one of the most useful plants in the herbalist's apothecary.

Botanically, catnip is known as *Nepeta cataria* and belongs to the mint family. Other common names for it are nep, catmint, catswort, and field balm. It is native to the British Isles, northern Europe, Siberia, and western Asia, and was introduced to North America over a century ago. Catnip is an herb that is green in color, with a downy, grayish white surface. Its stems are woody. They grow to an average height of two to three feet and have oblong leaves with scalloped edges. From June to September, catnip sprouts spikes of white flowers with purple or crimson spots. It has a distinct, mintlike smell, fresh or dried, and a pungent, slightly bitter flavor.

Medicinally, catnip is an important and reliable herb. It is a traditional home remedy for nervous tension, anxiety, and insomnia. Catnip has antispasmodic properties that can help stop hiccoughs and ease muscle spasms and cramps, even those that happen during menstrual periods. As a tea, it is gentle and safe. In fact, many of the "nighttime" teas use catnip as their primary ingredient, although it is an excellent daytime tranquilizer. Catnip tea promotes sweating to break fevers, is a mild painkiller, and works wonders on the symptoms of colds and flu. It is helpful to people with indigestion and gas. Catnip is used extensively for diarrhea and the symptoms of chronic bronchitis. Traditionally, catnip plasters, made of a paste of powdered catnip and water, have been used to soothe burns, bee stings, hemorrhoids, poison ivy, and swellings.

Catnip is used either fresh or dried. It is easy to grow in a sunny window, requiring only a small pot and protection from cats. Dried, catnip is sold in almost all health food and pet stores, and in many grocery stores. When buying dried catnip, it is a good idea to crush a few leaves and smell them. If there is no smell, reject the catnip. It is too stale to be of any use. Dried catnip is also available in capsule form and sometimes in teabags.

To make catnip tea, use one rounded tablespoon of the dried herb for every cup of boiling water. Pour the boiling water over the catnip. Do not boil the catnip itself. This will destroy the therapeutic action of the herb. Steep for five minutes and strain the tea before drinking. In place of loose leaves, the dried catnip can be enclosed in a homemade teabag (page 22). Since catnip is a mild sedative, it is a good tea to drink in the evenings or any time a tranquilizing effect is desired.

Cn

NAME
Capsicum.

PARTS USED
Fruit (whole pepper).

RECOMMENDED INTAKE
For treatment: Cayenne may be used daily.
For prevention: Cayenne may be used every other day.

FUNCTIONS
Cayenne is a vasodilator that can help relieve headaches.
It can alleviate nausea and stomach gas.
It can help in the treatment of thromboembolism, or blood clots.
In lozenge form, it can relieve sore throat
and hoarseness.
Topically, it can help relieve the
symptoms of rheumatism
and arthritis.

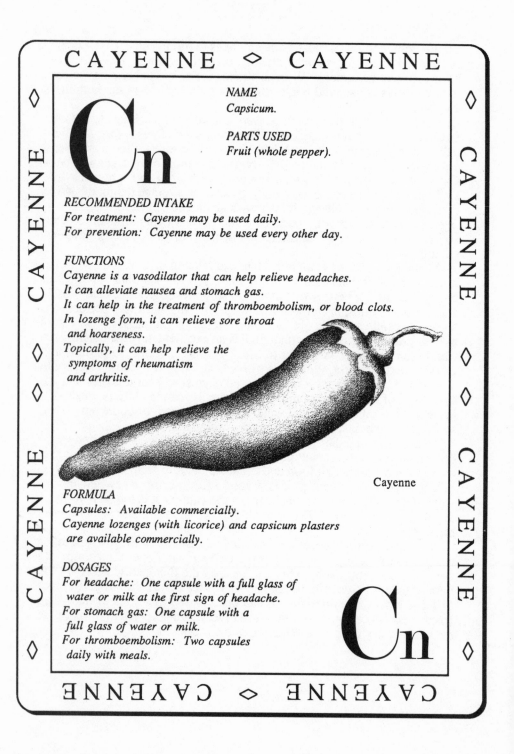

Cayenne

FORMULA
Capsules: Available commercially.
Cayenne lozenges (with licorice) and capsicum plasters
are available commercially.

DOSAGES
For headache: One capsule with a full glass of
water or milk at the first sign of headache.
For stomach gas: One capsule with a
full glass of water or milk.
For thromboembolism: Two capsules
daily with meals.

Cn

CAYENNE

Herbalists consider cayenne to be one of the purest and most dependable of the herbal stimulants. Known variously as capsicum, chili pepper, and red pepper, it is native to the Americas and tropical Asia. Cayenne is now cultivated on a worldwide basis and used extensively as a spicy condiment in preparing foods.

Cayenne is frequently called capsicum because this is the generic name used to cover a wide number of species of this plant. Along with the tomato, eggplant, potato, mandrake, and tobacco, capsicum is a member of the nightshade family. It grows as a small, spiky bush that is three to four feet high, with green, pointed, oval-shaped leaves. Capsicum produces white flowers that turn into two-to-five-inch long, conical, shiny, bright red or yellow fruit, referred to as peppers. The peppers are fleshy in texture and filled with air, dry pulp, and flat, kidney-shaped seeds that cling to the inner pulp. After ripening, the peppers are harvested in late summer, then dried and ground into powder for use. While the larger peppers are used primarily for cooking, the smaller, finger-sized ones are usually preferred for medicinal use.

Medicinally, cayenne is taken internally for indigestion and gas. It contains alkaloids that promote peristalsis and stimulate the secretion of gastric juices. It dispels nausea and acts as a stimulant, producing an overall feeling of well-being. It also acts as a vasodilator that can be useful in treating headaches. These qualities make cayenne an ideal remedy for many of the symptoms of a hangover. Cayenne is also used topically to ease joint stiffness from rheumatism and arthritis and to soothe sore, overworked muscles. It mildly irritates the surface of the skin, which increases the flow of blood through the affected area, removing built-up toxins and reducing inflammation. Many cultures have used cayenne powder to sterilize and speed the healing of wounds, with good results. In lozenge form, cayenne rapidly fights sore throats and hoarseness. It is often used by singers before a performance to clear their throats. Recent evidence indicates that cayenne, used therapeutically, may also counter the effects of thromboembolism, the development of dangerous blood clots in the cardiovascular system.

Cayenne is easy to purchase in grocery stores or health food stores, where it can be found in capsule form. For topical use, cayenne or capsicum plasters, called Back Plasters (Johnson & Johnson Products, Inc.), are available at most pharmacies. They are applied directly to the skin. Lozenges made of cayenne mixed with licorice, called Throat Discs (Marion Laboratories, Inc.) are also available in pharmacies. Not everyone can tolerate cayenne. Those who can, however, will gain health benefits from sprinkling it on their food at meals. Individuals who are taking anticoagulant medication should consult their physicians before using cayenne. It may affect their blood-clotting processes. Those using time-release medications should wait at least three hours before taking cayenne, as it may speed up the medication's release.

COMFREY ◇ COMFREY

COMFREY ◇ COMFREY ◇ COMFREY

COMFREY ◇ COMFREY ◇ COMFREY

Cy

NAME
Symphytum officinale.

PARTS USED
Root.

RECOMMENDED INTAKE
For treatment: Externally, comfrey may be used as needed. Internally, comfrey may be used for up to one week at a time, with a one-week break between regimens.

FUNCTIONS
Comfrey promotes the healing of sprains and broken bones.
It soothes and repairs mucous membranes.
Topically, it speeds the healing of wounds, burns, and sores.

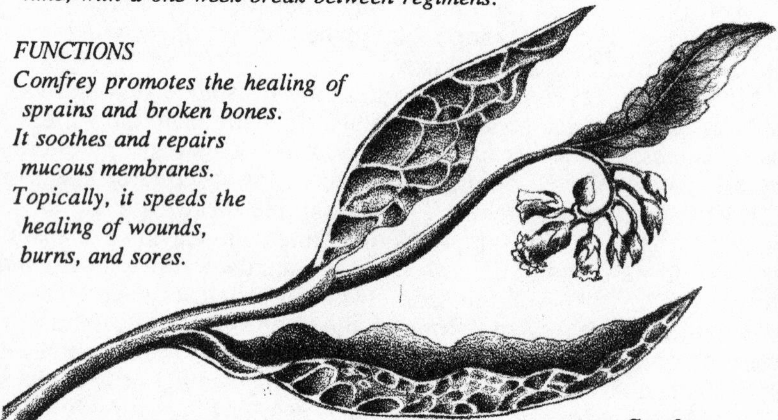

Comfrey

FORMULA
Capsules: Commercially available.
Plaster: Mix powdered comfrey root with warm water to make a paste.
Tea: One tablespoon of crushed root per two cups water. Cover and simmer ten minutes. Strain before drinking.

DOSAGES
For internal healing: One cup tea or one capsule, morning and night.
For sprains and bruises: Apply plaster, cover with bandage; change morning and night.
For burns, sores, and wounds: Apply paste; let dry to form scab. Do not bandage.

Cy

COMFREY ◇ COMFREY

COMFREY

Comfrey is a plant with many miraculous healing powers attributed to its roots and leaves. Its name is derived from the Latin *confervere*, meaning to heal or grow together. It has also been called bruisewort, healing herb, and knitbone, and is one of the most commonly used herbs in traditional European and American folk medicine.

Comfrey, *Symphytum officinale*, is a member of the borage family of plants. It is found in damp environments. Comfrey is native to Europe, western Siberia, and the British Isles. It grows to a height of three to four feet and has long, oval, deep green leaves covered with feltlike, sticky hairs. Comfrey sprouts mauve white clusters of bell-shaped flowers. Its root is bulbous, or beet-shaped, with a dark brown, almost black outer layer and a cream-colored interior. While young leaves of comfrey have been eaten as a substitute for spinach, it should not be consumed every day or for prolonged periods of time. Comfrey is often confused in the wild with foxglove, *Digitalis purpurea*, because of its similar appearance, a mistake that can have serious, even fatal, ramifications.

Comfrey root has been used to soothe the lining of the digestive tract and as a remedy for diarrhea. It is considered a good anti-inflammatory substance, and is most commonly used as a plaster applied to sprains. Comfrey root has been relied on to stop internal hemorrhaging, particularly uterine hemorrhaging, and actually seems to help broken bones heal faster; hence its folk name, knitbone. This last effect may be due to the presence, in both its root and its leaves, of a remarkable substance called allantoin, which has been shown to trigger the new growth of tissue in a short period of time. The allantoin in comfrey makes it useful as a topical substance that rapidly heals open sores, ulcers, burns, and wounds. Comfrey speeds the drainage and drying of abscesses and boils. It can work wonders as an astringent on skin eruptions from acne and eczema and, when added to bath water, is believed to help stimulate the growth of new skin. Like many medicinal plants, comfrey leaves and roots contain certain alkaloids that are considered toxic when ingested in large amounts over an extended period of time. The short-term use of comfrey root, however, is highly effective for treating quite a number of disorders.

Comfrey root and comfrey leaves are available in many health food stores, either fresh or dried, loose or in capsules. Dried comfrey root, which has a slightly sweet taste and no distinct odor, is the preferred form for teas and plasters. To make comfrey tea, put one rounded tablespoon of the crushed root into a pot containing two cups of water. Cover the pot and simmer for ten minutes. Comfrey tea is not one of the better-tasting of the herbal teas, but sweetened with honey, or steeped with a little peppermint, it is not unpleasant. To speed the healing of injuries, make a comfrey plaster by mixing powdered comfrey root with a small amount of warm water to form a paste. Apply it to the affected area.

G

NAME
Allium sativum.

PARTS USED
Bulb.

RECOMMENDED INTAKE
For treatment or prevention: Garlic may be used every day.

FUNCTIONS
Garlic has a positive effect on the immune system.
It lowers blood triglyceride and low density lipoprotein (LDL) levels
  while raising high density lipoprotein (HDL) levels, thus aiding
 in the prevention of cardiovascular disease.
It may help reduce blood pressure.
It may help fight tumor growth.

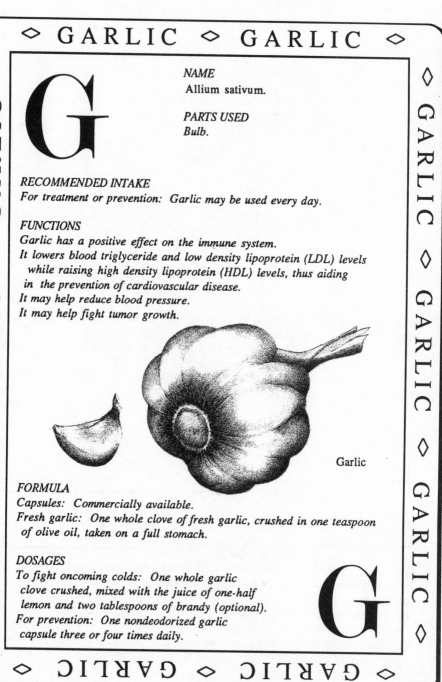

Garlic

FORMULA
Capsules: Commercially available.
Fresh garlic: One whole clove of fresh garlic, crushed in one teaspoon
of olive oil, taken on a full stomach.

DOSAGES
To fight oncoming colds: One whole garlic
 clove crushed, mixed with the juice of one-half
 lemon and two tablespoons of brandy (optional).
For prevention: One nondeodorized garlic
 capsule three or four times daily.

G

GARLIC

Garlic has been a principal food, flavoring, and medicinal botanical for thousands of years. It was used for myriad ailments by the ancient Chinese, Egyptians, Romans, Greeks, and Babylonians, and it is one of the important plants mentioned in the Bible. Referred to variously as the "herb of the common man" and the "stinking rose," garlic has a pungent flavor and such an unmistakably strong smell that it has been used to ward off vampires and other ardent, but undesirable, suitors.

Garlic, known botanically as *Allium sativum*, is a member of the onion family. Native to central Asia, it is now cultivated worldwide. Most of the garlic in the United States is grown in California. As a plant, garlic grows to a height of three to four feet, with purplish white flowers. After the plant has withered, the elongated parent root is dug up and the small bulblets, called heads or cloves, are cut off and stored for use. These heads are high in sulfur, potassium, and vitamins A, C, and niacin (as nicotinic acid). Garlic has active ingredients that perform antiseptic, antibacterial, and antifungal functions.

Medicinally, garlic has been shown to significantly lower levels of low density lipoproteins (LDLs), triglycerides, and serum cholesterol — all elements associated with heart disease — while increasing high density lipoproteins (HDLs), which are protective against heart disease. In this way, garlic helps protect against plaque deposits that cause narrowing of the arteries (atherosclerosis). Recent research indicates that garlic may help fight tumors. The National Cancer Institute has begun a series of studies to determine garlic's effects on preventing and treating certain types of cancer. Garlic can be used to kill many types of intestinal worms and is an excellent natural insecticide. It is believed to stimulate the immune system. It has been used effectively to fight colds, and it increases the body's resistance to infection. Garlic powder, in fact, was the penicillin of World War I.

Fresh cloves of garlic are available in most grocery and health food stores. Many health food stores also carry capsules of garlic oil. Fresh garlic, the best available form, can be chopped finely and spread on toast or mixed in many foods. People with sensitive stomachs will probably prefer the capsule form. While "deodorized" garlic oil is available, it may be less effective, since the elements that give garlic its distinctive smell are believed to be the precise elements needed for its medicinal effectiveness. Garlic is fairly nontoxic, and its odor can be removed from the hands by rubbing them with common table salt.

Herbalists consider garlic a natural antibiotic. Fresh garlic can be used to ward off a cold by crushing one clove in a teaspoon of olive oil, or by crushing one clove into a small glass and adding lemon juice, brandy, and the courage to swallow it. Neither of these remedies should be taken on an empty stomach. For cardiovascular or immunity conditioning, commercially available garlic capsules, containing approximately 1 mg. of nondeodorized garlic oil, should be used.

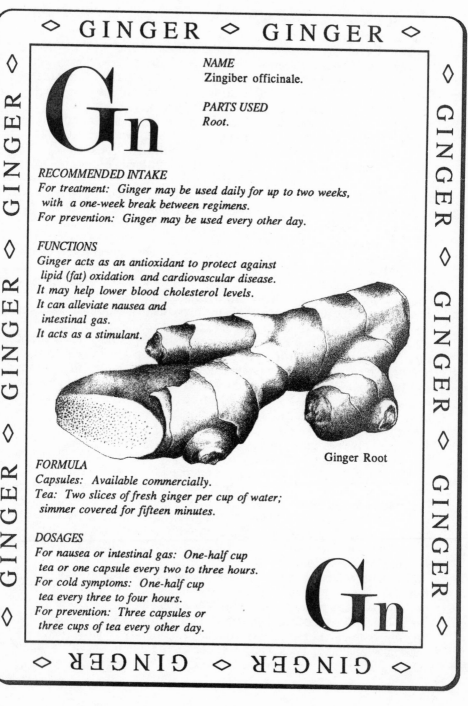

Gn

NAME
Zingiber officinale.

PARTS USED
Root.

RECOMMENDED INTAKE
For treatment: Ginger may be used daily for up to two weeks,
with a one-week break between regimens.
For prevention: Ginger may be used every other day.

FUNCTIONS
Ginger acts as an antioxidant to protect against
lipid (fat) oxidation and cardiovascular disease.
It may help lower blood cholesterol levels.
It can alleviate nausea and
intestinal gas.
It acts as a stimulant.

Ginger Root

FORMULA
Capsules: Available commercially.
Tea: Two slices of fresh ginger per cup of water;
simmer covered for fifteen minutes.

DOSAGES
For nausea or intestinal gas: One-half cup
tea or one capsule every two to three hours.
For cold symptoms: One-half cup
tea every three to four hours.
For prevention: Three capsules or
three cups of tea every other day.

Gn

GINGER

Ginger is an aromatic plant that lends its flowers' exotic scent to perfumes and its roots' spicy flavor to gingerbread and ginger ale. It was cultivated in India and China many centuries before Marco Polo described its uses in his travel diaries, firing the imaginations of Europeans eager to explore new lands, new medicines, and new tastes. The ginger plant was so easy to transport and propagate that it became one of the major commodities in the spice trade of the fourteenth and fifteenth centuries.

The ginger described by Marco Polo, and the one used commonly today, is the species *Zingiber officinale*. It is a three-to-four-foot-high tropical tuber with a bright green stem, narrow leaves shaped like the tip of a lance, and a torch-shaped, green stalk with purple-specked, light yellow flowers. After at least one year of growth, the plant is harvested for its light brown gray root, which is either used fresh or dried.

Medicinally, ginger is wonderful for colds or flu. It produces a feeling of warmth and alertness by stimulating the cardiovascular system. Furthermore, it encourages tense muscles to relax and clogged sinuses to drain. It also helps trigger the secretion of gastric juices in order to speed digestion, soothe an upset stomach, or dispel discomforting intestinal gas. Ginger has been used as a preservative for centuries. Recent studies indicate that ginger acts as an antioxidant, retarding fat spoilage, or lipid oxidation, in meats. Oxidized lipids are believed to increase the risk of developing heart disease in humans. This finding, coupled with evidence that ginger lowers cholesterol levels in rats, has focused attention on the use of ginger in preventing heart disease. There is some speculation that the frequent use of ginger in the Japanese diet may be a contributing factor to the relatively low levels of heart disease present there.

Dried ginger slices, powdered ginger (in bulk and in gelatin capsules), and fresh ginger root can all be found in most health food stores. Some stores will carry "wild" or "native" ginger. This is not *Zingiber officinale* but is similar in its effects. Grocery stores carry ginger powder in their spice sections. Many also carry fresh ginger root in their produce departments. Fresh ginger, whether refrigerated or not, will keep for many weeks. It can be stored for months on end in the refrigerator if kept in a tightly-sealed glass jar filled with sherry. Surprisingly, the sherry does not affect the taste or smell of the ginger root.

Ginger makes an excellent and tasty beverage, but since it acts as a stimulant, the tea or capsules should not be taken before bedtime. To use fresh ginger, bring a small pot of water to boil and add two slices of ginger for each cup of water. Cover the pot and simmer for fifteen minutes. Drink the ginger tea one-half cup at a time. Powdered ginger is just as effective as fresh ginger and can be purchased in capsule form. To discover ginger's remarkable effects as a stimulant, nibble on a slice of crystallized ginger, a delicacy found in most grocery store spice racks.

Gs

NAME
Panax ginseng,
Panax quinquefolius,
Panax schinseng,
Eleutherococcus senticosus.

PARTS USED
Root.

RECOMMENDED INTAKE
For treatment or prevention: Ginseng may be used every day.
Ginseng should not be taken before bedtime.

FUNCTIONS
Ginseng lowers blood triglyceride and cholesterol levels and increases
  heart-protecetive HDL (high density lipoprotein) levels.
It can help overcome fatigue.
It may help lower blood pressure.
It may help stimulate the immune system.
It may help promote cellular regeneration.

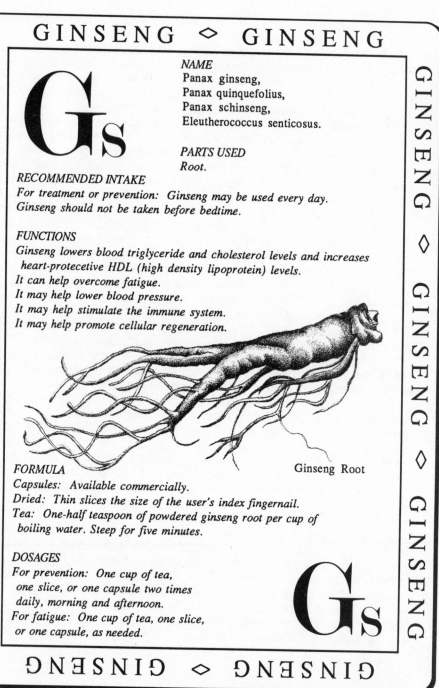

Ginseng Root

FORMULA
Capsules: Available commercially.
Dried: Thin slices the size of the user's index fingernail.
Tea: One-half teaspoon of powdered ginseng root per cup of
  boiling water. Steep for five minutes.

DOSAGES
For prevention: One cup of tea,
  one slice, or one capsule two times
  daily, morning and afternoon.
For fatigue: One cup of tea, one slice,
  or one capsule, as needed.

Gs

GINSENG

Ginseng means "manroot" in Chinese. It is the common name for two related plants that have roots bearing a resemblance to the human form. The first of these, *Panax schinseng* (often listed as *Panax ginseng*), commonly called Chinese, Korean, or white ginseng, is native to Asia, somewhat scarce, and, at several hundred dollars a pound, remarkably expensive. The second plant, *Panax quinquefolius*, known as American ginseng or brown ginseng, grows wild and is cultivated in Canada and the northern parts of the United States. Both plants have common medicinal properties and a sweet, mildly aromatic taste. Recently, a third type of ginseng, *Eleutherococcus senticosus*, has appeared in health food stores. Known as Siberian ginseng, it was one of the first herbs to go into outer space. In fact, Siberian ginseng is required for all Soviet Cosmonauts. Soviet and other research indicates that it may be protective against the effects of exposure to radiation such as X-rays.

Ginseng has had magical and supernatural properties ascribed to it for thousands of years. As it turns out, several of these properties have been scientifically validated by recent research. Considered an adaptogen, a substance that normalizes a wide range of physical and biochemical processes, ginseng seems to lower blood pressure in hypertensive animals, while raising it in hypotensive ones. In both animal and human studies published within the past two years, ginseng reduced blood triglyceride and total cholesterol levels and increased heart-protective high density lipoprotein (HDL) levels enough to change the risk category for cardiovascular disease from a high level to zero. Ginseng counteracts the effects of alcohol and depressants on the body. It appears to affect the functions of the brain and central nervous system, regulating certain neurotransmitters and fighting the effects of depression and fatigue. Animal studies indicate that ginseng may also stimulate the immune system, increasing resistance to infection, certain toxic chemicals, and even some forms of cancer. Traditionally, ginseng has been held to promote longevity and rejuvenation. While this may seem farfetched, there is new evidence, published in 1985, that ginseng can trigger the synthesis of DNA, RNA, and proteins, slow the breakdown of proteins already present, and stimulate the bone marrow to produce new blood cells.

All three varieties of ginseng root can be found in health food stores and Chinese apothecaries. "Red" ginseng is ordinary ginseng that has been steam treated. The roots come as powder, capsules, extracts, and elixirs. To make ginseng tea from powdered root, add one-half teaspoon of powder to a cup of boiling water. Allow the tea to steep five minutes and strain it before drinking. To make tea from the whole root, break it into pieces and add one-half teaspoon per cup to a pot of water. Cover the pot and simmer for twenty minutes. A simple way to take ginseng is to nibble a slice of the dried root that is about the size of the index fingernail (where it is attached to the finger). Since ginseng is a stimulant, it is best to take it early in the day. Pregnant women should not use ginseng as it contains strong alkaloids that may affect fetal health.

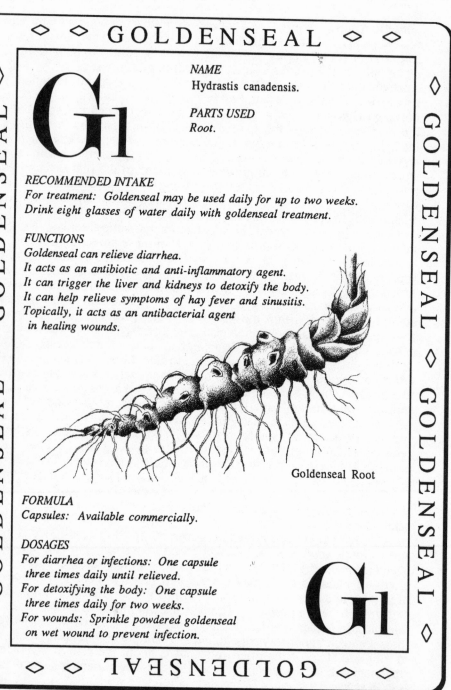

G1

NAME
Hydrastis canadensis.

PARTS USED
Root.

RECOMMENDED INTAKE
For treatment: Goldenseal may be used daily for up to two weeks.
Drink eight glasses of water daily with goldenseal treatment.

FUNCTIONS
Goldenseal can relieve diarrhea.
It acts as an antibiotic and anti-inflammatory agent.
It can trigger the liver and kidneys to detoxify the body.
It can help relieve symptoms of hay fever and sinusitis.
Topically, it acts as an antibacterial agent
in healing wounds.

Goldenseal Root

FORMULA
Capsules: Available commercially.

DOSAGES
For diarrhea or infections: One capsule
three times daily until relieved.
For detoxifying the body: One capsule
three times daily for two weeks.
For wounds: Sprinkle powdered goldenseal
on wet wound to prevent infection.

G1

GOLDENSEAL

Goldenseal has been used by Native Americans for centuries. It was one of the plants collected and used by Lewis and Clark on their explorations in search of a Northwest Passage. The Cherokee used goldenseal as a yellow dye for wool and a clear, green dye for cotton. It was one of their favorite medicinal plants. In the nineteenth century, goldenseal was used to treat malaria in place of quinine, as it did not trigger the violent side effects associated with concentrated quinine.

Goldenseal, *Hydrastis canadensis*, belongs to the buttercup family. Often called yellow root, jaundice root, or hydrastis, goldenseal was once plentiful in the woods of North America. Now it is rare in the wild. Its domestic cultivation is not easy, so it tends to be expensive. Goldenseal is a small plant, usually under a foot high, with two large, hand-shaped green leaves. When the plant is at least three years old, it is harvested for its small, thick, knotted root, which is gray brown on the outside and greenish yellow inside. The root is washed, dried, and later ground into a powder. It has a very bitter taste and a fairly disagreeable odor. It also produces a yellow saliva when chewed.

Goldenseal is considered a powerful, nonirritating antiseptic. It can be used topically to prevent infections in sores and for the relief of many skin problems. It is excellent for soothing inflamed tissues. One of its alkaloids, hydrastine, is used regularly in over-the-counter eyedrop preparations. Used internally, goldenseal stimulates the lymphatic system and fights bacterial infections. It is also an anti-inflammatory substance and has a strong astringent effect on mucous membranes, making it an easy, fast remedy for diarrhea. Goldenseal has been used to counter heavy menstrual periods. It used to be recommended, in small doses, for relief of morning sickness accompanying pregnancy. It should, however, be avoided by pregnant women, since it stimulates uterine muscles and, in large doses, it could cause miscarriage. Goldenseal acts as a mild stimulant for the liver and kidneys, helping them filter out and excrete toxins. It can be beneficial to people recovering from the effects of alcohol or opiates. Chemically, goldenseal's alkaloids are similar to codeine and morphine and may help relieve some of the discomfort of detoxification.

Goldenseal is available in most health food stores as dried slices, ground powder, capsules, and tea. The best way to avoid its bitter flavor is to take it in capsule form. Powdered goldenseal is handy to have around for topical first aid. Goldenseal should not be used for prevention. It should be taken only for specific reasons, such as to stop diarrhea, to overcome infections, or to help detoxify the body. It is used only for short periods of time — up to two weeks — as its alkaloids are excreted very slowly by the body. Those using codeine, morphine, or any of the opiate analogs should wait at least three hours after taking their medication before taking goldenseal, since it accelerates the narcotic effects.

J

NAME
Juniperus communis.

PARTS USED
Fruit (berries).

RECOMMENDED INTAKE
*For treatment: Juniper berries may be used as needed, but dependency
 on diuretics should be avoided.*
Drink eight glasses of water daily with juniper berry treatment.

FUNCTIONS
Juniper berries act as a diuretic.
*They can help in the treatment of
 bladder infections.*
*They can help manage high blood
 pressure by relieving edema.*
*They may help alleviate
 the symptoms of
 rheumatism and
 arthritis.*

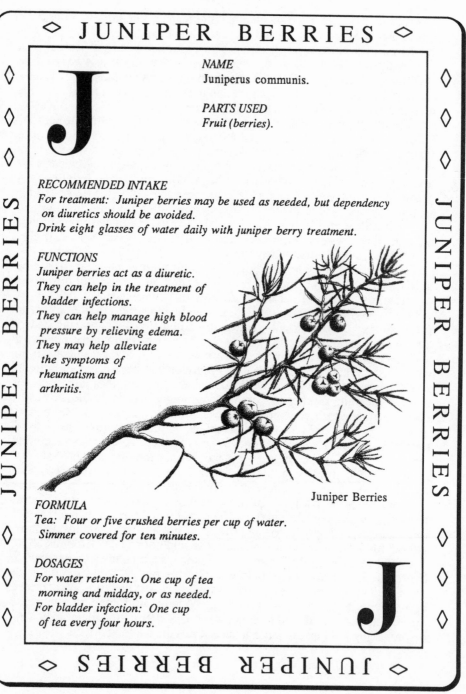

Juniper Berries

FORMULA
*Tea: Four or five crushed berries per cup of water.
 Simmer covered for ten minutes.*

DOSAGES
*For water retention: One cup of tea
 morning and midday, or as needed.*
*For bladder infection: One cup
 of tea every four hours.*

J

JUNIPER BERRIES

Juniper berries have been in use for thousands of years. Herbalists in ancient Greece, Rome, and Arabia used them medicinally and for their scent and flavor. They also employed them to tint hair and dye cloth. Marinades for wild game, such as venison or bear, often have a few berries added to cut the gamey undertaste of the meat, and it is juniper berries that give gin its distinctive flavor. From China, across Asia and Europe, and over to North America, juniper berries have been used to ward off evil spirits, bad magic, and other sociopathic elements. Their scent is frequently part of the incense used for the ceremonies of many religions, including Catholicism.

The plant that produces the berries is *Juniperus communis*, an evergreen shrub in the cypress family. It grows to heights ranging from six to fifteen feet and has long, narrow, sharply pointed leaves of deep green. Juniper blooms in the late spring and develops clusters of small, round, green fruits, each about the size of a large pea. The fruits ripen very slowly, taking a year or two to mature into bluish, bloom-covered berries ready to be picked. It is not unusual to see a juniper with berries of both colors, but only the ripe ones are harvested. As the berries dry, they turn blackish purple and become wrinkled, with a light brown or yellow pulp.

Medicinally, juniper berries are brewed into a tea and used for an assortment of urinary problems, particularly cystitis — a bladder disorder. The berries are an excellent, mild diuretic, helping to relieve and reduce edema, or water retention. They also give the urine a scent similar to that of violets. Tea brewed from juniper berries has been used with some success to relieve many of the symptoms of rheumatism, acting as both a mild painkiller and an anti-inflammatory agent. In fact, it was traditional to treat rheumatism by drinking the tea daily for six weeks each spring and fall. Recent medical research has found that some of the volatile oils in juniper berries reduce and inhibit tumor growth in many animals. They can act as antibacterial agents in infections, too.

Dried juniper berries are available in most health food stores and many gourmet or specialty food stores. When buying juniper berries in bulk, buy them carefully to be sure that they are not from plants called juniper mistletoe or American juniper. These plants are often confused with true juniper. They belong to the mistletoe genus, *Phoradendron*, and are listed by the U.S. Food and Drug Administration (FDA) as unsafe.

To make juniper berry tea, put four or five of the crushed or bruised berries into a pot containing one cup of water. Cover the pot and simmer for ten minutes. When brewed as tea, juniper berries have a bittersweet, resinous taste that can be improved by sweetening the tea with honey or by steeping a little peppermint in the boiled mixture. Because of its strong diuretic properties, women who are pregnant should not consume juniper berry tea, and individuals suffering from severe or chronic kidney disorders should also avoid it.

L

NAME
Glycyrrhiza glabra.

PARTS USED
Root.

RECOMMENDED INTAKE
For treatment: Licorice may be used daily for up to two weeks, with a one-week break between regimens.

FUNCTIONS
Licorice is an antispasmodic that helps suppress coughs.
It acts as an expectorant to clear lungs and bronchial tubes.
It can help heal gastric ulcers.
It acts as a mild stimulant.

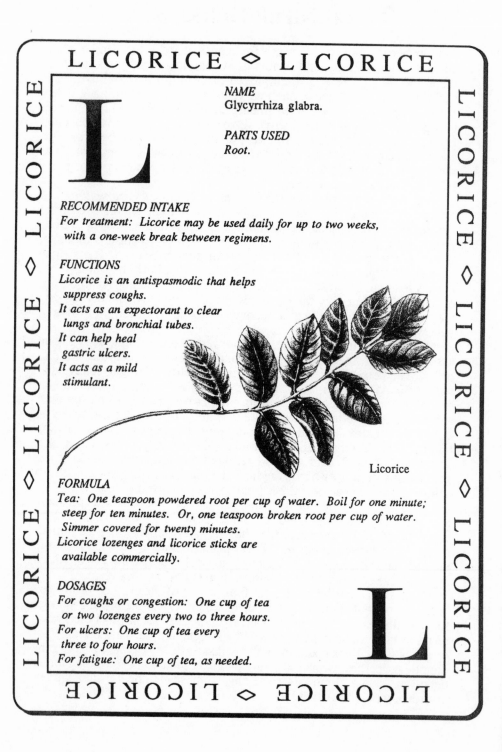

Licorice

FORMULA
Tea: One teaspoon powdered root per cup of water. Boil for one minute; steep for ten minutes. Or, one teaspoon broken root per cup of water. Simmer covered for twenty minutes.
Licorice lozenges and licorice sticks are available commercially.

DOSAGES
For coughs or congestion: One cup of tea or two lozenges every two to three hours.
For ulcers: One cup of tea every three to four hours.
For fatigue: One cup of tea, as needed.

L

LICORICE

Licorice has been used as a general curative agent for thousands of years in China and Egypt. When the tomb of Egyptian King Tutankhamen, who ruled around 1355 B.C., was discovered in 1922, sticks of dried licorice were found inside, attesting to the antiquity of this botanical's use. Known also as sweet root or sweet wood, licorice is used as a traditional flavoring for beverages, medicines, cigarettes, and candies. Recent research has determined that licorice contains a compound called glycyrrhizin, which is about fifty times sweeter than cane sugar. Unlike most other sweetening agents, such as sugar and honey, the sweetener in licorice does not increase thirst; instead, it helps quench it.

Licorice is a folk name that encompasses about fourteen different members of the genus Glycyrrhiza (Greek for "sweet root"), although the species generally referred to as "licorice" is *Glycyrrhiza glabra*. This member of the legume family is cultivated worldwide and has dark green leaves and spikes of blue or yellow flowers. Its root, with a brownish exterior and yellowish interior, is harvested for medicinal and other uses when the plant is about four years old. The root is washed and trimmed, then either used fresh or dried for later use.

Medicinally, licorice is used effectively for many throat and bronchial problems. It relieves sore throats, helps suppress coughs, and acts as an expectorant to bring out phlegm from the lungs and bronchial tubes. Considered one of the oldest, most efficient mild laxatives, licorice takes effect in just a few hours. It is soothing to the mucous membranes of the digestive tract and seems to help heal both gastric and mouth ulcers. Licorice contains substances that have recently been pinpointed as having cortisonelike behavior. They seem to stimulate the adrenal glands and act as anti-inflammatory agents and bronchodilators. As a result, licorice extract has been used in Europe, with some success, as a substitute for synthetic steroids to treat patients with Addison's disease, a hormonal disorder caused by improperly functioning adrenal glands.

Lozenges of licorice mixed with cayenne, called Throat Discs (Marion Laboratories, Inc.), are available in pharmacies. Dried licorice root, which requires no refrigeration and can be stored for long periods, is usually available in health food stores and can even be found in the spice racks of some grocery stores. It comes powdered, chopped, and as sticks, which are good to suck on for a sore throat or to help fight the urge to light a cigarette.

The best and most pleasant way to use licorice is to make a tea from the root. Bring water in a small pan to a boil and add one teaspoon of powdered root for each cup of water. Boil the mixture for one minute, then let it sit for about ten minutes before drinking. To use the whole root, break off and crush about one teaspoon per cup of water and simmer for twenty minutes in a covered pot. It is not a good idea to consume very large doses of licorice over an extended period of time, as it can contribute to water retention and raise blood pressure. Also, since licorice has steroidlike behavior, women who are pregnant or breast-feeding should avoid taking it.

121

Oo

NAME
Olea europaea.

PARTS USED
The derived oil of the fruit.

RECOMMENDED INTAKE
For treatment: Olive oil may be used every day.

FUNCTIONS
Olive oil can lower overall blood cholesterol
levels by reducing levels of dangerous
LDLs (low density lipoproteins).
It can help remove stored toxins
from the body.
It acts as a mild
laxative.

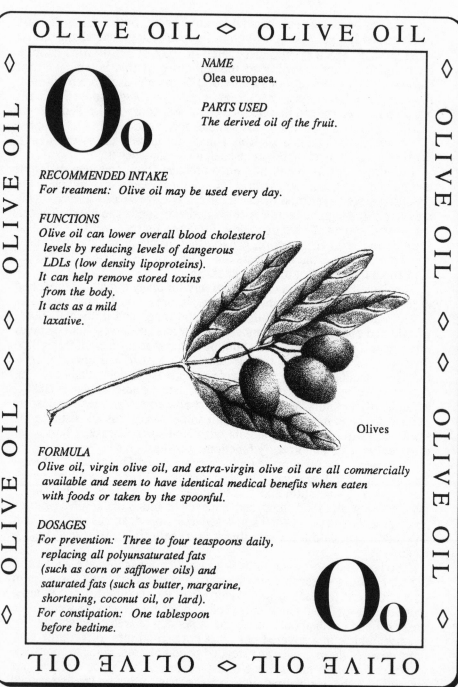

Olives

FORMULA
Olive oil, virgin olive oil, and extra-virgin olive oil are all commercially
available and seem to have identical medical benefits when eaten
with foods or taken by the spoonful.

DOSAGES
For prevention: Three to four teaspoons daily,
replacing all polyunsaturated fats
(such as corn or safflower oils) and
saturated fats (such as butter, margarine,
shortening, coconut oil, or lard).
For constipation: One tablespoon
before bedtime.

Oo

OLIVE OIL

The olive tree, whose branches are symbolic of peace, produces a fruit that contains oil in its pulp, as well as in its seed. For thousands of years, the fruit has been pressed for its pale yellow green oil, considered the essence of goodness and purity. Olive oil burned in the sacred lamps and anointed the warriors, champions, and kings of ancient Greece, Rome, and Egypt. It has been blended into fine soaps and cosmetics to soften the skin, and culinary artists depend on it to flavor dressings, sauces, and marinades.

Native to the Mediterranean area, the olive tree, *Olea europaea*, was introduced into Southern California by Franciscan Fathers at the end of the eighteenth century. It has been cultivated with success in other warm-weather areas of the world. The olive tree grows very slowly and does not develop fruit worth harvesting for oil until it is at least six years old. It may live for hundreds of years, growing a thick, gnarled, twisted trunk topped by thin leaves that are gray green on top and silvery underneath.

Traditionally, olive oil has been taken for indigestion, as it coats and soothes irritated mucous membranes in the digestive tract. It is also effective in treating mild constipation, as it seems to lubricate the intestines and encourage peristalsis. Although a great deal is known about olive oil's uses in preparing foods, and its topical uses in fighting dry skin, split cuticles, and dandruff, its health-protective values have been explored only recently. New research shows that olive oil can help the body rid itself of many insoluble pollutants that may be stored in body fats, including chlorinated hydrocarbons such as DDT and PCB. Olive oil attracts such pollutants, released from their storage areas in the body, and carries them to organs that can process and excrete them.

Olive oil, a monounsaturated oil, seems to be healthier to consume than polyunsaturated oils. Recent animal studies indicate that diets high in polyunsaturated oils may actually increase the risk for developing breast or colon tumors, while those high in olive oil pose a much lower risk. While polyunsaturated oils can lower total blood cholesterol levels, they do so by reducing the levels of both dangerous low density lipoproteins (LDLs) and heart-protective high density lipoproteins (HDLs). Olive oil, on the other hand, lowers overall blood cholesterol levels by specifically reducing LDL levels, while leaving the beneficial HDL levels relatively untouched. This means that olive oil may actually contribute to reducing the risk of developing cardiovascular diseases. It is interesting to note that two countries with relatively low rates of heart disease, Greece and Italy, are countries where olive oil plays a major dietary role.

Olive oil is widely available in health food and grocery stores. While there are many grades of oil and many methods for extracting it, the best for flavor and purity is virgin olive oil. Since it is an oil, it will turn rancid after a period of time, so refrigeration is a good idea. Substitute olive oil for all polyunsaturated oils, such as safflower and corn oils, and use it every day — uncooked whenever possible — on salads, for flavoring steamed vegetables, or by the teaspoonful with meals.

P s

NAME
Petroselinum crispum.

PARTS USED
Leaves.

RECOMMENDED INTAKE
For treatment: Parsley may be used every day.
Drink eight glasses of water daily with parsley treatment.

FUNCTIONS
Parsley acts as a mild diuretic and kidney cleanser.
It acts as a uterine stimulant.
It may have antibacterial
 properties.

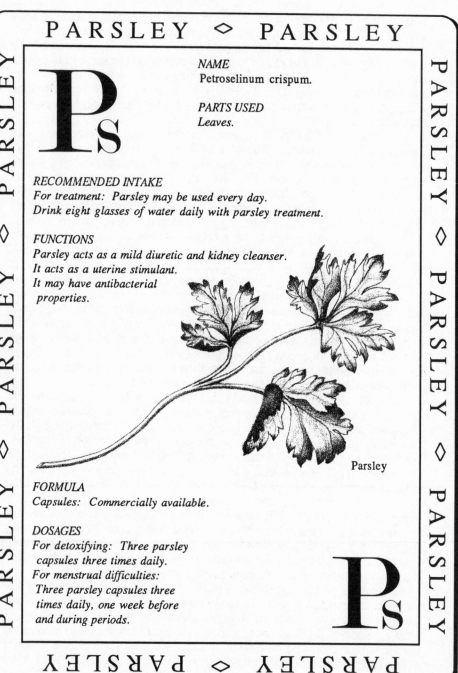

Parsley

FORMULA
Capsules: Commercially available.

DOSAGES
For detoxifying: Three parsley
 capsules three times daily.
For menstrual difficulties:
 Three parsley capsules three
 times daily, one week before
 and during periods.

P s

PARSLEY

A sacred herb in Greek mythology, parsley was used as a decorative garland for victors in athletic competitions. For centuries, parsley has been in use as an important flavoring and food in the Middle East, particularly in salads like tabouli. It was not used at the table in early Europe, however, because it was considered symbolic of death and oblivion. In later times, parsley garnered a reputation as a breath purifier, overcoming even garlic odors, and began to appear regularly at meals. Today, parsley is probably the most commonly used herb after coffee, tea, and tobacco.

Parsley, *Petroselinum crispum*, belongs to the same plant family as carrots. It is a shiny, dark green herb that grows up to three feet tall, with clusters of white or yellow green flowers. It has leaves with curly edges, a root resembling a small carrot, and is believed to be native to the eastern Mediterranean area. Today, parsley is grown worldwide and can be found in any basic kitchen garden.

High in minerals such as calcium and manganese, as well as vitamins A and C, parsley is a surprisingly good nutrient and nutritional supplement. Medicinally, parsley has had many effects credited to it over the years. Some of them involve countering poisons — probably based on parsley's remarkable reputation for overcoming strong odors — but these effects are, for the most part, only anecdotal. For the herbalist, parsley's primary use is as a mild diuretic that continuously encourages the flushing of the kidneys. The kidneys regulate fluid levels in the body, and they process many of the body's toxins and wastes. Flushing out the kidneys keeps them working at their full capacity, and ridding the body of wastes enhances its overall health. In addition, parsley has some antibacterial and antifungal properties that may help fight irritations of the bladder and urethra. Although parsley is an excellent urinary-tract stimulant, it should not be used when serious or chronic kidney disorders are present.

In women, parsley is believed to help ease certain menstrual problems, such as irregular periods and amenorrhea. Parsley acts as a uterine stimulant; and, in fact, a drink that is about eighty-five percent parsley leaf juice is used in the Soviet Union with great success to stimulate the uterine contractions of women in labor. For this reason, women who are pregnant should not ingest large amounts of parsley juice or any type of concentrated parsley extract. According to recent animal studies, dried parsley leaves seem to protect cells against the dangerous effects of some carcinogens, although further research is needed in this area.

Parsley, fresh or dried, is readily available in almost all grocery stores. Fresh parsley will keep for several days and can be air dried or dried in the oven at a very low heat. Health food stores carry parsley capsules and tablets made from dried parsley leaf. These are the best forms of parsley to take to achieve its kidney-cleansing functions. Because of mildly diuretic effects, at least eight glasses of water should be taken daily with dried parsley supplements.

Pp

NAME
Mentha piperita.

PARTS USED
Leaves.

RECOMMENDED INTAKE
For treatment: Peppermint may be used every day.

FUNCTIONS
Peppermint calms the digestive system.
It can help relieve nausea
and stomach gas.
It can help alleviate
congestion from colds.
It can help relieve the
symptoms of flu.

Peppermint

FORMULA
Tea: One cup boiling water poured over
one rounded tablespoon of dried leaves.
Steep five minutes; strain before drinking.

DOSAGES
For digestive problems or congestion:
One cup of tea every two to three hours.

Pp

PEPPERMINT

Peppermint, the most pungent of the mints, is one of the most extensively used herbs in the world today. Although thirteenth-century Icelandic records mention peppermint, European botanists did not recognize it as a distinct species until the middle of the seventeenth century. It was not commonly used until almost one hundred years later. Peppermint oil has been used to ward off rats, who dislike the smell. It is a component of many forms of ceremonial incense, perhaps because bad spirits are also thought to dislike the smell. Peppermint is currently used as a flavoring in candies, beverages, toothpastes, and chewing gums.

Peppermint, *Mentha piperita*, is also called brandy mint and balm mint. It is native to the British Isles and northern Europe, but it is now cultivated throughout the world, including Canada and the United States. Peppermint is a dark green plant with a purple tone to its leaves, which are slightly shiny and veined. It grows about two feet high and sprouts spikes of tiny, clumped, violet flowers. Peppermint is harvested at flowering time and either used fresh or dried for storage.

Medicinally, peppermint has been used with great success to calm indigestion and expel gas from the digestive tract. Peppermint has a slightly anesthetic effect on the nerves of the stomach, which helps decrease appetite, soothe stomach spasms, and quell nausea, particularly from motion sickness. For this reason, a cup of peppermint tea before a meal will decrease the appetite. A cup about ten minutes after a meal will ease digestion. Peppermint is a mild, refreshing stimulant, yet it calms jangled nerves and was once prescribed for insanity. Hot peppermint tea will warm the body on a cold night, while iced peppermint tea is a great restorative on a sweltering summer day.

Peppermint provides relief from the stuffiness caused by colds and soothes the irritations of the flu. Tradition holds that peppermint decreases the severity and duration of colds and flu. Recent biochemical research has shown that certain substances in peppermint do, indeed, seem to inhibit the activity of certain viruses that cause flu. There is even some preliminary evidence that these same substances may have a slight effect on herpes simplex, the virus that causes cold sores.

Both fresh and dried peppermint can be found in most health food and grocery stores. Both forms are effective, although fresh peppermint tastes better as an iced tea. Dried peppermint will keep for long periods of time and seems to make a tastier hot tea. It has a distinct smell and a slightly bitter taste that produces a cooling sensation. This cooling sensation is often perceived as a choking sensation by small children, so supervise them closely when serving peppermint tea. To brew peppermint tea, pour boiling water over crumbled peppermint leaves, using one tablespoon of crushed leaves or one teabag for every cup of water. Let the mixture steep for about five minutes, then serve hot or chill for later use. Never boil the peppermint leaves, as this will destroy their medicinal effects.

Va

NAME
Valeriana officinalis.

PARTS USED
Root.

RECOMMENDED INTAKE
For treatment: Valerian may be used every day.

FUNCTIONS
Valerian acts as a central nervous system
 depressant, or tranquilizer.
It acts as an antispasmodic that can
 relax muscle spasms.

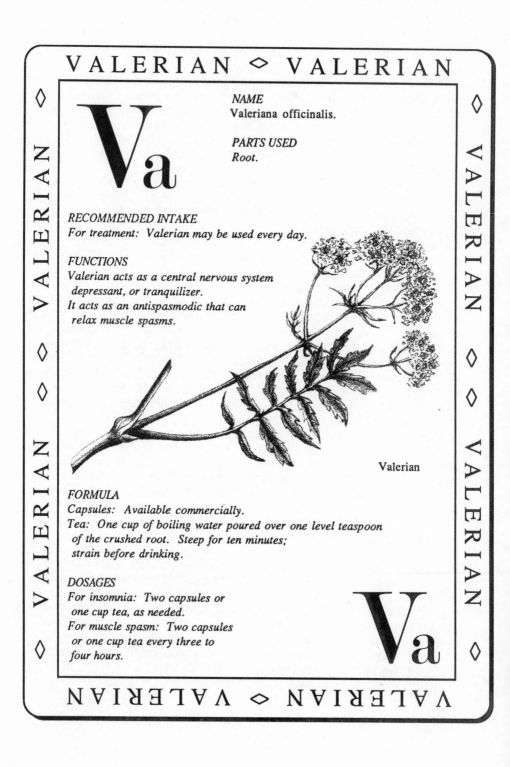

Valerian

FORMULA
Capsules: Available commercially.
Tea: One cup of boiling water poured over one level teaspoon
 of the crushed root. Steep for ten minutes;
 strain before drinking.

DOSAGES
For insomnia: Two capsules or
 one cup tea, as needed.
For muscle spasm: Two capsules
 or one cup tea every three to
 four hours.

Va

VALERIAN

Valerian was one of the primary medicinal plants cultivated by the Shakers, and, as far back as 1592, it was found to help alleviate certain forms of convulsions and epilepsy, triggered by emotional distress and fear. Valerian is considered alluring to rats. There is a traditional belief that the Pied Piper used not only his music but also valerian to lure the rats out of Hamelin. Valerian has been used to flavor tobacco, and it is considered valuable for releasing "woodsy" scents blended in perfumes.

Valerian, *Valeriana officinalis*, is also called setwall, amantilla, and garden heliotrope. It is a very pretty plant, often used as an ornamental, with white flowers that look like puffs of cotton from a distance. The flowers have a slight scent, as do the fresh yellow brown roots. As the roots dry, their volatile oils change, developing an odor that is unpleasant to many people, being likened to the smell of sweaty socks. This has caused valerian root to be referred to as "fu" or "phu." Cats, however, love the odor, fresh or dried, and will ecstatically destroy fresh valerian plants if the leaves or root become bruised.

Medicinally, valerian root has been used for thousands of years as a natural tranquilizer. Laboratory studies have shown that it does, indeed, have beneficial effects on the central nervous system and can relax muscle spasms. It is an excellent remedy for insomnia. It is also a safe, non-narcotic sedative for nervousness — safer than many of the commercially available tranquilizers. A cup of valerian root tea is a soothing way to unwind at the end of a stressful day, relaxing the body, calming a nervous stomach, and alleviating tension headaches. It was used in the eighteenth and nineteenth centuries for heart palpitations. New evidence shows that valerian root extracts have actually helped stabilize irregular heartbeat in animals.

Dried valerian root is available in most health food stores as a whole root, pieces of root, powdered root, or in capsules and tablets. Sometimes fresh valerian root is also available and is, of course, the preferable form to use. Be sure to purchase it from a reputable vendor. Use your nose to verify that it is the right plant: If it does not have a sweetish, oniony scent, buy the dried root instead. Fresh valerian root is usually shredded and soaked in cold water. Use two teaspoons of the root for every cup of cold water. Let the mixture stand for about eight hours to extract its medicinal substances. Strain the liquid and drink one warm cupful in the evenings. Dried valerian root should be crushed and steeped in boiling water. Use one teaspoon per cup of hot water and let it steep for about ten minutes. Drink one cup in the evenings. Do not boil valerian root. Boiling will destroy its useful substances. Valerian tea has a bitter-sweet flavor. The easiest way to take valerian root is in capsule form. Since valerian is a strong tranquilizer, take the capsules only before bedtime or during those times when a sedative effect is desired.

Ww

NAME
Salix alba.

PARTS USED
Bark.

RECOMMENDED INTAKE
*For treatment or prevention: White willow bark
may be used every day.*

FUNCTIONS
*White willow is an effective painkiller.
It acts as an anti-inflammatory agent.
It reduces fevers.
It acts as a blood thinner for
cardiovascular disease
management.*

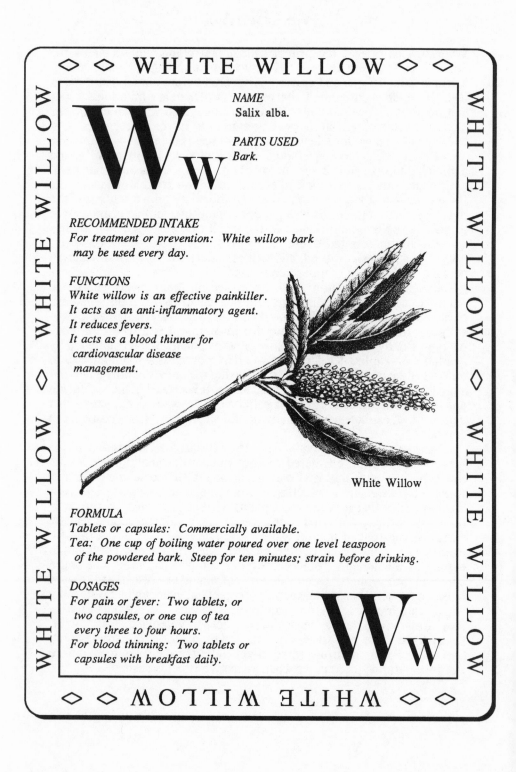

White Willow

FORMULA
*Tablets or capsules: Commercially available.
Tea: One cup of boiling water poured over one level teaspoon
of the powdered bark. Steep for ten minutes; strain before drinking.*

DOSAGES
*For pain or fever: Two tablets, or
two capsules, or one cup of tea
every three to four hours.
For blood thinning: Two tablets or
capsules with breakfast daily.*

Ww

WHITE WILLOW

White willow has been used in many ways over thousands of years. Its branches and twigs have been woven into graceful baskets and furniture. Its trunk has been fashioned into cricket bats and pulped to make paper. At one time, crushed charcoal was made from white willow wood and considered the finest available gunpowder. However, many of its most useful features come from its bark. As far back as A.D. 60, Greek physicians recognized the pain- and fever-relieving properties of the bark of the white willow tree.

White willow, *Salix alba*, is also called European willow and salicin willow. It is a tree native to wet areas of north Africa, central Asia, and Europe. The tree has been successfully introduced into the northeastern parts of the United States. White willow has long trailing branches and thin gray green leaves that are covered with a fine silvery down. Its bark is finely cracked into quill-shaped strips and colored grayish white, with a slightly glossy surface. The inside of the bark is cinnamon in color and smooth to the touch. The bark is peeled off in the summer, dried, and used for a variety of herbal purposes. In fact, modern-day wilderness explorers are taught to consider white willow one of the essential wilderness first-aid plants.

White willow bark contains several medicinal substances. Salicin is the most commonly known one. As early as 1830, salicin was extracted from white willow bark and used in a wide range of medicinal products. Several years later, a synthetic was produced, acetylsalicylic acid. It replaced white willow in everyday use. This synthetic substance is now known as aspirin. White willow shares the medical effectiveness of aspirin but may be preferable, since it contains alkaloids from the entire plant and is less acidic and irritating to the stomach. Like aspirin, white willow is effective in reducing fevers and relieving body aches caused by flu and colds. It reduces tissue inflammation. It also relieves the pain of rheumatism, arthritis, and neuralgia. Headaches are successfully treated with white willow, as are some digestive problems, particularly diarrhea. Irritations of the bladder and urethra will often respond to the astringent and antibacterial qualities of white willow. As cooled tea, it can be gargled to relieve sore throats.

White willow is available at most health food stores as dried-bark strips, powdered bark, and in capsule or tablet form. Many companies package the tablets exactly like aspirin, in handy, pocket-sized tins. For most purposes, white willow tablets are ideal. When tea is desired, however, put one teaspoon of the powdered root into a cup of boiling water. Better yet, put the powder into a homemade teabag (page 22), and steep for five minutes. If using loose powder, strain the tea before drinking. Those using white willow should not take aspirin at the same time. It could trigger overdose symptoms, such as ringing in the ears. White willow, like aspirin, acts as a blood thinner that can be a useful preventive for cardiovascular disorders. Those who are already taking blood-thinning medications, however, should check with their physicians before taking either white willow or aspirin.

Yd

NAME
Rumex crispus.

PARTS USED
Root.

RECOMMENDED INTAKE
For treatment: Yellow dock may be used daily for up to one week,
with a three-week break between regimens.
Drink eight glasses of water daily
with yellow dock treatment.

FUNCTIONS
Yellow dock stimulates liver functions,
which triggers the release of stored
toxins for elimination.
Thus, it helps the body
detoxify itself.

Yellow Dock

FORMULA
Capsules: Available commercially.

DOSAGES
For detoxifying: Two yellow dock
capsules three times daily
for one week only.

Yd

YELLOW DOCK

Yellow dock is considered one of the most persistent and troublesome weeds across the fields and pastures of Europe, the northern parts of the United States, and the southern parts of Canada. It is also considered the most medicinally useful member of the docks, a family of herbaceous plants that also includes sorrel, buckwheat, and rhubarb. Yellow dock has been in use since ancient times. Native Americans dried and ground its root into powder, which they applied to cuts, scrapes, and other wounds. European healers, until late in the nineteenth century, used yellow dock as a blood purifier and a cure for anemia.

Yellow dock, *Rumex crispus*, is also known as curly dock, sour dock, and garden patience. This last name is a comment on how difficult it is to eradicate the plant, once it has taken hold. It grows to a height of two to three feet, with large, curly-edged, light green leaves, and spikes of clustered greenish yellow flowers in the summer that turn to a rust color in the fall. Yellow dock has long been believed to grow only in soils rich in iron. It has a reddish brown, carrot-shaped taproot with a yellow orange interior. The darker the inside of the root, the stronger it is medicinally.

While both the leaves and root of yellow dock have been employed medicinally, the root is the preferred part. The leaves, a source of vitamin C, were once used to prevent scurvy. Their oxalic acid content is so high, however, that those using the leaves ran a serious risk of poisoning themselves. The root, usually dried and powdered, can be used topically to reduce the swelling and itching of sores and skin eruptions. Internally, the root was once used to slow the spread of intestinal cancer. It has been discarded in favor of more powerful chemotherapies. Yellow dock root triggers the release of bile from the gallbladder to stimulate digestive processes, which is particularly useful for breaking down fatty foods and stored fats. It is yellow dock's effectiveness in stimulating liver functions that makes it so important to herbalists today. The root, considered a body detoxifier, speeds metabolic processes and helps clear congestion in the liver. For this reason, yellow dock has been used at times to help ease some types of jaundice and posthepatitis flare-ups.

Dried yellow dock root is available in many health food stores — chopped, powdered, or in capsule form. Yellow dock will keep for several months, but, like all powerful herbs, it should be stored out of reach of small children. While the root may be brewed into a somewhat unpleasant-tasting tea, it is just as effective in capsule form. When yellow dock is taken for one or two days to stimulate the healing of localized infections, it acts fairly quickly. When it is used for several days or a week to detoxify the body, it may trigger short-term symptoms such as a mild rash, fatigue, or sour breath and sweat, as the toxins are eliminated from the body. Yellow dock should not be taken on a daily basis for more than seven days at a time.

Ym

NAME
Ilex paraguayensis,
Mate.

PARTS USED
Leaves.

RECOMMENDED INTAKE
For treatment: Yerba mate may be used every day. Treatment with
extra-strength tea should not be continued for more than two days.
Yerba mate should not be taken before bedtime.

FUNCTIONS
Yerba mate is a strong central
nervous system stimulant.
Is is a fast-acting laxative.
It is a vasodilator useful
in the treatment of headaches.
It can suppress
the appetite.

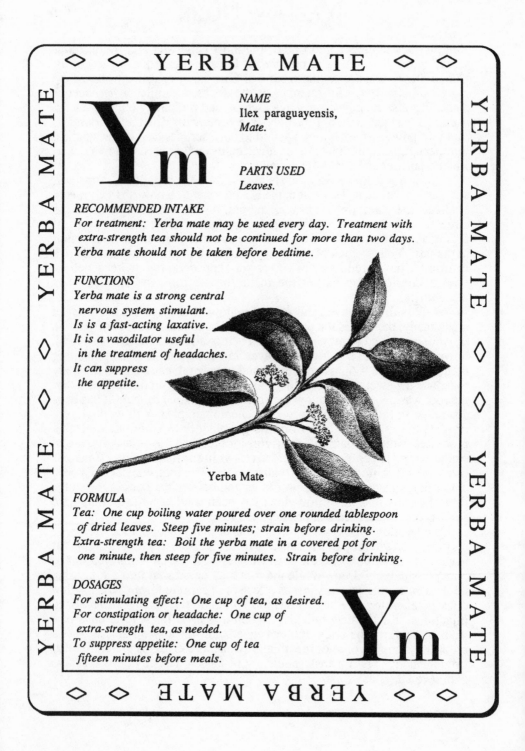

Yerba Mate

FORMULA
Tea: One cup boiling water poured over one rounded tablespoon
of dried leaves. Steep five minutes; strain before drinking.
Extra-strength tea: Boil the yerba mate in a covered pot for
one minute, then steep for five minutes. Strain before drinking.

DOSAGES
For stimulating effect: One cup of tea, as desired.
For constipation or headache: One cup of
extra-strength tea, as needed.
To suppress appetite: One cup of tea
fifteen minutes before meals.

Ym

YERBA MATE

Yerba mate is a South American plant. A tea called mate is brewed from its leaves. Sometimes called Paraguay tea, mate is commonly consumed as a beverage by millions of people in many of the central and southern countries of South America. Yerba mate was also cultivated by the Jesuits in the seventeenth century, and the brew was once referred to as Jesuit tea or missionary tea. Mate (pronounced "mah´ tay") is actually the Quechua word for "gourd." The tea is so named because it is usually brewed in gourds that have been grown into special shapes for this one function. Mate serves not only as a refreshing beverage, but also as a form of social interaction. The traditional way to drink it is to pass the gourd containing the brew among friends and coworkers, who suck it through a straw or thin reed.

Yerba mate is an evergreen shrub that looks a lot like a large orange tree. Its botanical name is *Ilex paraguayensis*, and it belongs to the holly family. Yerba mate sprouts white flowers and has pale green leaves that are harvested for later use. The leaves are dried as soon as they are picked to prevent them from fermenting. The leaf buds that have not yet opened are considered the finest, commanding higher prices than the more mature, fully-grown leaves. Most of the leaf buds are harvested for local consumption only. The yerba mate that reaches North American and European markets usually consists of the mature leaves.

Mate, the brew, is an excellent substitute for both coffee and tea, and not nearly as hard on the stomach as either of them. It contains caffeine and other alkaloids. It acts as a powerful stimulant, making it a perfect pick-me-up in the morning or at midday. Mate is also a mild diuretic and a fast-acting laxative. It has been used to treat morning stiffness and sore joints in the elderly. It is an excellent appetite suppressant. Mate is often taken along in parts of South America as the only form of sustenance for journeys of two to five days.

Yerba mate can be found in almost all health food stores and in most grocery stores that carry packaged herbal teas. It may be called simply "mate," and listed under the letter M. If stored in a dry, closed container, yerba mate will keep for several months. If it begins to grow moldy or ferment, it should be discarded immediately, as it was never properly dried. To brew mate, pour one cup of boiling water over one teaspoon of dried yerba mate, either as loose leaves or in a teabag. Steep for five minutes. For a stronger tea, boil the mixture for one minute in a covered pot, then let it stand for about five minutes. Its flavor is bitter, so it is usually mixed with lemon juice and sugar or honey. To make the mate taste more coffeelike, lightly toast the leaves in a skillet before brewing. Like coffee, mate's powerful stimulating effect can cause nervousness and anxiety if it is taken in excessive amounts.

CHAPTER FIVE

THE PROGRAMS

The Anti-Aging Program
The Cardiovascular Program
The Detox Program
The Fitness Program
The Immune-System Program
The Skin & Hair Program
The Stress Program
The Weight-Loss Program

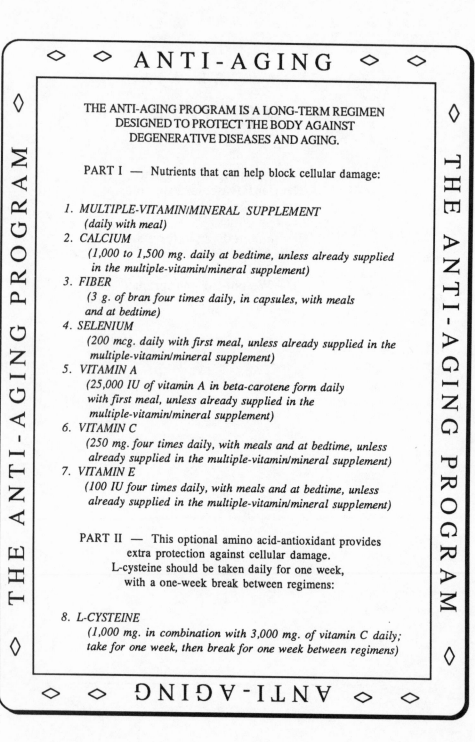

THE ANTI-AGING PROGRAM IS A LONG-TERM REGIMEN
DESIGNED TO PROTECT THE BODY AGAINST
DEGENERATIVE DISEASES AND AGING.

PART I — Nutrients that can help block cellular damage:

1. *MULTIPLE-VITAMIN/MINERAL SUPPLEMENT*
   (daily with meal)
2. *CALCIUM*
   *(1,000 to 1,500 mg. daily at bedtime, unless already supplied
   in the multiple-vitamin/mineral supplement)*
3. *FIBER*
   *(3 g. of bran four times daily, in capsules, with meals
   and at bedtime)*
4. *SELENIUM*
   *(200 mcg. daily with first meal, unless already supplied in the
   multiple-vitamin/mineral supplement)*
5. *VITAMIN A*
   *(25,000 IU of vitamin A in beta-carotene form daily
   with first meal, unless already supplied in the
   multiple-vitamin/mineral supplement)*
6. *VITAMIN C*
   *(250 mg. four times daily, with meals and at bedtime, unless
   already supplied in the multiple-vitamin/mineral supplement)*
7. *VITAMIN E*
   *(100 IU four times daily, with meals and at bedtime, unless
   already supplied in the multiple-vitamin/mineral supplement)*

PART II — This optional amino acid-antioxidant provides
extra protection against cellular damage.
L-cysteine should be taken daily for one week,
with a one-week break between regimens:

8. *L-CYSTEINE*
   *(1,000 mg. in combination with 3,000 mg. of vitamin C daily;
   take for one week, then break for one week between regimens)*

THE ANTI-AGING PROGRAM

THE ANTI-AGING PROGRAM

ANTI-AGING

THE ANTI-AGING PROGRAM

The Anti-Aging Program is designed to help prevent the accelerated aging of the body's cells caused by air pollution, chemicals in food and water, and normal metabolic processes. These can all damage the DNA in the nuclei of the cells, resulting in potentially hazardous mutations. These cellular mutations are believed to cause many of the diseases associated with aging: arthritis, cancer, arteriosclerosis, and the general signs of aging in the tissues of the skin and other organs. The Anti-Aging Program provides a broad spectrum of nutrient antioxidants that, when taken in adequate dosages, scavenge the bloodstream for free radicals. Free radicals are highly reactive, unwelcome molecules that can lodge in the cells, damaging their DNA. This prevents the cells from functioning normally or reproducing correctly. Some of these damaged cells can mutate into cancerous ones. When antioxidants are present in the bloodstream, they combine with free radicals, neutralize their reactiveness, and carry them safely out of the body.

WHO SHOULD FOLLOW THE PROGRAM — The Anti-Aging Program is designed especially for individuals who live in cities or highly polluted areas, frequently eat out in restaurants or consume processed foods, or drink more than two alcoholic beverages a day, as well as for cigarette smokers or those exposed to smokers.

HOW TO USE THE PROGRAM — The Anti-Aging Program is a selection of nutritional supplements to be taken each day to help prevent cellular damage. The Program is divided into two parts, based on how often the supplements are to be taken.

DIETARY GUIDELINES — Those who choose this program can enhance its effectiveness by drinking at least eight glasses of distilled water daily. In addition, they should also avoid, whenever possible, exposure to carcinogens such as sunlight, tobacco, excessive alcohol, and foods processed with nitrates or nitrites.

PART I

Part I lists nutrients that should be taken daily. While some vitamin/mineral formulas will contain adequate levels of the nutrients listed below, most will have to be supplemented to reach levels that can help block cellular damage.

1. MULTIPLE-VITAMIN/MINERAL SUPPLEMENT — (daily with meal)
A good multiple-vitamin/mineral supplement is essential to the Anti-Aging Program. A low dietary intake of certain vitamins and minerals can increase the body's vulnerability to lead, mercury, and other toxic metals. Choose a multiple-vitamin/mineral supplement that includes in its formula approximately 5 to 15 mg. of manganese, 100 to 150 mcg. of molybdenum, 18 to 20 mg. of iron, 25 to 30 mg. of zinc, and 2 to 3 mg. of copper. If possible, choose a multiple-vitamin/mineral supplement that does not contain any vitamin A in the retinol form. Look for a formula that supplies vitamin A in beta-carotene form only.

2. CALCIUM — (1,000 to 1,500 mg. daily at bedtime)
Calcium works with iron to protect against the adverse effects of lead, a particularly dangerous hazard in city environments. Recent research also shows that calcium can actually reverse mutations in the cells that line the colon. This means that calcium may help prevent one of the leading killers in the United States, colon cancer.

3. FIBER — (approximately 3 g. of bran four times daily, in capsules, with meals and at bedtime)
Evidence from epidemiological studies suggests that insoluble fiber, such as wheat bran, may contribute to the prevention of certain types of cancer, particularly of the colon. It can absorb carcinogenic substances and speed their excretion from the body. The amount of supplemental fiber required for prevention depends on the intake of dietary fiber. Those whose diets consist primarily of meats, dairy products, processed foods, and white bread are not getting adequate fiber.

4. SELENIUM — (200 mcg. daily with first meal of the day, unless already supplied in the multiple-vitamin/mineral supplement)
The antioxidant activity of selenium can help protect cells from irreversible damage caused by free radicals that come from heavy metals such as mercury, silver, and cadmium. Selenium works with vitamin E to protect the cells and their membranes. In animal studies, supplemental selenium lowered the risk of developing cardiovascular disease, inhibited many types of tumors, and countered the development of certain cancers. In humans, epidemiological surveys show a preventive relationship between dietary selenium and cancers of the breast, colon, and lung.

5. VITAMIN A — (25,000 IU of vitamin A in beta-carotene form daily, with first meal of the day, unless already supplied in the multiple-vitamin/ mineral supplement)

Vitamin A has the remarkable ability to interfere with certain carcinogens, such as those found in tobacco smoke and other pollutants. It prevents certain toxins from binding to the DNA in the cell. Women whose intake of vitamin A is less that 3,500 IU daily are three times more likely to develop serious cervical dysplasia or cervical cancer. A deficiency in vitamin A is also linked to cancers of the lung, larynx, and bladder. Vitamin A was recently shown to help reduce the incidence of lung cancer among smokers and also to have a preventive relationship to esophageal cancer. The beta-carotene form of vitamin A, not the retinol form, is believed to provide the vitamin's dynamic antioxidant properties.

6. VITAMIN C — (250 mg. four times daily, with meals and at bedtime, unless already supplied in the multiple-vitamin/mineral supplement)

Vitamin C is another vital antioxidant. Smokers, especially, need it to protect their cells from the damaging effects of cadmium, carbon monoxide, and other toxins found in cigarettes. A high intake of vitamin C is associated with a lower risk of esophageal and stomach cancers. Very high doses have been shown to reduce the incidence of rectal polyps, which are believed to be associated with colon cancer. Furthermore, women whose intake of vitamin C is less than 30 mg. daily have a seven-times higher incidence of cervical dysplasia, so they, particularly, should be certain to maintain strong levels of this nutrient. Vitamin C also inhibits the conversion of nitrates (often used as preservatives in foods and beverages) into nitrosamines, which are known carcinogens. Because this occurs during digestion, it is a good idea to take this vitamin in divided doses with meals.

7. VITAMIN E — (100 IU four times daily, with meals and at bedtime, unless already supplied in the multiple-vitamin/mineral supplement)

Vitamin E is a potent fat-soluble antioxidant that helps protect the body against the effects of air-pollution toxins such as ozone, mercury, and lead. It acts to maintain the stability of the cell membranes. It can help protect the cells lining the lungs from carcinogens in tobacco smoke. Vitamin E works in concert with selenium, so it is always a good idea to take both of them daily. Like vitamin C, vitamin E also helps to block the conversion of nitrates into nitrosamines. Nitrosamines are linked with stomach cancer; therefore, vitamin E, too, should be taken with meals.

PART II

Most of the antioxidants in Part I are scavengers of very specific free radicals. Part II of the Anti-Aging Program is an optional adjunct that provides additional nutrient insurance against cellular damage.

8. L-CYSTEINE — (1,000 mg. in combination with 3,000 mg. of vitamin C daily; take for one week, then break for one week between regimens)

L-cysteine is an amino acid that offers dramatic protection from toxic metals such as mercury and lead, as well as from aldehydes — toxic by-products of air pollution, tobacco, fats, alcohol, and preservatives such as formaldehyde. The sulfur in L-cysteine is believed to act as a scavenger for free radicals. It protects cells from them by inactivating their dangerous oxidizing properties. Those taking L-cysteine should boost their vitamin C intake to three times the amount of L-cysteine. This will prevent the conversion of L-cysteine into a related compound, cystine, a substance implicated in the formation of certain types of kidney stones. L-cysteine is commercially available already combined with the appropriate levels of vitamin C.

THE CARDIOVASCULAR PROGRAM IS A LONG-TERM REGIMEN
DESIGNED TO REDUCE THE RISK OF CARDIOVASCULAR DISEASE.

PART I — Nutrients that protect against the buildup of arterial plaques:

1. *CALCIUM & MAGNESIUM*
   (1,500 mg. of calcium with 600 mg. of magnesium daily at bedtime)
2. *CHROMIUM*
   (200 to 400 mcg. daily with first meal)
3. *SELENIUM & VITAMIN E*
   (200 to 400 mcg. of selenium with 400 IU of vitamin E daily)

PART II — Dietary elements that are helpful to those who have high
blood fat levels and need nutritional help to reduce them:

4. *FIBER*
   (3 g. of powdered psyllium, in capsules, three times daily with meals)
5. *GARLIC*
   (three capsules daily, one with each meal)
6. *GINGER*
   (three capsules every other day, one with each meal)
7. *GINSENG*
   (one capsule, one cup of tea, or one slice, morning and afternoon)
8. *L-CARNITINE*
   (250 mg. two times daily, with first and last meals)
9. *OLIVE OIL*
   (three teaspoons daily, with meals or alone)

PART III — Therapeutic nutrients for those who may already have a
certain amount of arterial blockage due to plaque buildup:

10. *CAYENNE*
    (three capsules every other day, one with each meal)
11. *EPA*
    *(1,000 to 1,200 mg. daily of a marine-lipid concentrate
    such as MaxEPA or Super EPA)*
12. *NIACIN*
    *(50 mg. of nicotinic acid four times daily for several days,
    increasing in 50 mg. increments over a two-month period until
    the desired range is reached — 1,500 to 3,000 mg. daily)*
13. *WHITE WILLOW*
    (two capsules daily, or before engaging in strenuous exercise)

THE CARDIOVASCULAR PROGRAM

Atherosclerosis is an epidemic of national proportion that will result in one and a half million heart attacks this year. The Cardiovascular Program provides a full spectrum of nutritional supplements that are specifically protective against heart disease. Those most at risk of developing heart disease are men who eat a high-cholesterol, high-fat, low-fiber diet. More specifically, this is a diet rich in meat, eggs, and dairy products, and poor in whole grains and fresh vegetables. When excess fats and cholesterol are consumed, they are dumped into the bloodstream, where they can stick to and harden on the inside of arteries, particularly those near the heart. The buildup of these fat deposits, called plaques, results in heart disease, or atherosclerosis. As the arteries narrow, the potential for a complete blockage, or heart attack, becomes more and more real. In order to prevent or halt cardiovascular disease, high-risk individuals must reduce their blood triglyceride levels and overall serum cholesterol levels. They must also increase their protective high density lipoprotein (HDL) levels, while reducing their damaging low density lipoprotein (LDL) levels. It sounds complicated, but it can be achieved through proper diet, regular exercise, and supplementary nutritional help.

WHO SHOULD FOLLOW THE PROGRAM — The Cardiovascular Program is designed for men and women who are concerned about the health of their circulatory systems, are overweight, have high blood pressure, or have a family history of heart disease.

HOW TO USE THE PROGRAM — The Cardiovascular Program is designed for those who are already taking a daily multiple-vitamin/mineral supplement. Part I is primarily preventive and includes a list of nutrients that are protective against the oxidation of fats and the buildup of plaques in the arteries. Part II is a list of nutrients that may be helpful to those who have high or imbalanced blood fat levels. Part III is therapeutic, and lists nutrients for those who already have some arterial blockage, and who have had limited success in reducing their cholesterol levels.

DIETARY GUIDELINES — The dietary guidelines that help prevent heart disease are quite clear. Avoid saturated fats from meats, dairy products, and coconut or palm oils. Substitute monounsaturated olive oil for all polyunsaturated oils. Research suggests that polyunsaturates do not reduce cholesterol in the ideal proportions. Avoid dietary cholesterol from egg yolks and meat. Cut out salt and processed foods. Increase dietary fiber by eating meals composed primarily of fruits, vegetables, and grains. Eat fish as frequently as possible for its protective lipids.

PART I

Part I consists of nutrients in dosages that may already be included in your multiple-vitamin/mineral formula. If they are not, purchase individual supplements to bring the formula into a range that is protective against cardiovascular disease.

1. CALCIUM & MAGNESIUM — (1,500 mg. of calcium with 600 mg. of magnesium daily at bedtime)

Recent studies have shown that a daily calcium intake in the range of 1,000 to 1,500 mg., coupled with a reduction in dietary sodium, can reduce high blood pressure in both men and women after only a few weeks. An imbalance between calcium and magnesium in the body, where there is not enough magnesium, may also play a role in high blood pressure, increasing the risk of developing cardiovascular disease. In addition, magnesium may decrease the incidence and severity of angina, chest pain caused by the blockage of a coronary artery. It may also protect against ischemic heart disease, a condition that occurs when the heart muscle does not get the oxygen it needs because of a spasm or narrowed, clogged arteries.

2. CHROMIUM — (200 to 400 mcg. daily with first meal)

Supplemental chromium helps lower overall serum cholesterol levels, reducing the chance of plaque formation. Furthermore, it reduces harmful low density lipoprotein (LDL) levels while increasing high density lipoprotein (HDL) levels. HDLs are believed to protect the arteries from becoming clogged by plaques.

3. SELENIUM & VITAMIN E — (200 to 400 mcg. of selenium with 400 IU of vitamin E daily, with first meal)

Epidemiological evidence indicates that low selenium levels are linked to increased incidences of stroke, heart disease, and other cardiovascular problems. Selenium is believed to work with vitamin E, the most potent of the fat-soluble antioxidants, to protect cells and their membranes from damage caused by oxidation, a common factor in many diseases of aging such as arteriosclerosis. Vitamin E acts to maintain the stability of cell membranes.

PART II

Part II describes additional nutrients and dietary elements that have demonstrated significant effectiveness as protective agents against cardiovascular disease. The following nutrients are not usually included in a multiple-vitamin/mineral supplement. Any or all of these elements, when added to the diet, can help reduce levels of dangerous blood fats, and/or prevent them from forming plaques on artery walls.

4. FIBER — (approximately 3 g. of powdered psyllium, in capsules, three times daily with meals)

A low-fiber intake has been associated with the increased incidence of cardiovascular problems. Soluble fiber, such as that found in oat bran or psyllium, has been shown in recent studies to reduce overall blood cholesterol levels. In addition, the increased fiber intake helped change the lipoprotein ratio in the blood: Levels of dangerous LDLs decreased, while levels of protective HDLs increased. There is also new evidence that an increased fiber intake may help lower the blood pressure of hypertensive patients.

5. GARLIC — (three capsules daily, one with each meal)

Garlic helps decrease the levels of LDLs that endanger the cardiovascular system. It increases the levels of HDLs that protect against plaque buildup. It also helps reduce the body's triglyceride and overall serum cholesterol levels. In addition, substances in garlic actually seem to decrease the chances of forming blood clots that can clog a plaque-lined artery. These active substances may even help dislodge blood fats from their deposit sites on arterial walls.

6. GINGER — (three capsules every other day, one with each meal)

There is some speculation that the frequent use of fresh ginger in the Japanese diet may be one of the contributing factors to the relatively low levels of heart disease in Japan. Recent studies seem to support this speculation. Ginger has been shown to lower cholesterol levels in rats. It acts as an antioxidant, reducing fat spoilage, or lipid oxidation, in meats. Oxidized lipids are believed to increase the risk of developing heart disease in humans.

7. GINSENG — (one capsule, one cup of tea, or one slice, morning and afternoon)

Both animal and human studies, published in 1984 and 1985, have shown that ginseng can increase protective HDL levels while it reduces blood triglyceride and overall cholesterol levels. Ginseng is considered an adaptogen, a substance that normalizes a wide range of physical and biochemical processes. In animal studies, ginseng's adaptogenic properties have lowered blood pressure in hypertensive animals and raised it in hypotensive ones.

8. L-CARNITINE — (250 mg. two times daily with first and last meals)

L-carnitine is vital to the production of energy for the heart and other muscles. It transports fatty acids into the part of the cell where they are burned for energy. Because of L-carnitine's function in fatty acid metabolism, it is becoming a promising nutrient in the treatment of cardiovascular disease. Recent studies have determined that when L-carnitine is taken by individuals with elevated blood fat levels, it reduced triglyceride levels while raising the HDL levels, thereby protecting the arteries from the buildup of plaques.

9. OLIVE OIL — (three teaspoons daily with meals or alone)
Olive oil has been shown to lower overall blood cholesterol levels. It leaves the heart-protective HDL levels relatively untouched, but reduces dangerous LDL levels. This means that olive oil, a monounsaturate, is much healthier to consume than polyunsaturated oils. Polyunsaturated oils reduce overall cholesterol levels by reducing *both* LDL and HDL levels, rather than changing the all-important ratio between them.

PART III

Part III consists of nutrients that may help individuals who have high cholesterol levels, coupled with a certain amount of arterial blockage due to plaque buildup. High blood pressure and, in more severe cases, occasional angina, or chest pain, may also be present. Individuals using medicines such as anticoagulants, to control any of these conditions should discuss the nutrients below with their physicians before using them. This will help prevent undesirable interactions.

10. CAYENNE — (three capsules every other day, one with each meal)
Cayenne is a vasodilator that increases the overall flow of blood in the cardiovascular system. Recent evidence indicates that cayenne may counter the effects of thromboembolism, the development of dangerous blood clots that can block an artery. Cayenne seems to break down clots already present in the cardiovascular system, too.

11. EPA — (1,000 to 1,200 mg. daily of a marine-lipid concentrate such as MaxEPA or Super EPA)
EPA is an omega-3 fatty acid that makes an important new contribution to decreasing the risk and preventing the development of cardiovascular disease. The supplemental intake of a marine-lipid concentrate containing EPA has been shown to lower serum cholesterol levels, decrease blood triglyceride levels, and help inhibit the formation of blood clots that could block a plaque-lined blood vessel.

12. NIACIN — (50 mg. of nicotinic acid four times daily for several days, increasing in 50 mg. increments over a two-month period until the desired range is reached — 1,500 to 3,000 mg. daily)
Large doses of niacin as nicotinic acid, not niacinamide, in ranges from 1,500 to 3,000 mg., can significantly reduce cholesterol and triglyceride levels in the blood. Nicotinic acid acts as a vasodilator to improve overall blood flow in the cardiovascular system. Because of side effects such as skin flushing and nausea, high doses of this form of niacin should be built up to gradually. It is a good idea to consult a physician or nutrition specialist before taking large doses of nicotinic acid. Also, the body's need for water will be increased, so be sure to include eight glasses of water daily in this regimen.

13. WHITE WILLOW — (two capsules daily, or before engaging in strenuous exercise)

White willow, like aspirin, is a mild blood thinner that can help prevent blood clots from forming in already narrowed arteries. It shares the therapeutic effectiveness of aspirin but may be preferable to it: White willow contains a variety of beneficial alkaloids and is less acidic and irritating to the stomach. Individuals using white willow should not take aspirin simultaneously, as it could trigger overdose symptoms such as ringing in the ears.

THE DETOX PROGRAM IS A TWO-WEEK-LONG REGIMEN THAT SHOULD
BE FOLLOWED NO MORE THAN FOUR TIMES YEARLY.
IT IS DESIGNED TO HELP THE BODY RID ITSELF OF STORED WASTES.

PART I — Nutrients and other substances to be used during the two-week
detoxification regimen:

1. *MULTIPLE-VITAMIN/MINERAL SUPPLEMENT*
   (daily with meals, in divided doses if possible)
2. *FIBER*
   *(approximately 2 g. of powdered psyllium and 2 g. of bran,
   in capsules, with each meal and at bedtime)*
3. *GOLDENSEAL*
   (one capsule before meals, three times daily)
4. *OLIVE OIL*
   (three to four teaspoons total, taken throughout the day)
5. *PARSLEY*
   (three capsules or tablets three times daily, with meals)
6. *VITAMIN C*
   *(500 mg. four times daily with meals and at bedtime, in addition
   to any vitamin C in the multiple-vitamin/mineral supplement)*
7. *WATER*
   *(eight to ten glasses of distilled or mineral-free water daily,
   especially before breakfast, before bedtime, and during the night)*

PART II — Add yellow dock during the second week, for one week only.

8. *YELLOW DOCK*
   (one capsule, morning and night)

PART III — Herbs that can help relieve any detoxification discomforts:

9. *CAYENNE*
   (for headache: one capsule with one glass of water, as needed)
10. *GINSENG*
    (for fatigue: one cup, one capsule, or one slice, as needed)
11. *PEPPERMINT*
    (for stomach distress: one cup of tea, as needed)
12. *VALERIAN*
    (for anxiety or sleeplessness: two capsules, as needed)
13. *WHITE WILLOW*
    (for body aches and pains: two capsules or tablets, as needed)

THE DETOX PROGRAM

Every day, in the air we breathe, in the food we eat, and in the water we drink, we ingest more toxic substances than our bodies can eliminate efficiently. As a result, these toxins are stored in the body's tissues. The liver and kidneys are the primary organs responsible for removing these wastes and toxins from the body. With a wholesome diet and a pure environment, these organs are able to eliminate toxins and wastes efficiently. But alcohol, processed foods, medications, chemicals, and preservatives present a set of metabolic problems that the body is not equipped to handle. Many food additives and pollutants have only been around for the past fifty years or so — too short a period of time for the body to have evolved tactics for surviving or eliminating these hostile substances. When the organs of elimination are confused, they tend either to hold the toxins or release them into the bloodstream to lodge elsewhere — usually in fat cells.

WHO SHOULD FOLLOW THE PROGRAM — The Detox Program is for healthy individuals who do not feel as alert and vital as they believe they should. It is a rigorous program, designed to cleanse the body of stored impurities and toxins. The Detox Program should not be used more than four times a year. A good time to detoxify the body is after vacations or holidays. Do not try to detox while ill or during convalescence from an illness, accident, or surgery. Individuals taking insulin or any other regular medications should consult with a nutrition specialist before using the Detox Program.

HOW TO USE THE PROGRAM — The Detox Program is a two-week long, daily regimen. One additional supplement, yellow dock, is added in Part II, at the beginning of the second week. Because detoxification releases stored toxins into the bloodstream, some individuals may experience minor discomforts such as headaches or muscle soreness during the first few days. Botanical medicines that can alleviate these problems are presented in Part III. Those who have access to a sauna can use it to enhance the Detox Program. Be sure to increase water intake accordingly.

DIETARY GUIDELINES — During the two weeks of the Detox Program, it is a good idea to limit or, better yet, eliminate any substances that make excessive demands on the liver or kidneys, such as alcoholic beverages, caffeine drinks, tobacco, and any unnecessary medications. During detoxification, water intake is very important to flush newly released toxins out of the body before they can be reabsorbed.

151

PART I

Part I is a selection of nutrients and other substances to be used during the two-week detoxification regimen. Although the majority of the nutrients listed may be taken indefinitely, goldenseal should be taken for only two weeks at a time.

1. MULTIPLE-VITAMIN/MINERAL SUPPLEMENT — (daily with meals, in divided doses if possible)

A very good daily multiple-vitamin/mineral supplement is essential to the Detox Program. When the body is detoxifying, it rapidly depletes its stores of nutrients. Without these nutrients, the detoxification processes can slow down or stop altogether. In addition, many of the toxins and the body's own metabolic systems often trigger the release of free radicals that can damage cells. Antioxidants help combat free radicals by scavenging them from the bloodstream, binding them, and carrying them out of the body. Many nutrients act as antioxidants and can help the body resist day-to-day free-radical damage. Choose a multiple-vitamin/mineral supplement that includes in its formula approximately 5 to 15 mg. of manganese, 100 to 150 mcg. of molybdenum, 18 to 20 mg. of iron, 25 to 30 mg. of zinc, and 2 to 3 mg. of copper. The formula should also include, or be supplemented with the following antioxidants:

Vitamin A — (25,000 IU of vitamin A in the beta-carotene form). Vitamin A has the remarkable ability to interfere with certain toxins found in tobacco smoke and other pollutants. Vitamin A can help prevent them from binding to the DNA in the cell. The beta-carotene form of vitamin A is the form that provides the vitamin's dynamic antioxidant functions.

Vitamin E — (200 to 400 IU). The most potent of the fat-soluble antioxidants, vitamin E helps protect the body against the effects of air-pollution toxins such as ozone, mercury, and lead. It is also essential to the functioning of the liver during detoxification.

2. FIBER — (approximately 2 g. of powdered psyllium [soluble] and 2 g. of bran [insoluble], in capsules, with each meal and at bedtime)

Fiber binds many toxic metals and other wastes, speeding their passage through the intestine and out of the body before they can be reabsorbed and stored. Psyllium, a soluble fiber, coats the intestines and inhibits the reabsorption of the supplementary olive oil (see below), which may be carrying many newly released, fat-soluble chlorinated hydrocarbons or other toxins. Wheat or rye bran, insoluble fibers, expand like a sponge and absorb water along with any water-soluble toxic substances it may contain. Both types of fiber help speed wastes out of the body.

3. GOLDENSEAL — (one capsule before meals, three times daily)

Goldenseal acts as a mild stimulant for the liver and kidneys, triggering their filtering and excretory functions. Goldenseal can also be beneficial to people recovering from the effects of alcohol or the opiates. Chemically, the alkaloids in goldenseal are similar to those in codeine and morphine, and may help relieve some of the discomfort of detoxification.

4. OLIVE OIL — (three to four teaspoons total, taken throughout the
    day)
Olive oil is effective for lubricating the intestines and encouraging the
rhythmic contractions that process wastes out of the body. In addition,
olive oil can help the body rid itself of many insoluble pollutants that may
be stored in body fats, including chlorinated hydrocarbons such as DDT
and PCB. Olive oil attracts the pollutants as they are released from their
storage areas in the body and carries them to organs that can excrete them.

5. PARSLEY — (three capsules or tablets three times daily, with meals)
Parsley is a mild diuretic that encourages the flushing of the kidneys.
Flushing the kidneys keeps toxins from building up in them and speeds
waste removal from the body, preventing the possible reabsorption of
impurities.

6. VITAMIN C — (500 mg. four times daily with meals and at bedtime,
    in addition to any vitamin C already in the multiple-vitamin/mineral
    supplement)
Vitamin C is an antioxidant that can protect cells from damage by newly
released toxins and reactive free radicals. Vitamin C also acts as a diuretic
that can help speed the body's excretion of toxins such as nicotine. As a
result, those who smoke will find that their nicotine cravings increase,
and they should be alert for this reaction. Those who wish to quit
smoking will find that this effect, which is very intense for the first few
days, will soon diminish and may actually shorten the overall period of
nicotine withdrawal.

7. WATER — (eight to ten glasses of distilled or mineral-free water
    daily, especially before breakfast, before bedtime, and during the
    night, when the body detoxifies most rapidly)
Water is possibly the most important nutrient in the Detox Program. The
body's water supply is depleted by the speeded-up metabolism during the
detoxification process. Water helps the skin eliminate impurities through
perspiration, and flushes out the toxins that are being processed by the
kidneys and other organs of excretion.

PART II

At the beginning of the second week of the Detox Program, continue the
nutrients listed in Part I, but add yellow dock to the daily regimen. This
combined regimen lasts for one week only.

8. YELLOW DOCK — (one capsule, morning and night)
Yellow dock is a powerful overall body detoxifier that speeds metabolic
processes. It helps clear congestion in the liver, one of the main organs
that processes toxic substances for elimination. Yellow dock also triggers
the release of bile from the gallbladder, stimulating digestive processes
particularly useful for breaking down fats.

153

PART III

Part III of the Detox Program consists of herbs selected to help relieve any discomforts that may occur during the detoxification process.

9. CAYENNE — (for headache: one capsule with one glass of water, as needed)
Cayenne is a vasodilator, a substance that dilates the blood vessels. It increases the overall flow of blood through the cardiovascular system and speeds the flushing of toxins that can trigger headaches.

10. GINSENG — (for fatigue: one cup, one capsule, or one slice, as needed)
Ginseng counteracts the effects of alcohol and depressants on the body. It seems to regulate certain neurotransmitters in the brain that fight the effects of fatigue and mild depression that may accompany detoxification.

11. PEPPERMINT — (for stomach distress: one cup of tea, as needed)
Peppermint tea has been used with great success to calm indigestion. It has a slightly anesthetic effect on the nerves of the stomach and can help soothe stomach spasms and quell nausea.

12. VALERIAN — (for anxiety or sleeplessness: two capsules, as needed)
Valerian is a natural tranquilizer, an excellent remedy for insomnia, and a safe, nonnarcotic sedative for nervousness. It is as effective as many commercially available tranquilizers.

13. WHITE WILLOW — (for body aches and pains: two capsules or tablets, as needed)
White willow reduces tissue inflammation and is effective for relieving body aches that may accompany detoxification. It is wonderful for combating headaches. White willow is as useful as aspirin, but without many of the stomach-irritating effects.

THE DETOX PROGRAM

THE DETOX PROGRAM

THE FITNESS PROGRAM IS DESIGNED TO ENHANCE THE HEALTH AND STAMINA OF INDIVIDUALS WHO EXERCISE STRENUOUSLY.

PART I — Supplements that replace depleted nutrients and protect the body from cellular damage:

1. *MULTIPLE-VITAMIN/MINERAL SUPPLEMENT*
   (daily with meal)
2. *CALCIUM*
   (1,200 to 1,500 mg. daily at bedtime, unless already provided in the multiple-vitamin/mineral supplement)
3. *CHROMIUM*
   (200 mcg. daily with first meal, unless already provided in the multiple-vitamin/mineral supplement)
4. *IRON*
   (18 to 25 mg. daily with first meal, unless already provided in the multiple-vitamin/mineral supplement)
5. *MAGNESIUM*
   (400 to 600 mg. daily at bedtime, unless already provided in the multiple-vitamin/mineral supplement)
6. *POTASSIUM CHLORIDE*
   (approximately 100 mg. after a workout, unless already provided in the multiple-vitamin/mineral supplement)
7. *VITAMIN C*
   (250 mg. four times daily, with meals and at bedtime)
8. *WATER*
   (eight to ten glasses of nondistilled water daily)

PART II — Supplements that enhance fat metabolism and tissue building:

9. *L-ARGININE WITH L-LYSINE*
   (1,500 mg. of each before bedtime, only on nights after a strenuous workout, up to three or four times per week)
10. *L-CARNITINE*
    (250 to 500 mg. with first and last meals)

PART III — Herbal aids that help increase stamina and repair tissues:

11. *COMFREY*
    (one capsule or one cup of tea after workout once each week)
12. *GINSENG*
    (one slice or one capsule, one-half hour before workout)

THE FITNESS PROGRAM

Individuals who exercise regularly without strategic nutrient replacement could be turning a healthful activity into a health-compromising one. The Fitness Program is designed to promote the results of any fitness regimen while protecting the body's health. During exercise, the body rapidly eliminates many of its water-soluble vitamins and minerals through perspiration. Other important nutrients are quickly depleted because the energy expended during exercise also causes the body's temperature to rise, which speeds the metabolic rate. As a consequence, the cells demand more nutrients as they perform more energy-releasing metabolic functions. Therefore, exercisers could be risking vitamin and mineral deficiencies. These deficiencies can affect the health of the immune system. In addition, strenuous exercise is believed to generate an increased number of cell-damaging free radicals, which must be neutralized through an increased antioxidant intake. Finally, strenuous exercise damages tissues at the cellular level, which is a normal part of muscle growth and fitness training. The faster these tissues heal or are replaced, the sooner stamina will increase and muscle tone will become apparent.

WHO SHOULD FOLLOW THE PROGRAM — The Fitness Program will not improve athletic performance, but it is designed to enhance the health, stamina, and appearance of those engaged in a regular fitness program.

HOW TO USE THE PROGRAM — Part I replaces those nutrients that are lost during strenuous exercise and adds others that can help exercisers reach their fitness goals healthfully. Part II introduces supplements that enhance fat metabolism, tissue growth and repair, and stamina.

DIETARY GUIDELINES — Wholesome low-fat, high-fiber meals are the key to a healthy, fit body. All the exercise in the world will not make up for an unhealthy diet. The fats will still go to the wrong places, especially to the arteries — and the toxins will still damage the cells.

PART I

Part I lists vitamin and mineral supplements that are important to those who exercise strenuously and frequently. Taken daily, these can help replace depleted nutrients, prevent muscle cramps, and protect the body from cellular damage caused by newly released free radicals.

1. MULTIPLE-VITAMIN/MINERAL SUPPLEMENT — (daily with meal)
Strenuous exercise speeds the body's basic metabolic processes, which depletes its nutrient reserves and triggers the release of free radicals. Free radicals can damage the structure of cells in ways that can actually age the body more rapidly. Antioxidants help clean up these newly released free radicals by scavenging them from the bloodstream, binding them, and then carrying them out of the body. Many nutrients act as antioxidants and can help the cells resist free-radical damage, so choose a multiple-vitamin/mineral supplement that includes vitamin A in beta-carotene form, vitamin E, and selenium. The beta-carotene form of vitamin A is the form that provides the vitamin's dynamic antioxidant functions, and vitamin E is a potent antioxidant that works in concert with selenium to protect cells and prevent their premature breakdown. The multiple-vitamin/mineral supplement should also contain all the B vitamins, especially vitamins B1, B2, niacin, and pantothenic acid. These vitamins are the most rapidly depleted during exercise, since they are used for the metabolic processes that release energy.

2. CALCIUM — (1,200 to 1,500 mg. daily at bedtime, unless already provided in the multiple-vitamin/mineral supplement)
Exercisers in general, and women in particular, require extra calcium. It is essential for muscle functions and the transmission of nerve impulses, triggering the flow of signals from nerve to nerve and between nerve and muscle. Calcium controls much of what passes in and out of the cells, and helps maintain the health and permeability of their membranes. Calcium also gives strength and rigidity to bones. It affects the body's immune system, the heartbeat, the maturation of collagen, and the release of many hormones, including some that affect blood pressure. It is also one of the minerals most depleted during exercise.

3. CHROMIUM — (200 mcg. daily with first meal, unless already provided in the multiple-vitamin/mineral supplement)
Strenuous exercise reduces chromium levels. Runners, especially, are at risk of chromium deficiency. Chromium is believed to affect cellular sensitivity to insulin. It may also influence how efficiently glucose is converted into energy.

4. IRON — (18 to 25 mg. daily with first meal, unless already provided in the multiple-vitamin/mineral supplement)
Iron is necessary to create healthy red blood cells, regulate and produce many of the brain's neurotransmitters, maintain the immune system, and create collagen — an important component of connective tissues. The

performance of the heart muscle requires iron. Iron is used for an assortment of enzymatic functions that trigger energy production in the body. Most of the body's iron is found in hemoglobin, the protein in red blood cells that transports oxygen from the lungs to the cells of the body. It is also present in myoglobin, the protein that transfers oxygen to the muscles. Sweating and the rupturing of red blood cells from the physical stress of strenuous exercise cause significant amounts of iron to be lost. This can lead to a condition known as sports anemia.

5. MAGNESIUM — (400 to 600 mg. daily at bedtime, unless already
   provided in the multiple-vitamin/mineral supplement)
Those who exercise strenuously need magnesium because it helps deliver oxygen to the muscles for peak performance. Magnesium is vital for converting glycogen into glucose for use as the body's fuel. Magnesium is also needed for transmitting nerve impulses, forming nucleic acids and proteins, keeping blood vessels well toned, and keeping the heart beating rhythmically. Like calcium, magnesium is stored primarily in the bones, and magnesium-calcium interactions are extremely important in the body. For example, when calcium passes into muscle cells, it triggers a set of reactions that cause the muscle to contract. The muscle then relaxes when the calcium leaves and is replaced by magnesium.

6. POTASSIUM CHLORIDE — (approximately 100 mg. after a workout,
   unless already provided in the multiple-vitamin/mineral supplement)
Potassium is an important electrolyte that, along with the electrolytes sodium and chloride, helps maintain the balance of water inside and outside of the cells. Potassium is needed for converting glucose in the blood into glycogen, which can be stored in tissues for later energy use. Sodium and calcium team up with potassium to regulate nerve-muscle interactions, to transmit signals in the nervous system, and to cause muscles to contract. Potassium is excreted in sweat and must be replaced. When not enough potassium is available, a condition called hypokalemia occurs, with symptoms that include muscle spasms and cramps.

7. VITAMIN C — (250 mg. four times daily, with meals and at bedtime)
Vitamin C levels are rapidly depleted during exercise, causing marginal deficiencies that produce symptoms of easy bruising, shortness of breath, and swollen, painful joints. Vitamin C is necessary for building and maintaining bones, teeth, and vascular tissue. It is essential for making collagen, the substance that acts as a "cement" in connective tissues such as tendons, cartilage, and spinal discs. Joggers and others engaged in exercise that stresses the spine should maintain high vitamin C levels. Vitamin C also makes iron available for the formation and maturation of red blood cells. It stimulates the adrenal glands, forming hormones such as cortisone, a natural anti-inflammatory substance, and epinephrine, a nerve stimulant commonly known by its trade name, Adrenalin.

8. WATER — (eight to ten glasses of nondistilled water daily)
Water with dissolved minerals helps replace the fluids and many of the minerals lost during exercise. These losses result in depleted body stores,

muscle dehydration, and electrolyte imbalances, causing muscle cramps and spasms. Water helps the skin, kidneys, and other organs of excretion flush out toxins that are released from cells as by-products of exercise. Replenishing and maintaining an adequate water level is vital to physical performance and overall health.

PART II

Part II describes the amino acids L-arginine and L-lysine, and an amino-acid-like substance, L-carnitine, that can enhance the metabolism of fats and the building of tissue. By taking these supplements in partnership with the nutrients in Part I, the time spent exercising could yield more dramatic results.

9. L-ARGININE WITH L-LYSINE — (1,500 mg. of each before bedtime on an empty stomach, only on nights after a strenuous workout, up to three or four times per week)

Recent research studies on animals, and preliminary findings on humans, indicate that taking supplemental L-arginine with L-lysine, in equal amounts, increases blood levels of hGH, the human growth hormone. The human growth hormone helps heal tissue by maintaining nitrogen balances in the body at levels that encourage new tissue growth. It also triggers cells to conserve the protein needed to rebuild tissues damaged during exercise.

10. L-CARNITINE — (250 to 500 mg. daily, with first and last meals)

L-carnitine is vital to the production of energy for use by the heart and other muscles. It transports fatty acids, the fuel that is burned to provide muscles with energy, into the part of the cell that acts as a chemical laboratory for this burning process. The energy released by the burning of fatty acids goes to the brain, muscles, and other tissues, making L-carnitine an ideal exercise-program adjunct. While L-carnitine has been cited as an aid to muscle building, research results so far indicate that this seems to happen only when the body has already suffered muscular problems directly due to a deficiency in L-carnitine. L-carnitine may, however, be useful in prolonging aerobic endurance during exercise. The body can manufacture L-carnitine, which it stores in the skeletal muscles. It may take a week or two of supplementation before these stores are increased and the beneficial effects from L-carnitine are experienced.

PART III

Part III lists herbal medications that can increase stamina and help soothe and repair muscle tissues stressed or damaged during workouts.

11. COMFREY — (one capsule or one cup of tea once each week after workout)

Comfrey is considered a mild astringent and anti-inflammatory agent. It has been relied on traditionally to stop internal bleeding, and it actually seems to help damaged tissues heal faster. This last effect may be due to the presence in comfrey of a remarkable substance called allantoin, which has been shown to trigger the rapid growth of new tissue. It can also work wonders on bruises and strained muscles when applied topically to the skin.

12. GINSENG — (one slice or one capsule, one-half hour before workout)

Ginseng is a stimulant that can increase the body's overall stamina. It is also an adaptogen, a substance that normalizes a wide range of physical and biochemical processes. New evidence, published in 1985, indicates that ginseng can trigger the synthesis of DNA, RNA, and proteins needed to build and repair exercise-damaged cells. Ginseng also seems to slow the breakdown of proteins and stimulate the bone marrow to produce new blood cells.

IMMUNE-SYSTEM

THE IMMUNE-SYSTEM PROGRAM IS A SHORT-TERM PROGRAM
DESIGNED TO HELP THE BODY FIGHT FLU, COLDS, AND INFECTIONS.

PART I — Nutrients that help maintain the body's immune system:

1. *MULTIPLE-VITAMIN/MINERAL SUPPLEMENT*
   (daily with meals, in divided doses if possible)

PART II — Nutrients to be used when illness is first felt:

2. *GARLIC*
   (two cloves of raw garlic or three capsules daily, in divided doses with meals, from first feeling of illness for one week)
3. *GOLDENSEAL*
   (one capsule three times daily, from first feeling of illness for one week)
4. *VITAMIN C*
   (500 mg. every four waking hours, from first feeling of illness through recovery, in addition to any vitamin C in the multiple-vitamin/mineral supplement)
5. *ZINC*
   (50 mg. zinc lozenges every four waking hours from first feeling of illness for three days, in addition to any zinc in the multiple-vitamin/mineral supplement)

PART III — Nutrients designed to speed recovery from illness and help eliminate toxins. Parts I and II should be continued, as well:

6. *FIBER*
   (approximately 3 g. of bran, in capsules, four times daily with meals and at bedtime, during illness, through recovery)
7. *L-ARGININE WITH L-LYSINE*
   (1,500 mg. of each, before bedtime, on an empty stomach, daily during illness, through recovery)
8. *WATER*
   (eight to ten glasses of nondistilled water, daily during illness, through recovery)

PART IV — Nutrients that can help restore vitality after illness:

9. *GINSENG*
   (one cup tea or one capsule, morning and afternoon)

THE IMMUNE-SYSTEM PROGRAM

It is the strength of the immune system that determines the health and longevity of the body. The Immune-System Program is designed to support the health of the immune system and promote its efforts in battling invading microorganisms, seeking out and destroying cellular mutations, and speeding the repair of damaged or overtaxed tissues and organs. When the body is threatened by an invasive element, the immune system triggers the formation of antibodies — substances designed to fight off specific diseases or infections. Once antibodies are formed, they rush to the threatened area to fight the invaders. Immunity, however, can be adversely affected when the body's physical condition is poor. Stress, exhaustion, exposure to pollutants, and a diet lacking protective nutrients can all weaken the immune system. To keep the body's immune responses alert and strong, and to trigger the rapid mobilization of lymphocytes — the army of the immune system — the body must receive full nutritional support.

WHO SHOULD FOLLOW THE PROGRAM — The Immune-System Program is for those individuals who are about to enter a stressful situation — travel, severe weather, emotional difficulties, a deadline at work, a contagious environment — or for those who feel that they are "coming down with something."

HOW TO USE THE PROGRAM — The illnesses addressed in the Immune-System Program are diseases such as the flu, colds, or infections that a strong or stimulated immune system can often circumvent. This four-part Program covers the time from just before illness through the time of recovery.

DIETARY GUIDELINES — During immune-compromising conditions, it is important to avoid substances that put a strain on the liver. The liver acts as the central clearinghouse for wastes and the switchboard for immune responses. Avoid excessive amounts of alcohol and caffeine, unnecessary drugs, and rich, high-fat foods. Eat and drink as simply and healthfully as possible.

PART I

Part I is a multiple-vitamin/mineral supplement that can help keep the body and its immune system in top form during times of stress or during exposure to immune-compromising conditions.

1. MULTIPLE-VITAMIN/MINERAL SUPPLEMENT — (daily with meals, in divided doses, if possible)

When the body calls on the immune-system to act in its defense, it puts a demand on its store of nutrients. Therefore, those individuals who want to protect and strengthen their immune systems, or who are actively fighting an illness, should take a daily comprehensive multiple-vitamin/ mineral supplement that includes in its formula 25,000 IU of vitamin A in its beta-carotene form, or 10,000 IU in its retinol form, along with 30 to 50 mg. of vitamin B6. The supplement should also contain adequate doses of the vitamins B12, C, and E, and the minerals iron, selenium, and zinc. These nutrients are vital to immune functions. A deficiency in any of them can compromise the actions of the immune system. Several of these nutrients, beyond having day-to-day functions in the immune system, also have special protective actions. Some are potent antioxidants that help maintain the stability of the cell membranes, protecting the body from toxic or carcinogenic substances, as well as from invading viruses or other microorganisms.

PART II

The nutrients in Part II are to be used when there is a feeling that disease may be near, at the very first sign of fatigue, unease, sore throat, swollen glands, diarrhea, headache, or sleeplessness. Part I should be continued, as well.

2. GARLIC — (two cloves of raw garlic or three capsules daily, in divided doses with meals, from first feeling of illness for one week)

Garlic is considered by herbalists to be a natural antibiotic. It has active ingredients that perform antiseptic, antibacterial, and antifungal functions, and can increase the body's resistance to infection. Garlic is used effectively to fight colds and to strengthen the immune system. Recent research indicates that garlic may also help fight tumors. The National Cancer Institute has begun a series of studies to determine garlic's effects on preventing and treating certain types of cancer.

3. GOLDENSEAL — (one capsule three times daily, from first feeling of illness for one week)

Goldenseal fights bacterial infections and stimulates the lymphatic system. When infectious microorganisms enter the body, the lymphatic system carries lymphocytes, small white blood cells, to the areas where they are needed. Once there, they produce antibodies to fight the invaders and neutralize their threat to the body's health. Goldenseal also acts as a mild stimulant for the liver and kidneys, helping them filter out and excrete toxins, wastes, and infectious matter.

4. VITAMIN C — (500 mg. every four waking hours, from first feeling of illness through recovery, in addition to any vitamin C already in the multiple-vitamin/mineral supplement)

Vitamin C has been shown to boost both the production and the activity of interferon, a substance that fights viruses such as those that cause colds and flu. Although recent studies indicate that vitamin C may not be really effective for preventing a cold, they do show that vitamin C, in the dosages recommended here, can minimize a cold's severity and even shorten its duration by almost one-third. In addition, vitamin C helps the body utilize iron, required for many immune-system functions.

5. ZINC — (50 mg. zinc lozenges every four waking hours, from first feeling of illness for three days, in addition to any zinc in the multiple-vitamin/mineral supplement)

Zinc lozenges allowed to dissolve in the mouth have been shown in recent studies to shorten the duration of colds. Zinc is known to stimulate the immune system and ward off infections. Higher doses of zinc actually increase the body's production of lymphocytes — the armed forces of the immune system. Recent studies indicate that supplemental zinc can reduce tissue-healing time by almost half. Furthermore, zinc helps the body metabolize vitamin A, a vitamin that, when mobilized, has the remarkable ability to fight viruses at the cellular level.

PART III

Once the illness is clearly present, the nutrients in Part III should be added to the diet. These nutrients are designed to speed recovery while rapidly eliminating toxins. Parts I and II should be continued, as well.

6. FIBER — (approximately 3 g. of bran, in capsules, four times daily with meals and at bedtime, during illness, through recovery)

Fiber plays a major role in maintaining the overall health and condition of the digestive system, which can significantly affect the health of the rest of the body. During illness, when the diet is often not as good as it should be, fiber helps keep things moving along. Insoluble fiber, such as bran, expands like a sponge to absorb wastes and speed their passage through the intestine and out of the body.

7. L-ARGININE WITH L-LYSINE — (1,500 mg. of each, before bedtime, on an empty stomach, daily during illness, through recovery)

L-arginine and L-lysine are two amino acids that work in combination. Research studies on animals, and preliminary findings on humans, indicate that taking supplemental L-arginine with L-lysine, in equal amounts, increases the blood levels of hGH, the human growth hormone. Because of this function, these amino acids are being investigated in their use for stimulating immune-system functions and speeding the healing of wounds. The human growth hormone helps maintain nitrogen balances in the body. It signals cells to conserve the protein needed to rebuild damaged tissue and promote the growth of new tissue.

8. WATER — (eight to ten glasses of nondistilled water, daily during illness, through recovery)
Water helps to quickly flush wastes from the liver and kidneys, which are engaged in the body's battle against illness. A higher intake of fluids helps rehydrate tissues overtaxed by speeded-up metabolic processes that occur when the body is fighting infections. Water also enhances the functioning of the skin, which, through increased perspiration, eliminates toxins from the body.

PART IV

After recovery is assured, Part IV provides support for fatigue and any lingering side effects or complications.

9. GINSENG — (one cup tea or one capsule, morning and afternoon)
Ginseng is considered an adaptogen, a substance that normalizes a wide range of physical and biochemical processes. It acts as a healthful pick-me-up tonic. Animal studies indicate that ginseng stimulates the immune system, increasing resistance to infection. New studies are also emerging which show that ginseng can trigger the synthesis of DNA, RNA, and proteins, slow the breakdown of proteins already present, and stimulate the bone marrow to produce new blood cells.

THE IMMUNE-SYSTEM PROGRAM

THE IMMUNE-SYSTEM PROGRAM

....
....
....
....
....
....
....
....
....
....
....
....
....
....
....
....

THIS PROGRAM IS A LONG-TERM REGIMEN
DESIGNED TO MAINTAIN
THE OVERALL HEALTH OF THE BODY WHILE ENHANCING
THE APPEARANCE OF THE SKIN AND HAIR.

PART I — Nutrients that protect the skin against
environmental pollutants and help detoxify
and nourish skin and scalp:

1. *MULTIPLE-VITAMIN/MINERAL SUPPLEMENT*
   (daily with meal)
2. *FIBER*
   (approximately 2 g. powdered psyllium [soluble]
   and 2 g. bran [insoluble], in capsules,
   with each meal and at bedtime)
3. *OLIVE OIL*
   (three teaspoons daily, with food or alone)
4. *PARSLEY*
   (three capsules or tablets three times daily, with meals)
5. *WATER*
   (eight to ten glasses of distilled or mineral-free water daily)

PART II — A regimen to be used one week of every month
for general body detoxification and
tissue rejuvenation:

6. *COMFREY*
   (one cup of tea each night for seven days)
7. *YELLOW DOCK*
   (two capsules three times daily, with meals, for seven days)

SKIN & HAIR

THE SKIN & HAIR PROGRAM

The nutrients in the Skin & Hair Program guard against tissue damage and aging caused by pollutants and ultraviolet radiation. They flush away infection-producing toxins stored in the body and skin and encourage skin-cell regeneration from within. The skin is the body's largest organ and is frequently the screen upon which the overall health of the body is displayed. When the body is ill, is over-exposed to pollutants or too much sunlight, or improperly nourished, the skin suffers visibly and ages rapidly. Because many chronic skin and scalp problems are the result of nutritional and environmental problems, rather than of specific diseases of the skin, the enlightened medical approach is to treat the whole body and not just its surface.

WHO SHOULD FOLLOW THE PROGRAM — The Skin & Hair Program is designed for individuals who feel that their skin looks dull and older that it should and for those who are plagued by chronic skin and scalp problems such as acne, dandruff, or psoriasis.

HOW TO USE THE PROGRAM — The Skin & Hair Program is a long-term program designed to keep the skin and scalp in peak condition. Part I lists all the nutrients upon which healthy, age-resistant skin is dependent. Part II is a one-week-per-month skin-detoxifying regimen that helps clear away accumulated wastes and stimulate new tissue growth. For best results, avoid ultraviolet radiation from sunlight and tanning lamps. They damage the DNA in the skin cells, causing them to lose their tone and elasticity.

DIETARY GUIDELINES — The diet always shows up in the skin. Alcoholic beverages dry the skin, regardless of how much water is consumed. High-fat, overly processed foods cause excessive elimination through the skin's pores, enlarging and clogging them. To enhance the effectiveness of the Skin & Hair Program, eat a simple diet that is high in fresh and raw foods.

169

PART I

Part I includes a comprehensive multiple-vitamin/mineral formula designed to protect the skin against environmental pollutants. It also contains nutrients that help detoxify and nourish the skin and scalp. Although this program should be followed every day, those who wish to may select from the nutrients listed and design their own daily regimen.

1. MULTIPLE-VITAMIN/MINERAL SUPPLEMENT — (daily with meal)
Air pollution, sunlight, chemicals in food and water, and the body's basic metabolic processes often accelerate the aging of the skin by triggering free-radical oxidation. Free radicals are highly reactive molecules that can lodge in a cell's nucleus and damage its DNA. The damaged DNA then sets off mutations that can slow the growth of new cells or alter their structure in ways that cause them to lose their elasticity and general tone. Antioxidants help combat free radicals by scavenging them from the bloodstream, binding them, and carrying them out of the body. Many nutrients act as antioxidants and can help the skin resist day-to-day free-radical damage. In addition, those who are suffering from skin problems such as acne, psoriasis, and nonspecific dermatitis (rashes that are caused by allergies or stress) have an increased demand in the body for nutrients. Any physical and emotional stress will speed cellular metabolism, depleting the body's nutrient reserves. Since the overall health of the skin is closely tied to the body's nutritional health, a daily multiple-vitamin/mineral supplement should be taken that includes the following antioxidants and other beneficial nutrients:

Calcium — (1,000 to 1,500 mg.). Calcium affects the health of the body's immune system and participates in the maturation of collagen — the connective tissue in the skin and body tissues. Calcium also works with iron to protect the body against the adverse effects of toxins such as lead, prevalent in city air.

Vitamin A — (25,000 IU in beta-carotene form, if possible). Vitamin A is an essential nutrient for the health and appearance of the skin. It has the remarkable ability to speed the regeneration of damaged tissue and the growth of fresh, new skin cells. The beta-carotene form of vitamin A is believed to provide dynamic antioxidant functions that interfere with many airborne pollutants and other oxidizing substances which damage skin. One of these is sunlight, which causes skin damage such as premature wrinkles, discolorations and scaly patches on the arms and hands, and skin cancer. Sunlight also speeds the breakdown of beta-carotene in the body, so this nutrient must be replenished daily to take advantage of its protective effects.

Vitamin B6 — (30 to 50 mg.). Cell division is dependent on the presence of vitamin B6 because of its role in metabolizing tissue proteins and synthesizing nucleic acids such as RNA and DNA. In fact, vitamin B6 is perhaps the most important of the B vitamins for a healthy body. A number of skin problems, such as premenstrual acne, can be controlled with vitamin B6 supplements.

170

Vitamin C — (1,000 mg.). Vitamin C is an important antioxidant that protects cells from damage by free radicals. It is essential for making collagen, the substance that acts as a "cement" in skin. The loss of collagen is one of the primary causes of wrinkles and an aged appearance of the skin.

Vitamin E — (200 to 400 IU). The most potent of the fat-soluble antioxidants, vitamin E acts to maintain the stability of cell membranes and prevent their premature breakdown. Recent studies have found that vitamin E seems to shorten the healing time of wounds, while a deficiency in vitamin E seems to speed the aging of tissues.

Zinc — (20 to 30 mg.). Zinc is believed to prevent or repair some of the cell damage that occurs as the body ages. It is a crucial element for the synthesis of DNA and RNA, the nucleic acids that build, reproduce, develop, and repair all cells. Zinc also helps stimulate the immune system. Recent studies indicate that supplemental zinc taken orally can reduce tissue-healing time by almost half.

2. FIBER — (approximately 2 g. powdered psyllium [soluble] and 2 g. bran [insoluble], in capsules, with each meal and at bedtime)
A mixture of soluble and insoluble fiber helps complete the detoxifying work done by the olive oil and water (see below). Insoluble fiber (bran) absorbs water and other fluids, along with any wastes they are carrying, and speeds them out of the body. Soluble fiber (psyllium) helps prevent the reabsorption from the intestines of the olive oil that may have sopped up toxins. A diet high in both soluble and insoluble fiber can help keep the skin clear, since fewer toxins need to be forced out of the body through its pores.

3. OLIVE OIL — (three teaspoons daily with food or alone)
Olive oil is effective in treating mild constipation, lubricating the intestines and encouraging the rhythmic contractions that process wastes out of the body. In addition, olive oil can help the body rid itself of many insoluble pollutants that may be stored in body fats, including the chlorinated hydrocarbons DDT and PCB. Olive oil attracts pollutants from their storage areas in the body and carries them to the intestines and out of the body.

Topically — Olive oil is the herbalist's indispensible topical for preventing and fighting a variety of skin problems. Dry skin, rashes, and split cuticles respond quickly to fresh, unheated olive oil. Dandruff can be controlled by applying olive oil directly to the scalp and leaving it on overnight.

4. PARSLEY — (three capsules or tablets three times daily, with meals)
Parsley's primary use by herbalists is as a mild diuretic that encourages the flushing of the kidneys, which process many of the body's toxins and wastes. Flushing the kidneys keeps toxins from building up in them and speeds watery wastes from the body, enhancing its overall health.

171

5. WATER — (eight to ten glasses of distilled or mineral-free water daily)

The health and appearance of the skin can be enhanced by drinking water every day. This helps flush out the skin through perspiration. It also helps speed toxins out of the body that have been processed by the kidneys and other organs of excretion. Dry skin may be the result of dehydration, so replenishing lost fluids and maintaining an adequate water level is very important to the appearance of the skin.

PART II

One week of every month is devoted to body detoxification and tissue rejuvenation. During this time, continue using the nutrients in Part I, but add the two herbs below for seven days. For best results, do not drink any alcoholic beverages during this time.

6. COMFREY — (one cup of tea each night for seven days)

Comfrey tea is a soothing, healing tonic for the skin. It is considered a mild astringent and anti-inflammatory agent. It contains a remarkable substance called allantoin, which has been shown to trigger the growth of new tissue in a short period of time.

Topically — A strong solution of comfrey tea, when cooled and applied like an astringent to the skin throughout the day and night, will help dry and heal skin infections. The allantoin in comfrey makes it useful as a topical for open sores, ulcers, and wounds. It also speeds the drainage and drying of abscesses and boils, and it can work wonders on skin eruptions caused by acne and eczema. When a quart of comfrey tea is added to the bath water, it is believed to help stimulate the growth of new skin.

7. YELLOW DOCK — (two capsules three times daily, with meals, for seven days)

Yellow dock is considered a good, general body detoxifier. It speeds the metabolic processes that help clear congestion in the liver. Yellow dock also triggers the release of bile from the gallbladder. This stimulates digestive processes and breaks down fatty wastes that affect the condition of the skin. The detoxifying process will begin at once, so skin conditions may get worse for a day or two as the body excretes stored toxins.

THE STRESS PROGRAM IS A LONG-TERM PROGRAM
DESIGNED TO MAINTAIN THE BODY'S HEALTH
DURING STRESSFUL WORKING OR LIVING CONDITIONS.

PART I — Nutrients that help maintain the body's health
during stressful times:

1. *MULTIPLE-VITAMIN/MINERAL SUPPLEMENT*
   (daily with meal)
2. *CALCIUM*
   *(1,000 to 1,500 mg. daily at bedtime, unless already included
   in the multiple-vitamin/mineral supplement)*
3. *MAGNESIUM*
   *(400 to 600 mg. daily at bedtime, unless this amount is already
   included in the multiple-vitamin/mineral supplement)*
4. *VITAMIN C*
   (250 mg. four times daily, with meals and at bedtime)

PART II — Herbal medicines that are effective in alleviating
some of the physical and emotional
symptoms of stress:

5. *CATNIP*
   (daytime tranquilizer: one cup or one capsule, as needed)
6. *GINSENG*
   *(daytime stimulant: one cup of tea, one capsule,
   or one slice, as needed)*
7. *VALERIAN*
   *(evening tranquilizer: one or two capsules
   or one cup of tea, as needed)*

THE STRESS PROGRAM

The significance of stress in the biological processes of life is quite a profound one. An astonishing fourteen hundred biochemical reactions occur throughout the human body at the very instant a stressful event is sensed. These reactions trigger muscle reflexes, immune responses, and the release of hormones. They also affect the functions of the cardiovascular, digestive, and reproductive systems. As a result, researchers now believe that such problems as asthma, eczema, diabetes, heart disease, ulcers, sexual impotence, backaches, migraine headaches, and behavorial disorders can be caused or influenced by stress.

The simple fact is, life is one of the most stressful physical and emotional conditions imaginable. The challenge, therefore, is to prevent stress from interfering with the body's health by either eliminating the cause of stress immediately or learning to peacefully co-exist with it. Most individuals are unable to do either — so in the end they internalize their responses and cope the best they can. It is this internal pressure that can lead to the development of many physical disorders. The Stress Program is designed to protect the body from the ravages of stress and provide buffers from its emotional and physical symptoms.

WHO SHOULD FOLLOW THE PROGRAM — The Stress Program is targeted toward those who are engaged in intensely stressful situations — divorce, illness or death of a family member, dislocation, project deadlines, fear — or those who are operating in an unrelentingly stressful environment — poverty, job pressures, unemployment, or boredom.

HOW TO USE THE PROGRAM — The Stress Program is in two parts. Part I is designed to replace nutrients that are depleted by stress. It will supplement the diet with nutrients that have a positive effect on certain physical problems associated with stress, such as high blood pressure. Part II provides plant-derived medications to help alleviate some of the symptoms of stress, such as nervousness or insomnia.

DIETARY GUIDELINES — Stress speeds cellular metabolism, which accelerates the breakdown and excretion of important nutrients, depleting the body's stores of them. Because there is an increased physical demand for nutrients, individuals under stress need to protect themselves from deficiencies that can compromise their health. The best dietary defense for stress is to drink plenty of water and eat three or four small but wholesome meals every day. Individuals under stress should guard against dependence on the cycle of stimulants and depressants, such as coffee and alcohol.

PART I

Part I provides nutrients that are necessary to maintain the body's health while engaged in stressful situations or difficult life transitions.

1. MULTIPLE-VITAMIN/MINERAL SUPPLEMENT — (daily with meal)
Nutrient deficiencies caused by stress can result in continued anxiety and nervousness, as well as promoting an overall health risk for the body. The B vitamins, particularly, are depleted rapidly by stress and must be replaced daily. Replacing these vitamins will not reduce stress, but preventing their deficiency can also prevent other problems that might aggravate already stressful conditions. Therefore, individuals under stress should take a comprehensive multiple-vitamin/mineral supplement daily.

2. CALCIUM — (1,000 to 1,500 mg. daily at bedtime, unless already included in the multiple-vitamin/mineral supplement)
Calcium affects the body's immune system, the heartbeat, and the release of many hormones, including some that affect blood pressure. Recent studies have shown that supplementary calcium intake, coupled with a reduction in dietary sodium, can reduce high blood pressure in both men and women after only a few weeks. It can also help reduce nervousness in some individuals, since calcium is necessary for the efficient transmission of nerve impulses, triggering the flow of signals from nerve to nerve and between nerve and muscle.

3. MAGNESIUM — (400 to 600 mg. daily at bedtime, unless already included in the multiple-vitamin/mineral supplement)
Magnesium has a beneficial effect on the nervous system. An imbalance between calcium and magnesium in the body, where there is not enough magnesium, may play a role in high blood pressure and may increase the risk of developing cardiovascular disease. Those who use alcohol to relieve stress should be aware that alcohol depletes the body's magnesium resources. Since some magnesium can be absorbed through the skin, a pleasant way to restore some of the body's magnesium is to relax in a warm bath of magnesium-rich Epsom salts (magnesium sulfate).

4. VITAMIN C — (250 mg. four times daily, with meals and at bedtime)
Stress depletes the body of vitamin C, a deficiency that can cause fatigue and anxiety, thereby continuing the stress cycle. Among other things, vitamin C is needed to stimulate the adrenal glands to form hormones such as cortisone, which is involved in stress reactions, and epinephrine, a nerve stimulant that is commonly known by its trade name, Adrenalin. In addition, vitamin C strengthens the immune system by boosting the production and activity of interferon, a substance that fights viruses.

PART II

Part II describes herbal medicines that are effective in alleviating some of the physical and emotional symptoms of stress.

5. CATNIP — (daytime tranquilizer: one cup or one capsule, as needed)
Catnip is a very effective, mild sedative that is gentle and safe, even for children, and good for calming frayed nerves and relaxing tense muscles. It can be taken throughout the day without causing excessive drowsiness.

6. GINSENG — (daytime stimulant: one cup of tea, one capsule, or one slice, as needed)
Ginseng is a stimulant that is beneficial to those under stress: It does not jangle nerves the way coffee and many other stimulants do, and it is an adaptogen, a substance that normalizes a wide range of physical and biochemical processes. Ginseng acts as an antidepressant and, in animal studies, has been shown to lower abnormally high blood pressure to near-normal levels.

7. VALERIAN — (evening tranquilizer: one or two capsules or one cup of tea, as needed)
Valerian is a natural tranquilizer that can bring symptomatic relief from stress. Laboratory studies have shown that it has beneficial effects on the central nervous system and can relax muscle spasms brought on by nervous tension. It is an excellent remedy for insomnia, and a safe, nonnarcotic sedative for nervousness — safer than many of the commercially available tranquilizers. A cup of valerian tea is a wonderful and soothing way to unwind after a stressful day, relaxing the body, calming nerves, and inducing sleep.

THE WEIGHT-LOSS PROGRAM IS DESIGNED TO HELP THE BODY LOSE WEIGHT HEALTHFULLY. IT MAY BE FOLLOWED FOR TWO WEEKS AT A TIME, WITH A ONE-WEEK BREAK BETWEEN REGIMENS.

PART I — Optional diuretic to help flush retained fluids:

1. *JUNIPER BERRIES*
   (one cup of tea in the morning about one-half hour before breakfast)

PART II — To suppress the appetite before meals:

2. *PEPPERMINT*
   (one cup of tea one-half hour before each meal)
3. *SOLUBLE FIBER*
   (approximately 3 g. of powdered psyllium, in capsules, with a full glass of water, one-half hour before each meal)

PART III — To help restore lost nutrients, provide metabolic energy, and eliminate food quickly from the body:

4. *MULTIPLE-VITAMIN/MINERAL SUPPLEMENT*
   (daily with meal)
5. *CALCIUM*
   (1,000 to 1,500 mg. daily at bedtime)
6. *INSOLUBLE FIBER*
   (approximately 3 g. of bran four times daily, in capsules, after meals and at bedtime)
7. *L-CARNITINE*
   (500 mg. two times daily, with first and last meals)

PART IV — To help with fat metabolism:

8. *L-ARGININE WITH L-LYSINE*
   (1,500 mg. of each before bedtime, at least two hours after eating)

PART V — To help dissolve and transport toxins and eliminate wastes:

9. *OLIVE OIL*
   (three to four teaspoons daily, with meals or alone)
10. *WATER*
    (eight to ten glasses of nondistilled or mineral water daily)

THE WEIGHT-LOSS PROGRAM

The Weight-Loss Program is strategically designed to suppress the appetite, help block the absorption of fats, and move food out of the body as quickly as possible. At the same time, it replaces many of the nutrients that may be lost during dieting. Most popular diets suggest drastically reduced caloric intake, with no supplementary nutritive support. These diets can seriously jeopardize the body's store of nutrients. Furthermore, the body tends to store the pollutants and chemicals that we eat, breathe, and drink in our fat cells, where they are relatively inert. As we lose weight, however, our fat cells shrink and simultaneously release these stored toxins, which must be captured and excreted from the body before they can cause permanent cell damage. The Weight-Loss Program includes substances that act as solvents to dissolve and capture toxins, or as antioxidants to incapacitate free radicals. In this way, the Program assures a comfortable and healthy loss of fatty tissue.

WHO SHOULD FOLLOW THE PROGRAM — The Weight-Loss Program is designed for individuals who plan to lose weight permanently. Those who tend to lose weight and then put it back on again should not be dieting at all. This cycle can cause a great deal of damage to the overall health of the body. The more this cycle is repeated, the faster the body ages. Unless the eating habits change, permanently, to a very low-fat, high-fiber format, it can be both pointless and dangerous to diet.

HOW TO USE THE PROGRAM — The Weight-Loss Program may be followed for two weeks, with a one-week break between regimens. It is divided into five parts that are used simultaneously. Part I is an optional morning diuretic to remove retained water. Part II is a before-meals appetite-suppression regimen. Part III includes after-meal supplements that replace nutrients, supply protective antioxidants, and speed food through the intestines. Part IV consists of amino-acid supplements that have shown promising results in weight-reduction programs. Part V adds nutrients that act as solvents to help dissolve and flush away toxins.

DIETARY GUIDELINES — The Weight Loss Program should be part of a lifetime readjustment to sound dietary values. Many popular diets with their "low-cal" menus are counterproductive to permanent weight loss, because they do not transform eating habits and instead create cravings which must be satisfied when the diet ends. The lean-body rules are eternal: Cut out fats; drink lots of water; eat fruits, vegetables, and grains; and walk, rather than ride, whenever possible.

PART I

Part I is an optional diuretic. While the Weight-Loss Program can be used without Part I, this diuretic will help flush away retained fluids and many of the toxins they might have carried to the kidneys.

1. JUNIPER BERRIES — (one cup of tea in the morning, about one-half hour before breakfast)
Juniper berry tea is an excellent mild diuretic that helps relieve and reduce edema, or water retention. The tea has a bittersweet, resinous taste: It can be improved by sweetening with honey or steeping a little peppermint in the boiled mixture. A large piece of lemon peel can also be added to the tea for both its detoxifying qualities and its flavor.

PART II

Part II is designed to suppress the appetite before meals. The ingredients are easy to carry and use anywhere.

2. PEPPERMINT — (one cup of tea one-half hour before each meal)
Peppermint tea produces a slightly anesthetic effect on the nerves of the stomach. For this reason, a cup of peppermint tea before a meal will help decrease the appetite, soothe stomach spasms, and expel gas from the digestive tract.

3. SOLUBLE FIBER — (approximately 3 g. of powdered psyllium, in capsules, with a full glass of water, one-half hour before each meal)
Soluble fiber such as psyllium is an excellent dieting aid because it increases in volume so dramatically when wet. It rapidly fills the stomach to overcome appetite and extends the time that it takes food to leave the stomach, which delays hunger. Psyllium also coats the digestive tract and helps reduce the amount of fat that is absorbed into the body.

PART III

Part III is a regimen to be used after meals. The supplements in this part help restore lost nutrients, provide metabolic energy, and add insoluble fiber to push the food just eaten through the intestines quickly.

4. MULTIPLE-VITAMIN/MINERAL SUPPLEMENT — (daily with meal)
A daily multiple-vitamin/mineral supplement is particularly important during the Weight-Loss Program because it increases the amounts of minerals available for the body's use. This will circumvent any potential mineral deficiencies due to the high-fiber intake recommended in this Program. Also, the metabolic processes in the body that accompany weight-loss often release free radicals, which trigger oxidation processes. These free radicals are highly reactive molecules that often lodge in a cell's nucleus and damage its DNA, setting off mutations that can alter the

structure of cells. Nutrients that act as antioxidants help combat free radicals by scavenging them from the bloodstream, binding them, and carrying them out of the body.

To compensate for lost minerals, choose a multiple-vitamin/mineral supplement that includes approximately 5 to 15 mg. of manganese, 100 to 150 mcg. of molybdenum, 18 to 20 mg. of iron, 25 to 30 mg. of zinc, and 2 to 3 mg. of copper. To scavenge newly released toxins and prevent oxidation damage to cells, be sure the formula contains or is supplemented with 1,000 mg. of vitamin C, 400 IU of vitamin E, and 25,000 IU of vitamin A in the beta-carotene form, all powerful antioxidants.

5. CALCIUM — (1,000 to 1,500 mg. daily at bedtime)
Calcium is more likely than any other mineral to be eliminated during a weight-loss regimen. It is particularly important for dieters to supplement with calcium in order to avoid any bone loss that may be triggered by a calcium deficiency. Furthermore, calcium protects the cells of the colon from damage during times of intense toxin elimination, such as during weight loss.

6. INSOLUBLE FIBER — (approximately 3 g. of bran four times daily, in capsules, after meals and at bedtime)
Insoluble fiber moves food very quicky through the digestive system, absorbing water and other fluids — and many of the toxic elements they contain. Recent epidemiological studies suggest that insoluble fiber such as wheat bran may contribute to the prevention of certain types of cancer, particularly of the colon, by either absorbing and diluting carcinogenic elements or by speeding their excretion from the body. The recommended dosage may be adjusted to meet individual needs.

7. L-CARNITINE — (500 mg. two times daily, with first and last meals)
L-carnitine increases the efficient burning of fatty acids and is vital to the production of energy in the body. As a result, L-carnitine may help quell the feelings of hunger and muscle weakness that frequently accompany reduced-calorie diets. The brain, muscles, and other tissues all benefit from the increased energy released when the body's metabolism of fatty acids is enhanced.

PART IV

Part IV is an amino-acid supplement that works best on an empty stomach. It should be taken at bedtime, two hours or more after eating.

8. L-ARGININE WITH L-LYSINE — (1,500 mg. of each before bedtime, on an empty stomach, at least two hours after eating)
L-arginine with L-lysine, in combination, increases the body's levels of human growth hormone (hGH), which speeds the burning of fatty acids from the body's fat tissues.

PART V

Part V provides nutritive elements that help dissolve and transport waste by-products and toxins that have been released during weight loss. These elements should be taken throughout the day.

9. OLIVE OIL — (three to four teaspoons daily, with meals or alone)
Olive oil can help the body rid itself of many insoluble toxins that may be stored in body fats, including chlorinated hydrocarbons such as DDT and PCB. Olive oil attracts these toxins from their storage areas in the body's fat cells and carries them safely out of the body. Psyllium, the soluble fiber that is taken before meals, helps prevent the reabsorption of the olive oil from the intestines.

10. WATER — (eight to ten glasses of nondistilled or mineral water daily)
Water, in ample quantities, helps flush away the wastes and toxins that are released during weight loss from their storage in fat cells. The toxic wastes are processed by the kidneys, liver, and other organs of excretion, and water flushes the wastes from these organs to help prevent their reabsorption. Water also helps in weight loss by giving bulk to fiber and providing a sense of fullness. The dissolved minerals in the water will help replace some of the minerals that can be difficult for the body to absorb when fiber intake is high.

NOTES

THE WEIGHT-LOSS PROGRAM

THE WEIGHT-LOSS PROGRAM

NOTES

Chapter Six

PROBLEM SOLVING

Aging
Alcohol Use
Anemia
Arthritis
Aspirin Use
Asthma
Backache
Bladder Disorders
Breasts
Bronchitis
Bruises
Burns
Caffeine Use
Cancer
Cold Sores
Colon Disorders
Common Cold
Constipation
Convalescence and Healing
Dental Problems
Depression
Diabetes
Diarrhea
Dieters
Diuretic Use
Ear Disorders
Edema
Eye Disorders
Fatigue
Flatulence
Flu
Forgetfulness
Hay Fever

Headache
Healing Wounds
Heart Disease
Hemorrhoids
High Blood Pressure
Indigestion
Infertility
Insomnia
Kidney Disorders
Leg Cramps
Liver Disorders
Loss of Smell or Taste
Menopause
Menstruation
Migraine
Motion Sickness
Muscle Cramps or Spasms
Nausea
Nervousness/Anxiety
Oral-Contraceptive Use
Osteoporosis
Phlebitis
Pollution
Pregnancy
Premenstrual Syndrome
Shingles
Sinusitis
Skin Disorders
Smoking
Sunburn
Ulcers
Varicose Veins
Vegetarians
Winter Weather

PROBLEM SOLVING

Recent research has demonstrated that there are a number of physical conditions that can occur through inadequate nutrient intake, or that can be treated with supplemental nutrients or herbs. Each listing that follows has a description of a condition or disorder, along with recommended nutrients for its treatment or prevention.

For treatment, the doses recommended are higher than normal, and they are usually temporary, lasting only a few days or weeks. Therefore, if you are already taking a daily multiple-vitamin/mineral supplement, you may want to subtract the amount of the recommended Problem-Solving nutrient from the dosages you normally take. For instance, if a treatment calls for two weeks of 600 IU of vitamin E, and you are already taking 400 IU daily, your Problem-Solving dosage would be an additional 200 IU. This formula for calculating your Problem-Solving dosages also applies if you are using any of the programs in this book.

To prevent certain physical disorders, increased dosages may be recommended for an indefinite period of time. Therefore, if you are already taking a daily multiple-vitamin/mineral supplement, you should be sure that the formula you choose reflects your nutritional goals. For example, the mineral calcium is rarely provided in multiple-vitamin/mineral supplements in the dosages necessary to prevent diseases like osteoporosis. Therefore, you will need to obtain calcium from additional supplements.

At the end of each listing is a botanical approach, using plant-derived medicines. These focus primarily on the treatment of disorders. The botanicals included in this section are intended to act quickly to relieve symptoms, as well as stimulate the body to employ its own healing mechanisms. These preparations may be used alone or in conjunction with any of the nutritional therapies.

AGING
(see also THE ANTI-AGING PROGRAM, page 138)

The elderly have special nutritional concerns. They are a particularly high-risk group for deficiencies because they eat less — resulting in reduced nutrition — and because their ability to absorb nutrients becomes increasingly inefficient with age. After middle age, the body actually requires a higher intake of nutrients. Many of the problems associated with old age — fragile bones, loss of appetite, headaches, insomnia, and depression — are often the result of nutritional deficiencies. Furthermore, these deficiencies impair immune-system functions, making the body more susceptible to disease. Older Americans — as many as one-third of the adults over the age of fifty — are deficient in vitamins A, B1 (thiamin), B2 (riboflavin), and C. The minerals iron, zinc, and calcium are also at insufficient levels in the diets of the elderly. Older individuals should take a multiple-vitamin/mineral supplement that includes at least 400 IU of vitamin D, 1,000 to 1,500 mg. of calcium, and 400 to 600 mg. of magnesium. The kind of supplement recommended is one that is taken with each meal, rather than the one-pill-a-day variety. In this way, unstored nutrients are available when the body needs them. Another nutrient frequently deficient in the elderly is water. Water deficiency, or dehydration, leads to a number of problems associated with aging, such as constipation. Because many of the elderly are taking medications, it is important to find out whether these medications are impaired by certain nutrients or, conversely, whether the medications are interfering with the effectiveness of specific nutrients.

BOTANICAL APPROACH — One botanical that has long been viewed as ideal for the elderly is ginseng. It can be taken in capsule form, in tea, or by nibbling a dried slice of the root itself. Ginseng is considered an excellent, uplifting tonic and antifatigue agent. Take one cup of tea, one capsule, or one slice of ginseng root first thing in the morning, before breakfast, and again in the mid-afternoon, if desired. Since ginseng has some stimulating effects, it is best not to take it before bedtime.

ALCOHOL USE
(see also THE DETOX PROGRAM, page 150)

For many Americans, alcoholic beverages are a part of social and business life and frequently a part of the evening meal. The American Heart Association recommends that alcohol intake be limited to about one and a half ounces daily, about one shot of liquor or two four-ounce glasses of wine. Yet even one glass of wine has specific effects on the body's nutritional balance, and those who drink two or more drinks a day will require some nutritional adjustments. Alcohol in the bloodstream interferes with the body's utilization of vitamins B1, B6, and folic acid. Moderate to heavy alcohol drinkers frequently show deficiencies in all the B vitamins, as well as in vitamins A, C, and D. To help remove alcohol toxins from the bloodstream, some nutritionists recommend taking 50 mg. of the nicotinic acid form of niacin, three times a day. Alcohol drinkers are also frequently deficient in the minerals zinc, iron, calcium, and magnesium. Drinkers who have more than two drinks daily are at risk nutritionally and should be certain to take a comprehensive multiple-vitamin/mineral supplement that contains adequate levels of the following nutrients:

ANTIOXIDANTS — The ethanol in alcohol triggers the release of free radicals that can do permanent damage to the cells. Antioxidants can help block some of that damage, so alcohol drinkers should take daily supplements of 1,000 mg. of vitamin C, 400 IU of vitamin E, and 25,000 IU of the beta-carotene form of vitamin A.

CALCIUM — Alcohol drinkers should supplement their diets with 1,000 to 1,500 mg. of calcium each day. Because the body's mineral status is compromised by alcohol, calcium deficiency is a common and health-defeating problem among heavy alcohol drinkers.

FOLIC ACID — Alcohol use is the number-one cause of folic acid deficiency in the United States. Folic acid deficiency can result in insomnia, a condition associated with alcoholism. Drinkers should take 400 to 800 mcg. of supplemental folic acid each day.

SELENIUM — Although all the scientific data is not in at this time, there is growing evidence that 200 mcg. of selenium daily may help prevent some of the liver damage or scarring that results from a moderate to heavy daily alcohol intake.

VITAMIN B1 (THIAMIN) — Deficiencies in vitamin B1 can trigger memory loss and psychotic behavior. A vitamin B1 loss coupled with insufficient magnesium is believed to be one of the culprits in the well-known hangover. Heavy alcohol drinkers need more vitamin B1 than do nondrinkers, at least 100 mg. daily.

WATER — Severe dehydration is a common problem for alcohol drinkers because the body's water supply is depleted as it metabolizes alcohol. In fact, among the suspected causes of hangover, dehydration is believed to be one of the primary ones. To help prevent dehydration and hangovers, drink one glass of water for every alcoholic beverage during the period you are drinking. Drink one glass of water before bed; and one glass during the night.

ZINC — Alcohol causes the body to excrete zinc and can interfere with its absorption. This can lead to chemical imbalances that trigger other problems such as depression, a frequent disorder among alcoholics. Alcohol users need daily supplements of zinc in the 25 to 50 mg. range, balanced with approximately 3 mg. of copper.

BOTANICAL APPROACH — To help detoxify the body after long-term alcohol use, herbalists recommend the following two-week program: Take two capsules of goldenseal root each morning for its detoxifying effect on the liver, and two valerian capsules early each evening to help relieve anxiety and to aid in sleeping. Also, drink eight glasses of water and take eight to ten parsley capsules throughout the day to help the body flush out stored toxins.

The botanical remedy for the dreaded hangover consists of the following: For nausea, fill a glass with sparking mineral water and a squeeze of lemon, and drink it with one cayenne capsule. For any accompanying headache pain, take two white willow tablets and go back to bed.

ANEMIA

Anemia is a blood disorder in which the level of hemoglobin, the compound in the blood that carries oxygen to body tissues, is low. This condition is most frequently due to deficiencies in iron, copper, vitamin B12, and/or folic acid. A low hemoglobin level means that the tissues are not getting the oxygen they need to function properly, which results in fatigue and shortness of breath. Individuals prone to anemia should take a comprehensive multiple-vitamin/mineral supplement every day to be sure that nutrient deficiencies are not contributing to the disorder.

ARTHRITIS

Arthritis is an inflammation of one or more joints in the body that may be the result of a variety of factors, including aging, obesity, and stress-related tension. Arthritis sufferers, in general, have overall nutrient concerns, since inflammatory disease taxes their body's store of antioxidants necessary to protect them from cellular damage. Such damage can be caused by pollutants, food additives, and the normal, but damaging, oxidation of molecules in the body. To make matters worse, this damage further contributes to the inflammatory response in arthritic joints. Therefore, arthritis sufferers should be certain to get a comprehensive multiple-vitamin/mineral supplement with strong levels of the following antioxidants: 25,000 IU of the beta-carotene form of vitamin A, 1,000 mg. of vitamin C, 400 IU of vitamin E, and 200 mcg. of selenium. Also important to arthritis sufferers are daily supplements of 1,500 mg. of calcium, 30 mg. of zinc, and 3 mg. of copper. Copper seems to play a role in the body's anti-inflammatory activity; and, since some minerals can be absorbed through the skin, do not discount the folk remedy of wearing a copper bracelet. Currently, some physicians are treating rheumatoid-arthritis patients with daily megadoses of 500 to 2,000 mg. of pantothenic acid, with limited, but promising, success. Such high doses, however, should be taken with the supervision of a nutrition specialist.

Bursitis, a painful inflammation of the fluid-filled sac, or bursa, that cushions the joint against friction, may also be helped with a regimen similar to that for arthritis. The elbows, shoulders, knees, hips, and ankles can all be affected by bursitis.

BOTANICAL APPROACH — For pain relief and to reduce tissue inflammation, arthritis sufferers may want to take white willow in tea form, one cup every three to four hours. For topical relief, cayenne plasters are available at most pharmacies. They are worn against the skin where joint stiffness occurs and cause a slight irritation that increases the blood circulation to that area. The increased circulation seems to help disperse the fluids causing inflammation.

ASPIRIN USE

Aspirin is probably the most commonly and frequently used drug in the world. Unfortunately, aspirin interferes with the absorption of a number of nutrients, including iron, vitamin B2 (riboflavin), folic acid, and vitamin C, so daily multiple-vitamin/mineral supplements that include these nutrients are a good health plan for long-term aspirin users. Aspirin may cause stomach irritation or bleeding, so do not take it within one hour of taking supplemental vitamin C, which could aggravate the condition. Furthermore, long-term aspirin users should be taking iron supplements to counteract any iron loss that may result from stomach bleeding.

BOTANICAL APPROACH — White willow, in tablets, capsules, or as tea, is a highly buffered organic form of the synthetic active ingredient of aspirin. It is therefore less likely to upset or irritate stomachs that are sensitive to strong acids. For those who take aspirin every day, such as arthritis sufferers, it may be more effective and soothing to take white willow in tea form.

ASTHMA

This condition is one of severe difficulty in breathing. It may be caused by allergies, emotional stress, or a number of other factors. Recent research indicates that a daily intake of 100 mg. of vitamin B6 decreases the frequency and severity of asthma attacks. Those considering increasing their vitamin B6 intake to this amount, however, should consult their physicians, as the dosage might affect the nervous system. Anyone suffering from traumatic physical stress will be compromised nutritionally and should be taking a comprehensive multiple-vitamin/mineral supplement that includes 1,000 mg. of vitamin C.

BOTANICAL APPROACH — Catnip is an excellent calming agent that can help relax the anxiety that often accompanies an asthma attack. Drink one cup of tea for quick relief, or take two capsules of catnip three times daily during stressful periods. Licorice and cayenne also contain substances that act as bronchodilators, so sucking on a licorice-cayenne lozenge may help relieve some asthma symptoms.

BACKACHE

Back pain, next to headache, is one of the most common physical complaints. Most middle- and lower-back problems are caused by muscle or disc injuries, poor posture, standing or sitting for long periods of time, tension, improper lifting, or improper exercise. Neck problems may be caused by injuries such as whiplash or can result from stress or from holding the head in an improper position (such as looking down at a desk) for a prolonged period. To speed the healing of injuries that involve a spinal disc, which is composed primarily of connective tissue, take 500 to 1,000 mg. of vitamin C three times daily.

BOTANICAL APPROACH — To help relieve pain, take two white willow tablets every three to four hours. To treat muscle soreness, wear a cayenne plaster over the affected area to increase circulation and provide soothing warmth. For muscle spasms, take two valerian capsules every three to four hours. Valerian is a strong antispasmodic and tranquilizer that may cause some drowsiness.

BLADDER DISORDERS

Most common bladder disorders are caused by minor bacterial infections, with symptoms of frequent and uncomfortable urination. Cystitis, an inflammation of the bladder, is one of the most frequent bladder problems. Those prone to bladder disorders and those trying to clear up minor infections should keep their urine slightly acidic. This can be most effectively accomplished by taking 250 mg. of vitamin C four to eight times daily, along with a full glass of water each time to help dilute the urine and flush the urinary tract until the symptoms disappear, usually in twenty-four to forty-eight hours. If a bladder infection does not improve in a day or two, a physician should be consulted.

BOTANICAL APPROACH — To flush the bladder, help fight bacteria,

191

and soothe irritated, burning sensations while treating bladder infections, brew a juniper berry and peppermint tea. Juniper acts as a mild diuretic to help flush the bladder, and peppermint is soothing to the urinary tract. Drink one cup every four waking hours.

BREASTS

The most common breast problems in women are swelling and soreness just before menstrual periods and during pregnancy, and fibrocystic condition, a general term that is usually used to describe the constant or intermittent presence of benign lumps in the breast.

BREAST TENDERNESS — Premenstrual tenderness may be helped with 50 to 100 mg. of supplemental vitamin B6 taken each day for one week before menstruation begins.

CANCER — Current research is focusing attention on early detection and prevention of breast cancer, a leading cause of death in women. Selenium, in daily doses of 200 mcg., is one mineral that seems to have a positive effect in the prevention of breast cancer. The antioxidant vitamins A, C, and E also seem to play a role in breast-cancer prevention. Those who are in a high-risk group for breast cancer should supplement their diets with a multiple-vitamin/mineral supplement that contains moderate dosages of these nutrients.

FIBROCYSTIC CONDITION — Millions of women suffer from painful, noncancerous breast lumps, usually cysts. Many types of fibrocystic conditions are now being successfully treated with 600 IU of vitamin E taken daily, usually for about eight weeks, until the condition improves. Over two-thirds of the women with fibrocystic condition who were studied reported a reduction in cyst size, pain, tenderness, and recurrence when treated with supplemental vitamin E.

BRONCHITIS

Bronchitis is an inflammation of the lining of the bronchial tubes, usually caused by bacterial or viral infections. Bronchitis often appears when the body's resistance to infection is lowered and is frequently a complication from a cold. Individuals who are deficient in vitamin A, a fairly common deficiency in the United States, seem to be more susceptible to bronchitis and respiratory infections. Those who are prone to bronchitis, or those who are currently treating it, should supplement their diets with 25,000 IU of the beta-carotene form of vitamin A, or 10,000 IU of the retinol form, to improve cellular immunity. While ill, it is a good idea to take 1,000 mg. of vitamin C to speed the respiratory healing process.

BOTANICAL APPROACH — Catnip tea is an antispasmodic that acts as an expectorant to help relieve congestion from bronchitis. It also induces perspiration, which helps remove wastes. Drink one cup of catnip tea every three to four hours. Those who tolerate garlic may also wish to take one garlic capsule three times daily to help increase the body's immune response and speed the relief of bronchitis symptoms.

BRUISES

Because of its role in the formation and strengthening of connective tissues, vitamin C can help with the healing of bruises. Those who bruise easily may have low levels of vitamin C and should take supplements of 500 to 1,000 mg. daily.

BOTANICAL APPROACH — To make bruises disappear quickly, mix powdered comfrey root with warm water to make a paste, apply it thickly to the skin, and wrap with gauze. Leave it in place overnight; repeat in the morning and continue as needed. Drink one cup of comfrey tea daily for up to seven days to speed the healing of internal tissues.

BURNS
(see also HEALING WOUNDS, SUNBURN)

Burns create physical stress and trauma, which increases the rate of metabolism of nutrients in the body, particularly of vitamins B1 (thiamin), B2 (riboflavin), and niacin. Therefore, the healing of burn injuries should be supported with a daily multiple-vitamin/mineral supplement that includes these nutrients, as well as 25 to 50 mg. of zinc. Additional vitamin C — 500 mg. four times a day — will help speed the healing process. There is no real proof that either vitamin E oil or lotions with pantothenic acid applied directly to healing burns will improve their appearance, but many anecdotal reports claim that this is the case. Vitamin E oil taken directly from a vitamin E supplement, or pantothenic acid in dexpanthenol form, may be applied several times daily to burns after they have closed. Whenever the body is engaged in healing, it is essential to keep fluid intake high. While healing from burns, drink no fewer than eight glasses of water daily.

BOTANICAL APPROACH — To soothe and quickly heal mild burns or burns that are no longer open, apply a comfrey plaster directly to the burned area. Mix powdered comfrey root with warm water to make a paste, let it cool, then apply it thickly to the skin and wrap it with gauze. Change the dressing three times daily until healed. For pain relief, take two white willow tablets as needed.

CAFFEINE USE

Caffeine is a strong diuretic and stimulant that achieves its effect by triggering the adrenal glands to release adrenalin. Coffee and cola drinkers should be aware that a frequent intake of caffeine throughout the day promotes the loss of the body's minerals and vitamins through the urine, particularly zinc and vitamin B1 (thiamin). A daily multiple-vitamin/ mineral supplement would be beneficial to caffeine users concerned about maintaining their nutrient levels. There have been several studies indicting high doses of caffeine as potential contributors to a variety of maladies, including arteriosclerosis and some cancers, but the results of these studies remain inconclusive at this time. Women who drink several caffeine-containing beverages daily, however, should take 1,000 to 1,500 mg. of supplemental calcium, since it is depleted by caffeine. A low calcium intake may lead to the development of osteoporosis.

BOTANICAL APPROACH — There are many healthful caffeine substitutes among the herbs. One flavorful tea is licorice, which is naturally sweet and stimulates the central nervous system, yet contains no caffeine. Ginger is another strong stimulant that works without caffeine. Ginseng can also be brewed into a tea, or its root can be sliced and nibbled for its stimulating effects. Rather than relying on a single stimulant, it is best to switch periodically. Each one causes the body to be stimulated by a different means, and switching intermittently prevents overtaxing any one bodily system.

CANCER
(see also THE IMMUNE-SYSTEM PROGRAM, page 162)

Currently, the best available methods for cancer prevention include avoiding carcinogens (such as pollutants, tobacco, and food additives), drastically reducing dietary fats (both saturated and polyunsaturated), and taking multiple-vitamin/mineral supplements strategically designed to reduce the risks of developing cancer. Some of the most important preventive nutrients are:

CALCIUM & FIBER — Calcium can actually reverse detrimental changes in the cells lining the colon, and, together, calcium and fiber, from both dietary and supplemental sources, are associated with the prevention of colon cancer. Take 1,000 to 1,500 mg. of calcium along with 10 to 12 g. of supplemental insoluble fiber, such as wheat bran, daily.

SELENIUM — Selenium is an antioxidant that works in concert with vitamin E. It has been shown epidemiologically to have a preventive effect on cancers of the breast, colon, and lung. Take 100 to 200 mcg. daily.

VITAMIN A — Vitamin A has the remarkable ability to interfere with certain cancer-causing agents, perhaps by preventing them from binding to the DNA in the cells they are invading. Deficiency in vitamin A is linked to cancers of the lung, throat, and bladder. Furthermore, women whose intake of vitamin A is less that 3,500 IU daily are three times more likely to develop serious cervical dysplasia or cervical cancer. To take advantage of vitamin A's many protective effects, take 25,000 IU of the beta-carotene form of vitamin A daily.

VITAMIN C — Vitamin C inhibits nitrates in foods from converting into nitrosamines, which have been shown to be carcinogenic. Because this conversion can occur in the digestive tract, it is a good idea to take this vitamin with meals. Therapeutic doses of 3,000 mg. daily of vitamin C have been shown to reduce the incidence of rectal polyps, which are believed to be associated with colon cancer. Furthermore, a high intake of vitamin C has been associated with a lower risk of cancers of the stomach and esophagus. Women whose intake of vitamin C is less than 30 mg. daily have a seven times higher incidence of cervical dysplasia, so they, especially, should be certain to maintain a high level of this nutrient.

Take 1,000 to 1,500 mg. of vitamin C daily for its antioxidant effects.

VITAMIN E — Vitamin E is an antioxidant that works with selenium to help protect cell membranes from damage by certain carcinogens. It also works with vitamin C to disarm nitrates in the digestive system. Take 100 IU of vitamin E four times daily with meals, or 400 IU once each day.

COLD SORES

Cold sores are caused by the virus herpes simplex, type I. They may be treated with 25 to 50 mg. of zinc along with 1,000 mg. of vitamin C daily until improved. Vitamin C has been shown to help cold sores heal in half the time, and zinc aids in the healing of wounds and in stimulating the immune system. Unfortunately, a related herpes virus, type II or genital herpes, has shown no such improvement with nutritional therapy. It is known, however, that people deficient in the B vitamins do have more frequently recurring outbreaks of either type of herpes simplex. Those prone to cold sores or genital herpes should take a daily multiple-vitamin/mineral supplement to correct any nutrient deficiencies they may have and to keep their immune systems in peak condition.

BOTANICAL APPROACH — To dry up and heal cold sores quickly, make a thick plaster with powdered comfrey root, goldenseal root, and warm water. Apply the plaster directly to the cold sore, where it will form a flexible scab. The brown scab will be unattractive, but not as unattractive as an open sore, and will be gone in a day or two, faster than a cold sore normally takes to heal.

COLON DISORDERS
(see also CONSTIPATION, DIARRHEA, FLATULENCE, HEMORRHOIDS)

Because the typical American diet is high in fat and low in fiber, we are particularly susceptible to many diseases of the large intestine, or colon, including colon cancer. In fact, colon cancer is the second most common killer among cancers in the United States. As a result, a great deal of research is focused on diseases of the colon, and a number of nutrients are showing great promise in both their prevention and treatment. Among these diseases are:

CANCER — Calcium and fiber, from both dietary and supplemental sources, are associated with the low incidence of colon cancer. Selenium has also shown a positive effect in colon-cancer prevention. To decrease the risk of developing colon cancer, take 200 mcg. of selenium, 1,000 to 1,500 mg. of calcium, and 10 to 12 g. of supplemental insoluble fiber, such as wheat bran, daily. Therapeutic doses of 3,000 mg. daily of vitamin C have been shown to reduce the incidence of rectal polyps, which are believed to be associated with colon cancer.

COLITIS — This painful abdominal condition is an inflammation of the colon. Colitis can interfere with the body's absorption of nutrients, particularly minerals, so a comprehensive multiple-vitamin/mineral supplement is very important for those suffering from this disorder. This supplement should include at least 1,000 mg. vitamin C, for its tissue-healing effect.

DIVERTICULITIS — Diverticulitis occurs when small pockets, or pouches, in the colon become infected or inflamed. Research has shown that many of those who suffer from diverticulitis have diets considerably lower in fiber foods, and higher in meat and dairy products, than those who manage to avoid the disease. Along with medical treatment, if any, diverticulitis can be significantly improved by increasing the overall dietary fiber intake and adding 10 to 12 g. of supplemental insoluble fiber, such as wheat bran, daily.

RECTAL POLYPS — Rectal polyps are abnormal tissue growths that occur inside the colon. Therapeutic daily doses of up to 3,000 mg. of vitamin C have been shown to reduce the incidence of rectal polyps, which are believed to be associated with colon cancer.

COMMON COLD
(see also FLU, BRONCHITIS, SINUSITIS)

This well-known infection is caused by a wide variety of viruses. Its symptoms include nasal congestion, sneezing, runny nose, muscle aches, coughing, and occasional fever. To date, there is no true preventive for colds except to maintain the immune system in top form. A multiple-vitamin/mineral supplement taken daily can prevent deficiencies that may compromise the immune system. Those treating a cold should take 10,000 IU of vitamin A in retinol form or 25,000 IU in beta-carotene form to help fortify the cells against further infection. Because vitamin C can decrease the length of time colds last by about one-third, as well as reduce their severity, it is a good idea to take 500 to 1,000 mg. with a full glass of water every four hours. Zinc lozenges have also shown promise in reducing the duration and severity of colds. Suck on a 30 to 50 mg. zinc lozenge every four waking hours for two or three days from the time the first cold symptom appears. Swallowing zinc lozenges does not seem to be very effective; they must be allowed to dissolve in the mouth. Colds are less severe and go away faster when the body's fluid levels are high. Drink eight full glasses of water daily and, rather than drinking juices full strength, dilute them to half strength with water.

BOTANICAL APPROACH — When a cold is first coming on, a strong dose of garlic may help trigger the immune system to fight it off. Crush one raw clove, mix it with one tablespoon of olive oil, and swallow the mixture. Do not do this on an empty stomach or indigestion may result. The following are remedies for a variety of cold symptoms:

CHILLS — Ginger tea creates a strong feeling of inner warmth in the body. Drink one-half cup every three hours, but not before bedtime, since ginger acts as a mild stimulant.

CONGESTION — Licorice-cayenne lozenges and one cup of catnip tea every three to four hours will act as expectorants to bring up mucus, open bronchial tubes, and help relieve congestion.

COUGH — Licorice tea or licorice-cayenne lozenges act as anti-spasmodics to help suppress coughs. Drink one cup of tea or suck on a licorice/cayenne lozenge every two to three hours. To promote sleep at night, take one or two capsules of valerian, which acts as both an anti-spasmodic and a tranquilizer.

FEVER — Two white willow tablets every three to four hours will bring down fevers.

SORE THROAT — Licorice-cayenne lozenges, available in most pharmacies, can relieve both sore throat and hoarseness.

CONSTIPATION

Constipation is the term that is used to describe difficult or sluggish bowel movements, often accompanied by gas and abdominal discomfort. Occasional constipation may be caused by dietary changes, stress, the absence of convenient toilet facilities, or dehydration. Chronic consti-pation may be caused by a low-fiber diet or may be the result of inade-quate nutrient levels, particularly among some of the B vitamins. To treat chronic constipation, increase daily fiber intake through dietary or supplemental means, add a good multiple-vitamin/mineral supplement, and drink eight full glasses of water every day.

BOTANICAL APPROACH — For relief of occasional constipation, drink one cup of yerba mate tea every two to three hours until relieved. This remedy is ideal for the morning, since yerba mate also acts as a stimulant. One teaspoon of olive oil just before bedtime will act as a mild laxative in the morning.

CONVALESCENCE AND HEALING
(see also HEALING WOUNDS)

Illness and trauma can rapidly deplete the body's store of nutrients. Yet, during convalescence, the body's nutrient needs may not be met due to restricted or otherwise altered diets, making it a risky time for nutrient deficiencies. Studies have demonstrated that patients do better and heal faster when they receive a comprehensive multiple-vitamin/mineral supplement. To help speed healing, take a supplement that includes 10,000 IU of the retinol form or 25,000 IU of the beta-carotene form of vitamin A, 1,000 mg. of vitamin C, and approximately 30 mg. of zinc. Vitamin A helps form new tissue, vitamin C increases collagen synthesis and helps fight traumatic stress, and zinc is associated with rapid tissue healing and the stimulation of the immune system. When surgery is involved, a good supplement can help recover mineral losses, typically potassium, phosphorus, and iron. If possible, it is a good idea while convalescing to choose a supplement that is taken in divided dosages with meals rather than the one-pill-a-day variety.

BOTANICAL APPROACH — Drink one cup of ginseng tea in the mornings as a general tonic during periods of convalescence. In the evenings, drink one cup of comfrey tea for up to seven days to soothe internal membranes and to promote tissue repair.

DENTAL PROBLEMS

There is a strong connection between healthy teeth and gums and the nutritional health of the individual. In general, individuals prone to oral or dental problems should be taking a multiple-vitamin/mineral supplement daily to rule out nutrient deficiencies as the cause of such problems. Some factors of oral health that can be affected by nutritional supplements are:

BLEEDING GUMS — Bleeding gums may be alleviated with supplements of 1,000 mg. of vitamin C taken daily.

MOUTH ULCERS — For treatment of mouth ulcers, suck zinc lozenges (30 to 50 mg.) every four waking hours until relieved. Recurring mouth ulcers may be prevented with supplements of 25 mg. of zinc, but it is best if the zinc is part of a daily multiple-vitamin/mineral supplement that also contains copper.

TOOTH DECAY — Use a toothpaste that contains fluoride and, if possible, a multiple-vitamin/mineral supplement that also incorporates molybdenum. If you live in an area without fluoridated water, or drink bottled water that does not have fluorine in it, make sure your multiple-vitamin/mineral supplement provides fluorine in a 2 to 4 mg. range.

BOTANICAL APPROACH — To treat bleeding gums, use a mouthwash in the morning and at night made of cooled peppermint and comfrey root tea. Together, these herbs will help reduce pain and inflammation. This mouthwash preparation may be stored in the refrigerator and used daily to prevent recurrence.

DEPRESSION
(*see also* MENOPAUSE, MENSTRUATION, NERVOUSNESS/ANXIETY, PREMENSTRUAL SYNDROME)

Depression can often be caused by nutritional deficiencies and chemical or hormonal imbalances in the body. The elderly are particulary at risk for nutritional deficiencies and imbalances because of their sparse diets and their bodies' impaired utilization of many nutrients. Frequently, when the minerals in the body are out of balance, such as high copper levels combined with zinc deficiencies, depression can result. A comprehensive multiple-vitamin/mineral supplement that incorporates at least 1,000 mg. vitamin C, 200 to 400 IU of vitamin E, 400 mg. of magnesium, and 30 to 50 mg. of zinc is especially important in fighting depression in the elderly and other high-risk individuals.

BOTANICAL APPROACH — Ginseng is an effective general tonic for the elderly and for individuals in emotionally stressful situations, and yerba mate tea is a good pick-me-up and mood elevator. Drink one cup of yerba mate tea in the morning before breakfast, and one cup of ginseng tea in the mid-afternoon. Since yerba mate and ginseng act as stimulants, do not take either before bedtime.

DIABETES

Diabetics often have low levels of vitamins A, B6, and C, as well as the minerals chromium, magnesium, and zinc. In addition, some reports indicate that many diabetics have problems with the metabolism and utilization of L-carnitine. Marginal deficiencies in any of these substances can cause many problems, perhaps even aggravating the diabetic condition. For example, deficiency in vitamin A and zinc can impair the immune system and slow the healing of wounds and infections, common problems among diabetics. Recent evidence indicates the many diabetics can actually be helped by certain nutrients. EPA has been shown to improve cellular sensitivity to insulin. Vitamin B6 may help regulate the glucose tolerance factor (GTF), and diets supplemented with chromium have shown substantial improvement of impaired GTF. In fact, chromium supplements have been reported to correct problematic GTF in children, perhaps by restoring the body's ability to use insulin effectively. In addition, research indicates that very high-fiber diets, with a daily intake of 65 g. of fiber, can cut the need for insulin by twenty-five to fifty percent in some patients. Since high-fiber diets tend to interfere with zinc utilization by the body, supplemental zinc is probably a good idea for diabetics. Before changing any aspects of their diabetes-management program, however, or embarking on any supplemental-nutrient program, diabetics should consult both their physicians and a nutrition specialist.

DIARRHEA

During periods of diarrhea, whatever the cause, vitamin and mineral loss is high and nutrient absorption is low, so a multiple-vitamin/mineral supplement should be taken. In the case of chronic diarrhea, a supplement will insure that the cause is not from a nutrient deficiency. Because dehydration is a particular risk for diarrhea sufferers, drink at least eight full glasses of water daily, preferably more, while ill, to replace lost fluids.

BOTANICAL APPROACH — When diarrhea comes from a reaction to a change in diet or occasional intestinal flare-up, take two goldenseal capsules daily, morning and evening, until the symptoms subside.

DIETERS
(*see also* THE WEIGHT-LOSS PROGRAM, page 178)

When caloric intake is reduced, nutrient intake is restricted as well. Therefore, all weight-loss diets that do not include vitamin and mineral supplements have the potential for causing marginal, even severe, nutrient deficiencies. These deficiencies, in turn, can trigger feelings of hunger as the body craves certain missing nutrients. In order for weight loss to be lasting, and to retain the health of the dieter, it is important to take a comprehensive multiple-vitamin/mineral supplement that incorporates 200 to 300 mcg. of biotin, 18 to 30 mg. of iron, 15 to 30 mg. of zinc, and 500 to 800 mg. of potassium chloride every day. Dieters should also realize that toxins are stored in body fat. As weight is lost and fat is burned, toxins are released and must be quickly flushed from the body before they lodge elsewhere. Therefore, dieters must drink at least eight full glasses of water daily, especially before meals, before bedtime, and during the night. Keep a glass of water handy by the bedside.

DIURETIC USE
(*see also* EDEMA)

Those who take diuretics for water-retention problems lose a great many minerals in their urine, which can cause marginal, sometimes severe, deficiencies. Furthermore, mineral deficiencies can make the body especially vulnerable to the toxic effects of food preservatives and pollutants. Diuretic users require extra calcium, magnesium, and zinc along with potassium — unless the diuretic is designed to conserve potassium. Diuretic users should be certain to take a daily multiple-vitamin/mineral supplement that incorporates adequate levels of these minerals into its formula.

EAR DISORDERS
(*see also* MOTION SICKNESS)

The ears are subject to many disorders. The outer ear is vulnerable to bacterial and fungal infections, while middle-ear problems are usually the result of upper-respiratory infections from viruses and bacteria. The inner ear is affected by allergies and infections, which may result in vertigo, nausea, tinnitus, and temporary or permanent hearing loss.

INFECTION — Infection of the ear is commonly an offshoot of respiratory-tract infections. Other causes include bacterial and fungal infections that enter the outer ear from water or other foreign matter. During illness, 10,000 IU of the retinol form of vitamin A, and 1,000 mg. of vitamin C, can help speed recovery of the respiratory tract and ear. Those prone to ear infections should strengthen their immune systems with a daily multiple-vitamin/mineral supplement.

TINNITUS — Some nutritionists report that people who suffer from tinnitus, particularly among the elderly, experience some improvement with zinc supplementation in the range of 25 to 50 mg. daily. Other nutrition specialists recommend taking 50 mg. of the nicotinic acid form of niacin, twice daily.

MENIERE'S DISEASE — Sufferers of Meniere's disease require a multiple-vitamin/mineral supplement to insure that they are not subject to nutrient deficiencies. Some nutritionists have successfully treated many of the symptoms of Meniere's disease with 100 mg. of the nicotinic acid form of niacin, four times daily.

EDEMA

Edema is a term that describes a condition wherein the body retains water, resulting in weight gain, bloating, and high blood pressure. Hormonal changes may cause edema, particularly in premenopausal women. Edema can also be triggered by excess dietary sodium from salt, which should be restricted in those prone to water retention. Mild edema may be alleviated by taking 1,000 mg. or more of vitamin C, which has a rapid diuretic effect. Those prone to edema should not drink fewer than six glasses of water daily, since restricting water may actually contribute to water retention. Severe or long-term edema can signal serious physical problems, and in such cases a physician should be consulted.

BOTANICAL APPROACH — One of the most effective herbal diuretics is tea made from juniper berries. Drink one cup in the morning and one again at midday, if desired.

EYE DISORDERS

There are many types of eye disorders, some permanent, and some temporary and thus treatable. The most common temporary eye problems are due to surface injuries, infections, weakened muscles, and overuse, especially under poor lighting conditions. Some eye disorders signal specific nutrient deficiencies.

BLOODSHOT EYES — Bloodshot eyes are usually caused by overuse, dehydration, allergic reactions, or irritants in the air. They can also be the result of a vitamin B2 (riboflavin) deficiency and can be helped with 10 mg. of vitamin B2 daily.

CATARACTS — Recent research indicates that vitamin C can delay oxidation in the eye that can lead to cataracts. To block the development of cataracts, the effective antioxidant dosage for vitamin C is 1,000 mg. daily.

EYESTRAIN — Excessive eye fatigue, or eyestrain, often results in headaches. Its causes include stress, overuse of the eyes in close work or at video or computer monitors, poor lighting, and incorrect eyeglass or contact-lens prescriptions. Occasionally, eyestrain comes from an oversensitivity to glare, which can signal a vitamin B2 (riboflavin) deficiency. To help prevent such a deficiency, the body should get 10 mg. of vitamin B2 daily.

NIGHT BLINDNESS — Night blindness, the eye's inability to adjust to darkness, can signal a vitamin A deficiency. Symptoms of night blindness can be reversed in under an hour with an injection of vitamin A. Night vision can also be restored, and night blindness prevented, by a daily oral intake of 25,000 IU of the beta-carotene form of vitamin A or 5,000 IU of the retinol form of vitamin A.

FATIGUE

Feelings of chronic tiredness may be caused by overwork, stress, or illness. Fatigue can also be a symptom of nutrient deficiencies. If there is no medical or emotional reason for fatigue, such as flu or boredom, then a comprehensive multiple-vitamin/mineral supplement will insure that such deficiencies do not exist. Choose a multiple-vitamin/mineral supplement that contains 20 to 50 mg. of pantothenic acid, 50 mg. of vitamin B6,

1,000 to 1,500 mg. of vitamin C, 200 to 400 IU of vitamin E, and 18 to 30 mg. of iron.

BOTANICAL APPROACH — Ginseng is an excellent general health tonic. One capsule, one dried slice the size of the nail on the index finger, or one cup of tea may be taken twice daily, once in the morning before breakfast and again in the afternoon. Ginseng may be taken indefinitely. Licorice tea is a mild stimulant that does not have a letdown, which tends to continue the fatigue cycle. Licorice tea may be taken several times daily for up to two weeks at a time, with a one-week break between regimens.

FLATULENCE
(see also INDIGESTION)

Flatulence is an uncomfortable condition caused by excess gas in the intestines. Flatulence can come from swallowing air or from eating certain high-fiber, gas-causing foods, such as beans. Since the health benefits of increased dietary fiber have come into the public eye, it is important to begin using fiber supplements or an increased-fiber diet slowly, because flatulence may result until the body adjusts to the higher fiber levels.

BOTANICAL APPROACH — Intestinal gas can be relieved with ginger tea. Drink one cup every two to three hours, but because ginger is a stimulant, not before bedtime.

FLU
(see also COMMON COLD)

Flu is usually the result of a viral infection. It may have symptoms similar to a cold, but it differs in the speed with which it attacks and in its severity. Flu may also carry symptoms of high fever, headache, muscle pain, nausea, or diarrhea. Vitamin A, vitamin C, and zinc can help the immune system fight virus infections. During flu, take 10,000 IU of the retinol form of vitamin A once a day, 1,000 mg. of vitamin C three times daily, and suck on a 30 to 50 mg. zinc lozenge every four waking hours. As with any infection, fluids are very important: Drink eight full glasses of water daily.

BOTANICAL APPROACH — Peppermint tea with lemon can help settle the stomach and soothe symptoms of fever and general malaise. Drink one cup every three hours. White willow tablets will help reduce fever and soothe headache pain and body aches. Take two tablets every three to four hours.

FORGETFULNESS

A lapse in memory is most commonly brought on by stress, a lack of attention, or exhaustion. It can also be triggered by deficiencies in specific nutrients, particularly vitamin B1 (thiamin), niacin, and vitamin B12. For general mental acumen, take a comprehensive multiple-vitamin/mineral supplement to insure that forgetfulness is not caused by any nutrient deficiencies. Due to limited dietary intake and an impaired ability to absorb nutrients, the elderly are highly susceptible to deficiencies in all the B vitamins, especially folic acid; this can cause apathy and the slowing of mental processes. This group should take a daily multiple-vitamin/mineral supplement that incorporates 400 mcg. of folic acid.

BOTANICAL APPROACH — For treatment of forgetfulness in the elderly, ginseng is an excellent general health tonic and mild central nervous system stimulant. Two capsules, one dried slice, or one cup of tea may be taken daily, once in the morning before breakfast and again in the mid-afternoon. Yerba mate tea is also a good mental stimulant.

HAY FEVER

Hay fever is a noncontagious allergic response to substances in the air, such as pollen or pollution. The symptoms of hay fever are usually seasonal and include inflamed eyes, sinuses, and nasal passages, with an occasional sore throat or irritated bronchial tubes. Those prone to hay fever may be helped with daily multiple-vitamin/mineral supplements. To help alleviate hay fever symptoms, take 500 mg. of vitamin C every four hours for its antihistamine effect and drink eight glasses of water daily.

BOTANICAL APPROACH — To relieve hay fever symptoms, sniff a pinch of goldenseal powder, just as you would take snuff, once in each nostril three times daily, or as needed.

HEADACHE
(see also MIGRAINE)

Painful sensations in the head or across the forehead are due to a variety of causes, including toxic reactions to alcohol or drugs, poor nutrition, tension in neck and shoulder muscles, vision problems, allergies, excessive noise, glaring light, and stress. Those who suffer from frequent headaches should take a good multiple-vitamin/mineral supplement daily, since headache is also a common symptom of many marginal nutritional deficiencies.

BOTANICAL APPROACH — Headaches caused by muscle tension can be treated with one capsule of cayenne, which acts as a vasodilator. Stress-related headaches can be treated with two valerian capsules, which sedate the central nervous system and cause drowsiness. For general headache pain, take two white willow tablets every three to four hours.

HEALING WOUNDS

Whenever the body is injured, it puts a demand on its store of nutrients to heal itself. In any injury, internal or external, a comprehensive multiple-vitamin/mineral supplement will insure that the body has what it needs to speed its healing processes.

INTERNAL HEALING — Healing time can be reduced with a daily intake of 1,000 mg. of vitamin C. Daily supplements of zinc in ranges of 20 to 30 mg., along with 3 mg. of copper, are essential to the body's ability to use other nutrients for healing. For best results, take a multiple-vitamin/mineral supplement that includes all these nutrients, along with 10,000 IU of the retinol form of vitamin A and 10 to 50 mg. of vitamin B2 (riboflavin), which are also essential to tissue repair. Additional supplements of L-arginine and L-lysine can also help speed the healing of wounds. Take 1,500 mg. daily of each at bedtime, preferably on an empty stomach, until healing is complete.

EXTERNAL HEALING — Topical vitamin E oil is believed by many to speed the healing of wounds when applied two or three times daily after the wound has closed. Pantothenic acid comes in a topical formula, Panthoderm, which is also believed to speed external healing.

BOTANICAL APPROACH — Internal healing can be aided with comfrey tea, which is soothing to internal membranes and stimulates tissue repair. Take one cup in the morning until healing is complete. To reduce the potential for infection in external wounds, sprinkle them with powdered goldenseal root. To form an unsplitable scab after the wound is closed, apply a paste of comfrey root powder mixed with warm water. Do not bandage.

HEART DISEASE
(see also THE CARDIOVASCULAR PROGRAM, page 144)

Heart disease, or atherosclerosis, is caused by a buildup of plaque in the arteries leading to the heart. The plaque narrows the arteries and creates the potential for a complete blockage, or heart attack. Plaque is caused by excess lipids, or fats, that enter the bloodstream, cling to the inside of arteries, and harden. Those who have heart disease, or are genetically prone to it, should reduce their overall serum cholesterol levels; increase their HDL (high density lipoprotein) levels, while reducing their LDL (low density lipoprotein) levels; and lower their triglyceride levels. This can often be accomplished through a low-fat, high-fiber diet and regular exercise. Many who are at risk, however, need additional medical or nutritional help. Those nutrients which have the greatest effect in reducing the levels of dangerous blood fats in individuals suffering from heart disease include:

FIBER — When water-soluble fiber intake is increased to 50 g. or more daily, either through pills, powders, or intense dietary changes, a ten- to fifteen-percent reduction in blood cholesterol levels has been noted. When dietary fiber is increased, it is a good idea to also take a multiple-vitamin/mineral supplement to insure that mineral levels remain adequate.

L-CARNITINE — Recent research indicates that daily supplements of 1,000 mg. of L-carnitine can increase HDL levels while reducing overall blood fat levels. It has also been used with some success in managing ischemic heart disease.

NIACIN — Large doses of niacin as nicotinic acid, not niacinamide, ranging from 1,500 mg. to 3,000 mg. daily, can significantly reduce cholesterol and triglyceride levels in the blood. Because of side effects such as skin flushing and nausea, high doses of niacin should be built up to gradually, beginning with 50 mg. four times daily for several days, and increasing in 50 mg. increments over a two-month period until the desired range is reached. It is a good idea to use this treatment under the supervision of a physician or nutrition specialist. This will probably increase the body's need for water, so be sure to drink at least eight glasses daily.

BOTANICAL APPROACH — White willow bark, like aspirin, is a mild blood thinner that can help prevent blood clots from forming in already narrowed arteries. If you are not taking any other blood-thinning drugs, take two white willow tablets or capsules daily.

HEMORRHOIDS

Hemorrhoids are varicose veins of the rectum and anus. They are usually considered harmless, unless infection is present or they rupture, but they can be quite painful. Hemorrhoids, also known as piles, are often aggravated by constipation, pregnancy, and the repeated use of strong laxatives. To heal and strengthen the connective tissue in the veins, take 500 mg. of vitamin C in the morning and again in the evening. A daily intake of 10 to 12 g. of supplemental insoluble fiber, such as wheat bran, will keep the stools soft and moving. Water is especially important for the management of hemorrhoids. Drink eight full glasses daily.

BOTANICAL APPROACH — To treat hemorrhoid pain, use white willow tea, cooled, for a rectal wash or in a sitz bath. Its astringent quality tones and cools the affected tissues. To help heal tissues and reduce the swelling of severe hemorrhoids, make a poultice by boiling one-half pound of broken comfrey root until soft, about twenty minutes. Let the mixture cool slightly, and strain it into a muslin bag. Sprinkle the comfrey with powdered goldenseal, close the bag, and sit on it for an hour or two while reading or watching television.

HIGH BLOOD PRESSURE
(*see also* THE CARDIOVASCULAR PROGRAM, page 144)

High blood pressure is a condition in which the heart is forced to pump harder to provide proper circulatory functions. High blood pressure has a variety of causes, including hereditary predisposition, obesity, stress, diseases of the heart, kidney disorders, and disturbances in glandular functions. Some of the symptoms of high blood pressure are dizziness, nausea, and headaches. Anyone suffering from high blood pressure should promptly consult a physician for help in controlling it. Medications can usually bring high blood pressure down when taken regularly, and dietary changes can also help. Studies have shown that a daily intake of 1,500 mg. of supplemental calcium, coupled with a decrease in sodium intake, can help lower some types of high blood pressure in just a few weeks. Total daily sodium intake should not exceed 3,000 mg., about as much as is in a level teaspoon of salt.

BOTANICAL APPROACH — One cup of juniper berry tea, taken daily in the morning, can help alleviate water retention, a condition associated with high blood pressure. The ideal stimulant for individuals with high blood pressure is ginseng. One cup of tea, one slice, or one capsule of ginseng is an invigorating tonic that acts to help reduce blood pressure in hypertensive individuals. If stress is a contributing factor to high blood pressure, two valerian capsules in the afternoon or evening will soothe the central nervous system.

INDIGESTION
(see also NAUSEA, ULCERS)

Indigestion is a general term for abdominal discomfort during or just after eating. It is sometimes caused by stress or the improper functioning of one or more of the organs in the digestive system. Taking vitamin or mineral supplements on an empty stomach can also cause digestive discomfort. Frequent or unrelieved indigestion could indicate conditions requiring medical attention.

BOTANICAL APPROACH — For those prone to general indigestion, one cup of ginger tea, taken one-half hour after meals, but not before bedtime, will help regulate the digestive processes and soothe possible upsets. Stomach gas can be relieved with cayenne capsules, which stimulate the release of gastric juices. Take one capsule after meals or when stomach gas occurs.

INFERTILITY

To keep the reproductive system in peak condition, both men and women should take a multiple-vitamin/mineral supplement each day that includes vitamin A as 10,000 IU of retinol or 25,000 IU of beta-carotene. An adequate vitamin A level in the body is critical to the cells that reproduce frequently, such as sperm in males and fertilized eggs in females. Women who experience infertility should consult with their gynecologists, since the most common causes are hormonal imbalances and blocked Fallopian tubes.

The most common cause of infertility in men is poor sperm production. Zinc is a very vital component of sperm production, and zinc supplements have been shown to increase male fertility. Zinc should be supplemented in the range of 20 to 50 mg. daily, along with 1,000 mg. of vitamin C, which aids in the utilization of zinc and enhances sperm motility.

BOTANICAL APPROACH — Angelica tea is considered a menstrual regulator. Women trying to regulate their menstrual cycles in order to predict their ovulation times may find drinking one cup of angelica tea daily to be helpful.

INSOMNIA
(see also THE STRESS PROGRAM, page 174)

Insomnia has many causes, including stress and the overuse of caffeine or other stimulants. It can also be a sign of nutrient deficiency, particularly in the B vitamins and certain minerals such as calcium and magnesium. Those suffering from insomnia should take a comprehensive multiple-vitamin/mineral supplement daily that incorporates 1,000 to 1,500 mg. of calcium and 400 to 600 mg. of magnesium to rule out nutrient deficiencies as a cause.

BOTANICAL APPROACH — Valerian root is a strong herbal sedative. Take two capsules, or drink one cup of valerian tea, in the evening or whenever sleep is desired. Catnip tea also helps fight insomnia; drink one cup in the evening, but not if you are taking valerian.

KIDNEY DISORDERS

The kidneys regulate the fluids in the body and purify the blood by removing solid waste matter. The inability of the kidneys to perform their waste-removal and water-balancing functions may be caused by a variety of factors, including stress, infection, or a chemical imbalance in the body. Kidney disorders can be life-threatening and should not be left medically untreated.

INFECTION — Kidney infections may be caused by bacteria or by toxic materials in the blood. Pain in the lower back that is not caused by muscle strain is frequently the first indication of kidney infections. If left medically untreated, these infections can result in permanent damage. Those prone to kidney infections should be certain to drink eight glasses of water daily to keep the kidneys flushed of toxins.

KIDNEY STONES — Kidney stones precipitate out of the fluids that filter through the kidneys. While the chemistry of kidney stones varies, the most common are formed from calcium salts or excessive uric acid that has crystallized. Kidney stones can be very painful, especially if they become lodged in the ureters or the urethra as they are being passed out of the body. Furthermore, they can block the flow of urine, producing dangerous, sometimes life-threatening, complications. Those prone to kidney stones should take 50 mg. of vitamin B6 and 400 mg. of magnesium daily, which seems to prevent or cut down on their recurrence. The magnesium helps dissolve calcium and reduce calcium levels in the urine, and the vitamin B6 complements the action of the magnesium. Kidney stone sufferers should also drink four quarts of water daily to help prevent their recurrence by diluting the minerals that may crystallize to form stones.

LEG CRAMPS

This painful condition is caused by sudden and involuntary tightening of the muscles of the lower limbs, especially the calf muscles. Its causes include fatigue, strain, and, most commonly, nutritional deficiencies. Some success in preventing leg cramps has been reported when 400 IU of vitamin E is taken daily before retiring. It may also be a good idea to take a multiple-vitamin/mineral supplement that incorporates both magnesium and potassium chloride in its formula. Also helpful are daily supplements of 1,000 to 1,500 mg. of calcium and 500 to 1,000 mg. of vitamin C.

LIVER DISORDERS

The liver is the laboratory of the body, performing over five-hundred vital biochemical functions. The inability of the liver to perform its wide-ranging functions may be caused by infections, by exposure to toxic substances, or by obstructions. Signs of serious liver trouble include jaundice — yellowish skin and eyes from too much bile in the blood — or abnormal, light-colored stools. Liver disorders should not be taken lightly and should not be left medically untreated.

CIRRHOSIS — This degeneration of the cells of the liver, with their replacement by fibrous scar tissue, results in obstructed blood flow through the liver and disruption of liver functions. Cirrhosis can be induced by repeated exposures to toxins, by chronic alcoholism, by infections such as hepatitis, by certain forms of cardiovascular disease, or by poor nutrition. If caught in its early stages, cirrhosis can be treated medically and nutritionally. Sufferers of cirrhosis of the liver utilize many nutrients poorly and need a daily multiple-vitamin/mineral supplement that includes the fat-soluble vitamins A, D, E, and K, as well as the minerals copper and iron.

HEPATITIS — This inflammation of the liver comes from a number of causes, including viral or bacterial infections and exposure to toxic substances such as arsenic, alcohol, poisonous mushrooms, and carbon tetrachloride. Because of impaired liver functions, hepatitis sufferers should take, along with their medication, a daily multiple-vitamin/mineral supplement. There have been some reports that high doses of vitamin C, 500 mg. every four hours, may help speed recovery from hepatitis.

LOSS OF SMELL OR TASTE

Zinc and vitamin A deficiencies can cause a loss of smell or taste, which is particularly common among the elderly. To avoid deficiencies that may result from variable dietary habits, take a comprehensive multiple-vitamin/mineral supplement daily. Improvement has also been observed in some individuals with daily supplements of zinc, in the 25 to 50 mg. range, and vitamin A, as either 25,000 IU of the beta-carotene form or 10,000 IU of the retinol form.

MENOPAUSE

Menopause is the span of time in a woman's life when her menstrual cycles diminish and eventually stop, ending her childbearing abilities. During menopause, the ovaries slow or stop their estrogen production. Some of the problems women suffer during menopause include hot flashes, sudden weight gain or loss, insomnia, depression, heart palpitations, and the loss of bone calcium due to hormonal changes. Those who are taking estrogen-replacement medication during menopause should increase their vitamin C intake to 1,000 mg. daily, because supplemental estrogen increases the copper level in the body, causing an increased need for vitamin C. The best approach for balancing the body's higher copper levels is to take, along with the vitamin C supplement, a multiple-vitamin/mineral supplement that incorporates approximately 30 mg. of zinc in its formula. Some symptoms of menopause that can respond to nutrient supplementation include:

BLOOD LOSS — Because of sporadic bleeding, menopausal women should take additional iron, approximately 15 to 20 mg. daily, along with 1,000 mg. of vitamin C to help with iron utilization.

BONE LOSS — Menopausal women should be sure to take 1,500 mg. of supplemental calcium and 400 IU of vitamin D daily to help prevent bone loss. Recent studies indicate that estrogen therapy may be an important factor in preventing bone loss, and that calcium, alone, may not be effective during actual menopause.

DEPRESSION — Depression due to the effects of menopause may be helped with daily supplements of 400 IU of vitamin E and 50 to 100 mg. of vitamin B6. For best results with this nutritional approach, it is a good idea also to take a daily multiple-vitamin/mineral supplement.

HOT FLASHES — A daily intake of 100 IU of vitamin E with each meal, or 400 IU total, has been reported to help alleviate hot flashes.

POSTMENOPAUSE — After menopause, it is still necessary to take 1,000 to 1,500 mg. calcium daily. New evidence indicates that calcium supplements may reduce the amounts of estrogen used for post-menopausal estrogen therapy. Do not take more than the U.S. RDA of supplemental iron, however. If you are postmenopausal and have an iron deficiency, it could point to the presence of other problems, so consult a nutrition specialist and your physician.

BOTANICAL APPROACH — Angelica is used by herbalists as a hormone regulator in women. Drink one cup in the morning and one before retiring. For relieving intermittent anxiety or insomnia, take one or two valerian capsules.

MENSTRUATION
(see also PREMENSTRUAL SYNDROME, SKIN DISORDERS)

There are a number of symptoms that are related to menstrual cycles. These include premenstrual tension, painful menses, water retention, swollen breasts, and backache. Since menstruating women lose iron each month, they should be sure to supplement their iron levels, either through conscientious nutritional practices or through iron supplementation.

BLOOD LOSS — To insure efficient hemoglobin production, women should take daily supplements of approximately 18 to 25 mg. of iron, along with 1,000 mg. of vitamin C to help in iron utilization. A good multiple-vitamin/mineral supplement that incorporates these nutrients along with vitamin E, folic acid, and vitamin B12 will also aid women who menstruate.

BREAST TENDERNESS — Breast tenderness happens when the breasts retain excess fluid and swell. This painful condition is caused by hormonal changes that are part of the menstrual cycle. Daily supplements of vitamin B6 in ranges of 50 to 100 mg. have been used successfully to alleviate breast tenderness when taken for one week before menstruation.

CRAMPS — Cramps are caused by the sudden contraction of the uterus and sometimes the surrounding abdominal, back, or thigh muscles. The causes of menstrual cramps include poor nutrition, lack of calcium, a narrow or bent cervix, stress, and exhaustion. Those prone to menstrual cramps should be taking 1,000 to 1,500 mg. of supplemental calcium and 400 to 600 mg. of magnesium daily.

DEPRESSION — Depression is a common condition associated with menstruation. Premenstrual depression has been successfully treated with supplements of 50 to 100 mg. of vitamin B6 and 200 to 400 IU of vitamin E daily. Some women may require higher dosages and should consult their physicians or a nutrition specialist

BOTANICAL APPROACH — Angelica tea is considered a good overall menstrual tonic. To help regulate menstrual periods, drink one cup of angelica tea daily. To help soothe and alleviate menstrual discomfort, take three parsley capsules three times daily, starting one week before and continuing through to the end of the period. Parsley is high in calcium, which helps relieve cramping. It is also a uterine stimulant, which can help bring on a period, and a diuretic, which helps flush excess water out of the body. To ease menstrual cramps and the mild anxiety that often accompanies a period, drink one cup of catnip tea three times daily for the duration of the period.

MIGRAINE

A migraine is a severe form of headache that usually affects only one side of the head. It is often preceded by flashes of light, a spot, or a flickering in the center of the field of vision, and is frequently accompanied by nausea and dizziness. Causes of migraine are still unknown, but it is believed to be triggered by disturbances in blood circulation in the brain. Stress, exhaustion, glandular imbalances, allergies, and cardiovascular problems such as high blood pressure may be contributing factors. Techniques for controlling migraines are largely individual. Some doctors report that 100 to 300 mg. of the nicotinic acid form of niacin, taken at the first sign of migraine, may help abort those headaches. Daily supplements of 400 mg. of magnesium may also help to reduce the frequency of migraines in some individuals.

BOTANICAL APPROACH — Cayenne and yerba mate are powerful vasodilators and have been used to abort migraine headaches, particularly those brought on when fatigued. Take one cayenne capsule or drink one cup of yerba mate tea at the first sign of a migraine. Those who wish to sleep should avoid yerba mate, which is a stimulant, and, instead, take two capsules of valerian as soon as symptoms of migraine appear.

MOTION SICKNESS

Motion sickness is not a disturbance of the digestive system but a temporary disorder of the inner ear. It is most commonly prevented with antihistamines, which keep channels in the inner ear open. In addition, the incidence of motion sickness is greatly reduced when the stomach is full.

To help fill the stomach, take 2 to 3 g. of psyllium fiber with a full glass of water.

BOTANICAL APPROACH — To help prevent or treat nausea, drink one cup of peppermint tea, warm or cold, every two to three hours.

MUSCLE CRAMPS OR SPASMS
(see also LEG CRAMPS)

Painful muscle cramps or involuntary muscles spasms, particularly the small muscles of the face, are frequently caused by mineral imbalances in the body. This condition may be corrected by taking a comprehensive multiple-vitamin/mineral supplement that includes potassium chloride and vitamin D. In addition, it may be helpful to take daily supplements of 1,000 to 1,500 mg. of calcium along with 400 to 600 mg. of magnesium.

NAUSEA

Nausea is the unpleasant sensation that often precedes vomiting. The causes of nausea are many and include digestive problems, stress, balance problems, and certain infectious diseases such as flu.

BOTANICAL APPROACH — To help relieve nausea, drink one-half cup of ginger tea or one cup of peppermint tea every two to three hours, depending upon which one has the most agreeable taste during nausea. Sucking on a mint-flavored toothpick may provide some relief. Eating ice can also help relieve nausea quickly by numbing the stomach.

NERVOUSNESS/ANXIETY
(see also THE STRESS PROGRAM, page 174)

Prolonged anxiety and stress can severely deplete the body's store of nutrients, compromising the immune system and opening the way to disease. These nutrient deficiencies, in turn, can result in continued anxiety and nervousness. Therefore, those who suffer from anxiety are particularly at risk for developing health problems and should take a comprehensive multiple-vitamin/mineral supplement each day. Nutrients that are especially important for reducing stress include:

CALCIUM — Supplements of calcium in the 1,000 to 1,500 mg. range can help reduce nervousness in some individuals.

MAGNESIUM — Magnesium has a beneficial effect on the nervous system. Those suffering from anxiety need 400 to 600 mg. of magnesium each day. If you use alcohol to relieve anxiety, keep in mind that it depletes the body's magnesium resources, which will then continue the anxiety cycle. One helpful way to restore magnesium levels is by relaxing in a warm bath of Epsom salts (magnesium sulfate), since some magnesium is absorbed through the skin.

VITAMIN C — Nervousness and stress can deplete the body of vitamin C, and such a deficiency can cause further anxiety and fatigue, so a daily supplement of at least 1,000 mg. is recommended.

BOTANICAL APPROACH — Valerian root acts as a central nervous system depressant, and one or two capsules can bring symptomatic relief from anxiety and will trigger sleepiness. Catnip tea is an effective daytime sedative. Drink one cup every three to four hours. Do not take valerian and catnip together.

ORAL-CONTRACEPTIVE USE

Oral-contraceptive users are subject to a variety of nutrient imbalances. Many women who take oral contraceptives show reduced levels of the vitamins B1, B2, B6, B12, niacin, and folic acid. In addition, oral contraceptives can cause copper levels in the blood to rise, causing a corresponding demand in the body for zinc and vitamin C. Users who do not get ample folic acid in their diets may develop megaloblastic anemia; they are also frequently deficient in vitamin C, which triggers the excretion of vitamin B6. To protect the health of the body from this complicated nutritional imbalance, oral-contraceptive users should take a daily multiple-vitamin/mineral supplement that incorporates ranges of 6 to 30 mcg. of vitamin B12, 400 mcg. of folic acid, 200 to 400 IU of vitamin E, 1,000 mg. of vitamin C, and 30 mg. of zinc. They should also take 50 to 100 mg. of vitamin B6 as an additional supplement if their multiple-vitamin/mineral supplement does not supply that much. Vitamin B6 can help with the mood swings and depression associated with the use of oral contraceptives.

OSTEOPOROSIS
(see also MENOPAUSE)

Nearly twenty million Americans are subject to osteoporosis, a degen-erative condition during and after menopause wherein the body loses stored calcium, mostly from the bones, making them brittle and easily broken. To prevent this condition, it is important for women in their twenties, thirties, and forties to take at least 1,200 to 1,500 mg. of calcium every day. Although this amount of calcium is available in a diet rich in dairy products, vegetable greens, or bony fish, it is not always possible or desirable to eat this way. Therefore, calcium supplements are very important to women who hope to block the development of osteoporosis. For best results, it is a good idea to take, along with the calcium, a multiple-vitamin/mineral supplement that provides 400 IU vitamin D and, if it is not contained in the drinking water, 2 to 4 mg. of fluorine.

PHLEBITIS

Phlebitis is the inflammation of a vein, particularly a vein in the leg. It is usually caused by a clot that has formed in the vein due to slow circulation or injury. Along with medical treatment, those prone to phlebitis can help prevent its recurrence with daily supplements in the range of 400 to 600 IU of vitamin E.

BOTANICAL APPROACH — To treat existing blood clots and help

prevent the formation of new ones, nutritionists have had success with cayenne. Take two cayenne capsules daily with meals. Also, white willow acts as a painkiller and blood thinner. Take two white willow tablets at least once a day, or as needed for pain.

POLLUTION
(see also THE ANTI-AGING PROGRAM, page 138)

It is important for those who live in cities or high-pollution areas to take a comprehensive multiple-vitamin/mineral supplement that has above-average levels of antioxidants. City dwellers will benefit from taking the following nutrients:

CALCIUM — Calcium supplements in the 1,000 to 1,500 mg. range work with iron to protect against the adverse effects of lead, a particularly dangerous hazard in city environments.

SELENIUM — Approximately 200 mcg. of supplemental selenium daily reduces the potential toxicity of mercury, silver, and cadmium. Selenium works in concert with vitamin E.

VITAMIN A — Vitamin A, in beta-carotene form, can protect the body from a number of pollutants and carcinogens. Approximately 25,000 IU should be taken each day, in the beta-carotene form only, not the retinol form.

VITAMIN C — Daily supplements of 1,000 mg. of vitamin C can protect the body against carbon monoxide, cadmium, and other toxic substances.

VITAMIN E — Vitamin E in the 300 to 400 IU range can help protect the body against ozone and nitrogen dioxide, as well as against the toxic effects of mercury and lead.

ZINC — Daily supplements of zinc in the 15 to 30 mg. range can protect cells from a number of pollutants, including lead.

PREGNANCY

Women who are pregnant will find that their nutrient needs undergo many changes. They will probably need increased amounts of certain vitamins, such as the B vitamins and vitamin C, as well as minerals, particularly iron and calcium. To keep their bodies in peak condition, pregnant women should consult their obstetricians and nutrition specialists about a specialized nutrition program that will meet their individual needs. Pregnant women are strongly advised to avoid using any internal botanical supplements, especially ginseng and goldenseal. These botanical supplements, like many medications, contain strong active alkaloids that may affect fetal health and development.

PREMENSTRUAL SYNDROME
(see also MENSTRUATION)

There are many uncomfortable symptoms related to menstrual cycles, including water retention, emotional tension, and depression. At its most chronic and severe level, this problem is known as premenstrual syndrome, or PMS. PMS is believed to be caused by the disorderly secretion of certain hormones, such as progesterone. Certain vitamin and mineral deficiencies seem to play a role in triggering PMS symptoms, so women prone to PMS should take a daily multiple-vitamin/mineral supplement that incorporates the following nutrients:

MAGNESIUM — A common symptom of PMS, depression, may be alleviated by a daily intake of 400 to 600 mg. of magnesium.

VITAMIN B6 — Shifts in hormone levels can deplete the body's supply of vitamin B6 and trigger anxiety or depression. A daily intake of 50 to 100 mg. of vitamin B6 will insure that a deficiency is not causing or aggravating PMS symptoms.

VITAMIN C — Low vitamin C levels can trigger the excretion of vitamin B6. This can be prevented by taking 1,000 mg. of vitamin C daily.

VITAMIN E — Recent evidence indicates that a daily intake of 200 to 400 IU of vitamin E can help relieve mood swings associated with PMS.

BOTANICAL APPROACH — For alleviating water retention, juniper berry tea is an excellent diuretic. Drink one cup in the morning and again in the mid-afternoon. Valerian capsules can help reduce anxiety and relieve insomnia. Take one or two capsules when needed or just before retiring. Valerian is a sedative and may cause drowsiness.

SHINGLES

Shingles are a painful viral infection of the nerve endings, often triggered by stress and sometimes accompanied by blisters. The shingles virus, herpes zoster, happens to be the same one that causes chicken pox. To help fight off any virus, it may help to get plenty of vitamin C — between 2,000 and 3,000 mg. daily, during the initial outbreak. Those prone to shingles should take a comprehensive multiple-vitamin/mineral supplement to maintain the body's immune system in top form.

BOTANICAL APPROACH — White willow is an anti-inflammatory substance that can help relieve many of the symptoms of shingles. Drink one cup of white willow tea or take two white willow tablets every three to four hours for relief. Since stress can aggravate shingles, take one or two valerian capsules as needed to relax.

SINUSITIS

Sinusitis is an inflammation of the mucous membranes that line the sinuses. Frequently, sinusitis triggers the sinuses to fill with pus. Some of its causes are allergies, exposure to pollutants, exposure to temperature extremes, and upper-respiratory-tract infections. Those prone to sinusitis should take a comprehensive multiple-vitamin/mineral supplement to maintain their immune system in top form. They should also consult a physician in the event antibiotic treatment is needed.

BOTANICAL APPROACH — There are a number of botanical preparations that can help relieve some of the symptoms of sinusitis. To reduce the membrane inflammation, mix one-half teaspoon of goldenseal powder in one-half cup of distilled water and sniff the solution in the nostrils with a nasal-spray bottle or dropper. Also, it may help to take one cayenne capsule and a glass of sparkling mineral water with a squeeze of lemon to relieve the spacey feeling that sometimes accompanies sinus problems. For pain, take two white willow tablets every three to four hours; and to help stimulate the immune system, eat one clove of raw garlic with each meal, or take one garlic capsule every three to four hours, until the symptoms are gone.

SKIN DISORDERS
(see also THE SKIN & HAIR PROGRAM, page 168)

The skin is the body's largest organ. Because it is an organ of excretion, the health and appearance of the skin can be enhanced by drinking eight glasses of purified water every day. Often the skin is the first place that health problems in the body become apparent. A large number of skin problems can be helped with nutritional therapy and many come about as the result of nutrient imbalances.

ACNE — Acne is most frequently the result of temporary glandular imbalances, improper diet, or localized infection. For continuous outbreaks of acne, it is a good idea to nutritionally balance the body by taking a daily multiple-vitamin/mineral supplement that includes 5,000 to 10,000 IU of vitamin A in retinol form and 15 to 30 mg. of zinc. Premenstrual acne may be controlled with 50 mg. of vitamin B6 taken daily for one week before the menstrual period begins. Zinc comes in a topical formula available in pharmacies, which is good for drying up acne outbreaks.

DANDRUFF — This scalp disorder can sometimes be caused by nutrient deficiencies. Those suffering from dandruff should take a multiple-vitamin/mineral supplement to insure that a nutrient deficiency is not contributing to their dandruff problem. Topical applications of selenium have shown some beneficial effects on dandruff. Shampoos containing selenium sulfide are available at pharmacies.

DRY SKIN — Dry skin can be caused by poor nutrition, harsh chemicals, dehydration, or glandular imbalances. A multiple-vitamin/ mineral supplement that contains vitamin A in both beta-carotene and retinol form, along with all the B vitamins, can help insure that the skin's nutritional needs are met. There have been numerous anecdotal reports that vitamin E applied topically can help eliminate dry skin. Those suffering from dry skin may be dehydrated and should drink at least eight glasses of water every day — especially in the morning and during the night.

PSORIASIS — Psoriasis has responded well to treatments with topically applied vitamin A in the form of retinoic acid. This requires a prescription from a physician. Again, the overall health of the skin is closely tied to the body's nutritional health, so a good multiple-vitamin/mineral supplement is recommended to sufferers of psoriasis and related skin disorders.

BOTANICAL APPROACH — Comfrey tea is a soothing, healing tonic for the skin, both internally and externally. During a period of skin disorders, drink one cup before bedtime for up to seven days. Another excellent solution for dry skin and rashes is olive oil, the herbalist's indispensible topical ointment. Apply fresh, unheated olive oil as frequently as needed to soothe and heal troubled skin. To quickly eliminate dandruff, apply olive oil directly to the scalp and leave it on overnight.

ACNE — For acne, make a strong solution of comfrey tea and add one-fourth teaspoon goldenseal powder. Allow it to cool, apply it to the skin, and let it dry. This may be done throughout the day and night and will help dry and heal acne infections.

DETOXIFYING — The skin is an organ of excretion, so chronic or persistent problems such as eczema, boils, or pimples could suggest a general toxicity in the body. To detoxify the body through the skin, take two yellow dock capsules three times daily with meals, and drink at least eight glasses of water daily. Because the detoxifying process will begin at once, skin conditions may get worse for a day or two before improvement begins. Continue treatment for two weeks.

BOILS — To bring a boil to a head and draw out the infected matter, make a paste of goldenseal powder and warm water. Apply it to the boil and cover with a bandage. Change the dressing three times daily.

ITCHING — For chronic itching, rub the problem area with olive oil.

POISON IVY OR POISON OAK — To dry up poison ivy or poison oak outbreaks, make a comfrey root plaster by making a paste of comfrey powder and warm water. Apply a thick layer of the plaster to the affected areas and cover with bandages or gauze. Do not let the area get wet for at least two days. The comfrey plaster will form a protective scab that will fall off by itself when the skin is healed.

SMOKING
(see also THE ANTI-AGING PROGRAM, page 138)

Tobacco smokers take in many dangerous carcinogens and other toxic substances, including acetaldehyde, carbon monoxide, nicotine, and nitrogen dioxide, some of which cause irreversible respiratory damage. Furthermore, a number of the body's nutrients are depleted by smoking, particularly vitamins B1, B6, and B12. Those who expose themselves (or are exposed) to tobacco smoke should take a multiple-vitamin/mineral supplement each day that includes adequate levels of all the B vitamins, along with 30 mg. of zinc and 3 mg. of copper. In addition, there are a number of other nutrients that can, in larger dosages, help protect smokers and their families and coworkers against the damaging effects of tobacco smoke. Among these are:

L-CYSTEINE — L-cysteine is an amino acid that seems to protect the body against the carcinogenic and toxic effects of tobacco smoke when taken in doses of 1,000 mg. daily.

SELENIUM — The antioxidant activity of this nutrient can help protect cells from the irreversible damage of free radicals when taken in a range of 200 to 400 mcg. Selenium works in concert with vitamin E and has

216

demonstrated a positive effect in the prevention of lung cancer.

VITAMIN A — In several studies, the effects of the carcinogens in tobacco smoke have been impaired by a daily intake of 25,000 IU of the beta-carotene form of vitamin A, and vitamin A has been found to reduce the incidence of lung cancer in smokers.

VITAMIN B12 — A recent study indicates that a daily intake of 600 mcg. of vitamin B12 can actually reverse cellular damage in the lungs caused by smoking. Folic acid levels in the study were increased to 8 mg. daily. It is a good idea to consult a nutrition specialist before taking prolonged high doses of these nutrients.

VITAMIN C — Each cigarette smoked depletes the body's level of vitamin C. In fact, studies show that heavy smokers have forty-percent lower blood-plasma levels of vitamin C than nonsmokers. Ironically, vitamin C is a vital antioxidant for smokers, necessary to protect the body from the damaging effects of specific toxins. A number of nutritionists recommend that smokers increase their vitamin C intake to 2,000 mg. by taking 500 mg. four times daily.

VITAMIN E — Vitamin E is an antioxidant that acts to maintain the stability of the cell membranes. This can help protect the cells lining the lungs from carcinogens in tobacco smoke, some of which can cause irreversible respiratory damage. A daily intake of 400 IU of vitamin E has been shown to be protective.

BOTANICAL APPROACH — Those trying to eliminate the smoking habit can suck licorice roots or sticks, which provide a mild stimulating effect. Anxiety can be controlled with valerian capsules, one or two at a time, which act as a central nervous system tranquilizer. Valerian may cause some drowsiness.

SUNBURN

To speed the healing of sunburn, take 500 mg. of vitamin C three times daily. Supplemental zinc in the range of 25 to 50 mg. is also helpful when taken during the healing process. Some individuals report that vitamin E applied topically and/or taken orally in doses of 200 IU three times daily is soothing and healing to sunburn. While the sunburn is healing, drink one full glass of water every two hours.

To prevent sunburn, apply zinc oxide to the nose, lips, shoulders, and other easily-burned areas. Zinc oxide is available at most pharmacies. Although it appears in many vitamin formulas, PABA, para-aminobenzoic acid, has no effect in the human body when taken orally, but it acts as an effective sunscreen when applied topically and continuously. Sunscreens with PABA are available at most health food stores and pharmacies.

New reasearch has shown that beta-carotene can help protect the skin from some of the damaging effects of sunlight, such as the rapid aging of the skin and, possibly, skin cancer. Those who plan to expose themselves to ultraviolet radiation should take a multiple-vitamin/mineral supplement that incorporates 25,000 IU of the beta-carotene form of vitamin A. This must be taken each day, since beta-carotene, an important antioxidant stored in the body, is, in turn, destroyed by exposing the skin to sunlight.

BOTANICAL APPROACH — To relieve the chilled feelings and pain that often accompany sunburn, take two white willow tablets every four hours until symptoms subside.

ULCERS

An ulcer is an open sore that is inflamed and slow to heal. The most common ulcers are peptic ulcers — areas of erosion on the mucous lining of the stomach, esophagus, or intestine. Exactly what triggers digestive ulcers is still not known, but stress seems to play a role. Those prone to ulcers may be helped by increasing their vitamin E intake to 600 IU daily. In treating gastric ulcers, studies show that those who take 50 to 150 mg. of zinc daily find that their ulcers heal three times faster than normal.

BOTANICAL APPROACH — Ulcer sufferers should drink licorice tea during the day rather than other beverages. It acts as a demulcent, soothing to the mucous membranes of the digestive tract.

VARICOSE VEINS

Distended, swollen veins, usually visible just below the surface of the skin on the legs, are known as varicose veins. Varicose veins often appear knotted and make the legs feel fatigued, sore, and prone to cramps and swelling. They can be aggravated by long periods of standing or sitting in one position. Varicose veins are associated with low-fiber diets, so those prone to varicose veins should increase their daily insoluble fiber intake, through dietary or supplemental means, to 30 to 60 g. This increased fiber intake should be accompanied by eight full glasses of water. Vitamin E, in the range of 400 to 600 IU daily, has been shown to help prevent phlebitis, or inflamed veins, and 1,000 mg. of vitamin C daily can help strengthen connective tissues.

VEGETARIANS

Those who do not eat meat but do eat dairy products, eggs, or fish, are known in the United States as vegetarians. Those who eliminate all types of animal tissues and products from their diets and eat only fruits, grains, nuts, seeds, and vegetables, are known as vegans. Vegans who do not take a daily multiple-vitamin/mineral supplement that includes vitamin B12, vitamin D, iron, zinc, and calcium, may be at some risk nutritionally. Some vitamins have inadequate nonanimal sources and some minerals are not absorbed as well when dietary fiber levels are very high. In fact, to take full advantage of an otherwise optimally healthy diet, all vegetarians should take daily vitamin and mineral supplements.

WINTER WEATHER
(*see also* COMMON COLD, FLU)

In the winter months, in cold climates, it is especially important to take a daily multiple-vitamin/mineral supplement that incorporates the following: vitamin A, for withstanding colder temperatures; vitamin D, because sunlight is infrequent; vitamin C, because fresh fruits and vegetables may not be readily available; and all the B vitamins, for stress due to cold weather and an enclosed environment. Residents in winter areas should also drink at least eight glasses of water daily, as both cold air and heated air are very dehydrating to the body.

BOTANICAL APPROACH — For chills or mild hypothermia, drink one cup of ginger tea, which warms and stimulates the body.

APPENDIXES

Product Reviews
Reference Sources

PRODUCT REVIEWS

The vitamin products reviewed in the pages that follow are commercially available supplements with well-structured formulas that are reasonably close to the recommended dosage ranges in The Vitamin Power Formula. The approximate cost of using these products was calculated at the time of publication. This cost does not include additional supplements that may be required to reach The Vitamin Power Formula dosages.

BROAD SPECTRUM™
NutriGuard Research, Encinitas, California
Cost: approximately $0.33 per day

This formula is among the best that we could find. Its dosage ranges fall very close to those recommended in The Vitamin Power Formula. Broad Spectrum™ is not available in stores. NutriGuard Research is a mail-order company, so this supplement may only be ordered directly from: NutriGuard Research, P.O. Box 865, Encinitas, CA 92024. Tel.: (619) 942-3223. Six tablets daily provide:

Vitamin A (as beta-carotene)	25,000 IU
(as retinyl palmitate)	5,000 IU
Vitamin B1 — Thiamin	10 mg.
Vitamin B2 — Riboflavin	10 mg.
Niacin (as niacinamide)	100 mg.
Pantothenic Acid	50 mg.
Vitamin B6 — Pyridoxine	50 mg.
Vitamin B12	30 mcg.
Folic Acid	400 mcg.
Biotin	100 mcg.
Vitamin C	1,000 mg.
Vitamin D	400 IU
Vitamin E	400 IU
Vitamin K	100 mcg.
Calcium	1,000 mg.
Chromium	200 mcg.
Copper	3 mg.
Iodine	150 mcg.
Iron	18 mg.
Magnesium	400 mg.
Manganese	10 mg.
Molybdenum	150 mcg.
Selenium	200 mcg.
Zinc	30 mg.

Other Ingredients:	
Choline	250 mg.
Silicon	20 mg.

FORTIFIED VITAMIN & MINERAL INSURANCE FORMULA®
Bronson Pharmaceuticals, La Cañada, California
Cost: approximately $0.36 per day

Bronson Pharmaceuticals puts out a number of formulas and individual supplements that they sell primarily through mail order and, to a lesser degree, in health food stores. The Fortified Vitamin & Mineral Insurance Formula® comes quite close to the self-defense ranges of The Vitamin Power Formula, although it is unusually high in biotin and vitamin C. Neither nutrient, however, is harmful in these dosages. Those who use this formula, particularly women, exercisers, and those with high blood pressure, will need to supplement it with approximately 1,000 mg. of calcium. This formula may also be ordered directly from: Bronson Pharmaceuticals, 4526 Rinetti Lane, La Cañada, CA 91011. Tel. in continental U.S.: (800) 521-3322; in California (only): (800) 521-3323. Six tablets daily provide:

Vitamin A (as beta-carotene)	7,500 IU
(as retinyl palmitate)	7,500 IU
Vitamin B1 — Thiamin	20 mg.
Vitamin B2 — Riboflavin	20 mg.
Niacin (as niacinamide)	200 mg.
Pantothenic Acid	150 mg.
Vitamin B6 — Pyridoxine	30 mg.
Vitamin B12	90 mcg.
Folic Acid	400 mcg.
Biotin	3,000 mcg.
Vitamin C	2,500 mg.
Vitamin D	400 IU
Vitamin E	400 IU
Vitamin K	100 mcg.
Calcium	250 mg.
Chromium	200 mcg.
Copper	2 mg.
Iodine	150 mcg.
Iron	30 mg.
Magnesium	200 mg.
Manganese	10 mg.
Molybdenum	200 mcg.
Selenium	100 mcg.
Zinc	30 mg.

Other Ingredients:	
Choline	500 mg.
Inositol	500 mg.
PABA (para-aminobenzoic acid)	30 mg.
Phosphorus	250 mg.
Rutin	200 mg.

SUPER MAXICAPS™
Wm. T. Thompson Co., Carson, California
Cost: approximately $0.46 per day

Thompson products are widely available in health food stores. For a two-pill formula, Super Maxicaps™ comes reasonably close to The Vitamin Power Formula and is right on target with its use of beta-carotene for vitamin A. Those who choose this formula should supplement it with 1,000 mg. of calcium, 200 mcg. of chromium, and 200 mcg. of selenium. The vitamin C range is not very high, but certainly acceptable. It, too, can be supplemented if desired. Two soft gelatin capsules daily provide:

Vitamin A (as beta-carotene)	25,000 IU
Vitamin B1 — Thiamin	60 mg.
Vitamin B2 — Riboflavin	60 mg.
Niacin (as niacinamide)	60 mg.
Pantothenic Acid	60 mg.
Vitamin B6 — Pyridoxine	60 mg.
Vitamin B12	60 mcg.
Folic Acid	400 mcg.
Biotin	60 mcg.
Vitamin C	300 mg.
Vitamin D	600 IU
Vitamin E	400 IU
Vitamin K	none
Calcium	200 mg.
Chromium	15 mcg.
Copper	1 mg.
Iodine	150 mcg.
Iron	18 mg.
Magnesium	50 mg.
Manganese	15 mg.
Molybdenum	15 mcg.
Selenium	15 mcg.
Zinc	15 mg.
Other Ingredients:	
Choline	30 mg.
Hesperidin	5 mg.
Inositol	30 mg.
Lecithin	80 mg.
Lemon Bioflavonoid Complex	10 mg.
PABA (para-aminobenzoic acid)	30 mg.
Phosphorus	50 mg.
Potassium	15 mg.
Rutin	5 mg.

TWINSPORT™ ENDURANCE MULTI VITAMIN FITNESS PAK
Twin Laboratories, Inc.
Ronkonkoma, New York
Cost: approximately $0.67 per day

Although Twin Laboratories promotes this formula as a "fitness formula," it happens to come very close to the ideal health-protective ranges and seems to be a good all-around supplement. It is high in a few nutrients and, curiously, quite low in iron, one of the minerals most at jeopardy during exercise. Generally, however, it seems to be a well-structured formula that is available in convenient take-along packets. Twinsport™ can be found in many health food stores and some pharmacies. Seven hard gelatin capsules daily provide:

Vitamin A (as beta-carotene)	15,000 IU
(as retinol acetate)	10,000 IU
Vitamin B1 — Thiamin	50 mg.
Vitamin B2 — Riboflavin	50 mg.
Niacin (as niacinamide)	50 mg.
Pantothenic Acid	50 mg.
Vitamin B6 — Pyridoxine	50 mg.
Vitamin B12	50 mcg.
Folic Acid	400 mcg.
Biotin	50 mcg.
Vitamin C	1,000 mg.
Vitamin D	400 IU
Vitamin E	400 IU
Vitamin K	none
Calcium	1,000 mg.
Chromium	200 mcg.
Copper	2 mg.
Iodine	150 mcg.
Iron	10 mg.
Magnesium	500 mg.
Manganese	10 mg.
Molybdenum	500 mcg.
Selenium	200 mcg.
Zinc	30 mg.

Other Ingredients:

Choline	50 mg.
Inositol	50 mg.
PABA (para-aminobenzoic acid)	50 mg.
Potassium	99 mg.

This particular formula is among the best of the many one-pill-per-day supplements available in pharmacies and grocery stores. It will need to be supplemented to reach the ideal health-protective levels of some nutrients, but many people prefer to design their own regimens and choose from some of the best individual supplements. To reach nutritional self-defense levels, add these individually available supplements: 15,000 to 25,000 IU of beta-carotene; 1,000 mg. of vitamin C (250 mg. four times daily is a good way to take this nutrient); 400 IU of vitamin E; 1,000 mg. of calcium; 200 mcg. of chromium; and 200 mcg. of selenium. Women should also add 25 to 50 mg. of vitamin B6. One tablet daily provides:

Vitamin A (as retinol acetate)	9,000 IU
Vitamin B1 — Thiamin	10 mg.
Vitamin B2 — Riboflavin	10 mg.
Niacin (as niacinamide)	20 mg.
Pantothenic Acid	20 mg.
Vitamin B6 — Pyridoxine	5 mg.
Vitamin B12	10 mcg.
Folic Acid	400 mcg.
Biotin	45 mcg.
Vitamin C	90 mg.
Vitamin D	400 IU
Vitamin E	30 IU
Vitamin K	25 mcg.
Calcium	70 mg.
Chromium	15 mcg.
Copper	3 mg.
Iodine	150 mcg.
Iron	30 mg.
Magnesium	100 mg.
Manganese	7.5 mg.
Molybdenum	15 mcg.
Selenium	15 mcg.
Zinc	15 mg.
Other Ingredients:	
Phosphorus	54 mg.
Potassium	8 mg.

REFERENCE SOURCES

Abraham, G. E., and Hargrove, J. "Effect of vitamin B6 on premenstrual symptomatology in women with premenstrual tension syndromes: a double-blind cross-over study." *Infertility* 3(1980):155-57.

Abraham, G. E., and Lubran, M. M. "Serum and red cell magnesium in patients with premenstrual tension." *American Journal of Clinical Nutrition* 34(1981):2364.

Ackley, S., et al. "Dairy products, calcium, and blood pressure." *American Journal of Clinical Nutrition* 38(1983):457-79.

Adams, J. S., et al. "Vitamin D synthesis and metabolism after ultraviolet irradiation of normal and vitamin D-deficient subjects." *New England Journal of Medicine* 306(1982):722.

Adams, P. W., et al. "Effect of pyridoxine hydrochloride (vitamin B6) upon depression associated with oral contraceptives." *Lancet* 1(1973):899-904.

——. "Vitamin B6, depression, and oral contraception." *Lancet* 2(1974):516-17.

Ahmad, F., and Bamji, M. S. "Vitamin supplements to women using oral contraceptives." *Contraception* 14(1976):309-18.

Aikman, L. *Nature's Healing Arts: From Folk Medicine to Modern Drugs.* Washington, D. C.: National Geographic Society, 1977.

Albert, M. J., et al. "Vitamin B12 synthesis by human small intestinal bacteria. *Nature* 283(1980):781.

Alhadeff, L., et al. "Toxic effects of water soluble vitamins." *Nutrition Reviews* 42(1984):33-40.

Allen, L. H., and Lindsay, H. "Calcium bioavailability and absorption." *American Journal of Clinical Nutrition* 35(1982):783.

Altura, B. M., and Altura, B. T. "Magnesium and contraction of smooth muscle: Relationship to vascular disease." *Federation Proceedings* 40(1981):2672.

Anderson, B. M., Gibson, R. S., and Sabry, J. H. "The iron and zinc status of long-term vegetarian women." *American Journal of Clinical Nutrition* 34(1981):1042-48.

Anderson, R., and van Rensburg, A. J. "The effects of increasing weekly doses of ascorbate on certain cellular and humoral immune functions in normal volunteers." *American Journal of Clinical Nutrition* 33(1980):71.

Anderson, T. W., and P. B. Reid. "A double blind trial of vitamin E in angina pectoris." *American Journal of Clinical Nutrition* 27(1974):1174-77.

Anderson, T. W., Surany, G., and Beatson, G. H. "The effect on winter illness of large doses of vitamin C." *Canadian Medical Association Journal* 111(1974):31.

Angier, B. *Field Guide to Medicinal Wild Plants.* Harrisburg, Pennsylvania: Stackpole Books, 1978.

Anon. "An introduction to free radicals." *Vitamin and Nutrition Information Service Backgrounder* 1(1986):1-4.

——. "Benefits of eating fish." *Tufts University Diet and Nutrition Letter* 3(1985):1-3.

——. "Calcium, colon cancer, and high blood pressure." *Tufts University Diet and Nutrition Letter* 3(1986):1.

——. "Cholesterol, cancer, and stroke." *Nutrition and the M.D.* 8(1982):1.

——. "Do chillies influence duodenal ulcer healing?" *Lawrence Review of Natural Products* 6(1985):15-16.

——. "Garlic." *Lawrence Review of Natural Products* 5(1984):21-24.

——. "Ginseng." *Lawrence Review of Natural Products* 6(1985):1-4.

——. "How much sodium is coming from your tap?" *Tufts University Diet and Nutrition Letter* 4(1986):1-2.

229

———. "Iron overload a threat to body's vital organs." *Health Scene* 1(1986):9.

———. "Is ginseng the root to good health?" *Tufts University Diet and Nutrition Letter* 3(1986):2.

———. "It's not fishy: Fruit of the sea may foil cardiovascular disease." *Journal of the American Medical Association* 247(1982):11.

———. *Nutrition Common Sense and Cancer*. New York: American Cancer Society, 1984.

———. *Nutrition and Cancer: Cause and Prevention*. New York: American Cancer Society, 1985.

———. "Oral zinc and immunoregulation." *Nutrition Reviews* 40(1982):12.

———. "Season gingerly to retard rancidity." *Science News* 129(1986):137.

———. "The medicinal uses of parsley." *Lawrence Review of Natural Products* 5(1984):37-38,.

———. "Vegetarian diet and B12 deficiency." *Nutrition Reviews* 36(1978):243-44.

———. "Vitamin C at work in the eye." *Science News* 129(1986):410.

———. *Vitamin interactions.* Vitamin and Nutrition Information Service pamphlet, May 1985.

Ansell, J. E., et al. "The spectrum of vitamin K deficiency." *Journal of the American Medical Association* 238(1977):40-42.

Antonious, L. D. "Zinc and sexual dysfunction." *Lancet* 1(1980):1034.

Archer, J. "Vitamin E." *Journal of the American Medical Association* 247(1982):29.

Arlette, J. P. "Zinc and the skin." *Pediatric Clinics of North America* 30(1983):583-96.

Armstrong, B., and Doll, R. "Environmental factors and cancer incidence and mortality in different countries, with special reference to dietary practices." *International Journal of Cancer Research* 15(1975):617.

Avioli, L. V., and Haddad, J. G. "The vitamin D family revisited." *New England Journal of Medicine* 311(1984):47-49.

Ayers, S., and Mihan, R. "Nocturnal leg cramps (systremma): A progress report on response to vitamin E." *Southern Medical Journal* 67(1974):1308-12.

———. "Vitamin E as a useful therapeutic agent." *Journal of American Academy of Dermatology* 7(9182):521-25.

Barbul, A., and Seifter, E. "Wound healing and thymotropic effects of arginine: A pituitary mechanism of action." *American Journal of Clinical Nutrition* 37(1983):786.

Barbul, A., Rettura, G., et al. "Arginine: A thymotropic and wound-healing promoting agent." *Surgical Forum* 28(1977):101.

———. "Arginine stimulates lymphocyte immune response in healthy human beings." *Surgery* 90(1981):244.

Barna, P. "The case of ginseng." *Lancet* 2(1985):548.

Basu, T. K., and Williams, D. C. "The thiamine status of cancer patients." *International Journal of Vitamin and Nutrition Research* 44(1974):53.

Bazzato, G., and Ciman, M. "Myasthenia-like syndrome after DL- but not L-carnitine." *Lancet* 2(1981):1209.

Belizan, J. M., et al. "Reduction of blood pressure with calcium supplementation in young adults." *Journal of the American Medical Association* 249(1983):1161.

Berkow, R., ed. *The Merck Manual*. 14th ed. Rahway, New Jersey: Merck & Co., Inc., 1982.

Beyer, P. L., and Flynn M. A. "Effects of high-/low-fiber diets on human feces." *Journal of the American Medical Association* 72(1978):271-76.

Bickle, D. D. "Calcium absorption and vitamin D metabolism." *Clinical Gastroenterology* 12(1983):380-94.

Bierenbaum, M. L., et al. "Long term human studies on the lipid effects of oral calcium." *Lipids* 7(1972):202.

Bieri, J. G., et al. "Medical uses of vitamin E." *New England Journal of Medicine* 308(1983):1063.

Binder, H., et al. "Tocopherol deficiency in man." *New England Journal of Medicine* 283(1965):1289-97.

Bjelke, E. "Dietary vitamin A and human lung cancer." *International Journal of Cancer Research* 15(1975):561-65.

Blake, D. R., and Gutteridge, J. M. C. "The importance of iron in rheumatoid disease." *Lancet* 1:(1981)1142.

Bollag, W. "Vitamin A and retinoids: From nutrition to pharmacotherapy in dermatology and oncology." *Lancet* 1(1983):860-63.

Bordia, A. "Effects of garlic on blood lipids in patients with coronary heart disease." *American Journal of Clinical Nutrition* 34(1981):2100.

Borum, P. R., and Broquist, H. P. "Carnitine." *Journal of Nutrition* 107(1977):1209.

Bougneres, P. F., and Assan R. "Hypolipidemic effect of carnitine in uremic patients." *Lancet* 1(1979):1401.

Bowerman, S. J., et al. "Nutrient consumption of individuals taking or not taking nutrient supplements." *Journal of the American Dietetic Association* 82(1983):401-04.

Brace, L. "The pharmacology and therapeutics of vitamin K." *American Journal of Medical Technology* 49(1983):457-63.

Bright, S. E. "Vitamin C and cancer prevention." *Seminars in Oncology* 10(1983):294-98.

Brunner, D. J., et al. "Serum cholesterol and high density lipoprotein cholesterol in coronary patients and healthy persons." *Atherosclerosis* 33(1979):9-16.

Bull, R. J. "Health effects of drinking water disinfectants." *Environmental Science and Technology* 16(1982):554.

Burkitt, D. P. "Dietary fiber and disease." *Journal of the American Dietetic Association* 229(1974):1068.

Burton, G. W., and Ingold, K. U. "Beta-carotene: An unusual type of lipid antioxidant." *Science* 224(1984):569-573.

Butterworth, C. E., and Krumdieck, C. L. "Improvement in cervical dysplasia associated with folic acid therapy in users of oral contraceptives." *American Journal of Clinical Nutrition* 35(1982):73.

Cameron, E., and Pauling, L. "Supplemental ascorbate in the supportive treatment of cancer: Prolongation of survival times in terminal human cancer." *Proceedings of the National Academy of Science* 73(1976):3685-3689.

Carlson, L. A., et al. "Effect of oral calcium upon serum cholesterol and triglycerides in patients with hyperlipidemia." *Atherosclerosis* 14(1971):391.

Check, W. A. "And if you add chromium, that's even better." *Journal of the American Medical Association* 247(1982):3046.

Cheraskin, E., et al. *The Vitamin C Connection.* New York: Harper & Row, 1983.

Chipperfield, B., and Chipperfield, J. R. "Magnesium and the heart." *American Heart Journal* 93(1977):679.

Cho, J. M., and Cho, H. G. "The effect of red ginseng on chemical carcinogenesis." *Journal of Dental Research* 65(1986):600.

Chow, C. K. "Dietary vitamin E and cellular susceptibility to cigarette smoking." *Annals of the New York Academy of Science* 393(1982):96-108.

Connor, W. E., and Gallo, L. L. "Lymphatic absorption of shellfish sterols and their effects on cholesterol absorption." *American Journal of Clinical Nutrition* 34(1981):507.

Cordova, C., et al. "Influence of ascorbic acid on platelet aggregation in vitro and in vivo." *Atherosclerosis* 41(1982):15-19.

Coulehan, J. L. "Ascorbic acid and the common cold." *Postgraduate Medicine* 66(1979):153.

Crary, E. J., and McCarty, M. F. "Potential clinical applications for high-dose nutritional antioxidants." *Medical Hypotheses* 13(1984):77.

Creagan, E. T., et al. "Failure of high dose vitamin C (ascorbic acid) therapy to benefit patients with advanced cancer: A controlled trial." *New England Journal of Medicine* 301(1979):687-90.

Crouse, S. F., et al. "Zinc ingestion and lipoprotein values in sedentary and endurance-trained men." *Journal of the American Medical Association* 252(1984):785.

Culbreth, D. M. R. *A Manual of Materia Medica and Pharmacology*. Philadelphia: Lea & Febiger, 1927.

Darby, W. J., et al. "Niacin." *Nutrition Reviews* 33(1975):289-97.

Davis, R. E., and Icke, G. C. "Clinical chemistry of thiamin." *Advances in Clinical Chemistry* 23(1984):163-216.

DeCosse, J. J. "Effect of ascorbic acid on rectal polyps of patients with familial polyposis." *Surgery* 78(1975):608-12.

DeLuca, H. F. "Some new concepts emanating from a study of the metabolism and function of vitamin D." *Nutrition Reviews* 38(1980):169.

———. "New developments in the vitamin D endocrine system." *Journal of the American Dietetic Association* 80(1982):231.

Deugun, M. S., and Cohen, C. "Vitamin D nutrition in relation to season and occupation." *American Journal of Clinical Nutrition* 34(1981):1501.

DiPalma, J. R., and Ritchie, D. M. "Vitamin toxicity." *Annual Review of Pharmacology & Toxicology* 17(1977):133-48.

Disorbo, D. M., and Litwack, G. "Vitamin B6 kills hepatoma cells in culture." *Nutrition and Cancer* 3(1982):216-22.

———. "Pyridoxine resistance in a rat hepatoma cell line." *Cancer Research* 42(1982):2362-70.

Dubick, M. A. "Dietary supplements and health aids — A critical evaluation. Part 2: Macronutrients and fiber." *Journal of Nutrition Education* 15(1983):88.

Duchateau, J. et al. "Beneficial effects of oral zinc supplementation on the immune response of old people." *American Journal of Medicine* 70(1981):1001.

Dustan, H. P. "Is potassium deficiency a factor in the pathogenesis and maintenance of hypertension?" *Arteriosclerosis* 3(1983):307-09.

Dyckner, T., et al. "Effect of magnesium on blood pressure." *British Medical Journal* 286(1983):1847-49.

Dyerberg, J., and Schmidt, E. B. "Omega-3 polyunsaturated fatty acids and ischemic heart disease. *Lancet* 2(1982):614.

———. "Eicosapentanoic acid and the prevention of atherosclerosis." *Lancet* 2(1978):117.

Dworken, H. J. "Vitamin E reconsidered." *Annals of Internal Medicine* 98(1983):253-54.

Eby, G. A., et al. "Reduction in duration of common colds by zinc gluconate lozenges in a double-blind study." *Antimicrobial Agents in Chemotherapy* 25(1984):20.

Ehud, B. H., and Fuller, S. "Effect of *Panax ginseng* saponins and Eleutherococcus senticosus on survival of cultured mammalian cells after ionizing radiation." *American Journal of Chinese Medicine* 9(1981):48-56.

Elwood, P. C., et al. "A randomized controlled trial of the therapeutic effect of vitamin C on the common cold." *Practitioner* 218(1977):133.

Epstein, O., and Sherlock, S. "Vitamin D, hydroxyapatite, and calcium gluconate treatment of cortical bone thinning." *American Journal of Clinical Nutrition* 36(1982):426.

Ershoff, B. H. and Marshall, W. E. "Protective effects of dietary fiber in rats fed toxic doses of sodium cyclamate and polyoxyethylene sorbitan monostearate (Tween 60)." *Journal of Food Science* 40(1975):358.

Evans, D. L., et al. "Organic psychosis without anemia or spinal cord symptoms in patients with vitamin B12 deficiency." *American Journal Psychiatry* 140(1983):218-21.

Fernandez, R., and Phillips, S. F. "Components of fiber bind iron in vitro." *American Journal of Clinical Nutrition* 35(1982):100.

Fletcher, D. C. "Vitamin K content of various foods." *Journal of the American Medical Association* 237(1977):1871.

Fliegel, S. E. G., et al. "Evidence for a role of hydroxyl radicals in immune-complex-induced vasculitis." *American Journal of Pathology* 115(1984):375-382.

Francis, T. T. "Golden root of the Cherokee: Golden seal." *The Herbalist* 3(1979):4-5.

——. "Valerian." *The Herbalist* 4(1979):17-18.

Freedland-Graves, J. H., and Young, R. "Effect of zinc supplementation on plasma HDL cholesterol." *American Journal of Clinical Nutrition* 35(1982):988.

Fregly, M. J. "Estimates of sodium and potassium intake." *Annals of Internal Medicine* 98(1983):792-99.

Gallagher, J. C., and Riggs, B. L. "Nutrition and bone disease." *New England Journal of Medicine* 298(1978):193.

Garland, C., et al. "Dietary vitamin D and calcium and risk of colorectal cancer: 19-year prospective study in men." *Lancet* 1(1985):307.

Garmon, L. "Zones of goiter: Drinking water connection?" *Science News* 23(1983):230.

Gerber, L. E., and Erdman, J. W., Jr. "Effect of dietary retinyl acetate, beta carotene, and retinoic acid on wound healing in rats." *Journal of Nutrition* 112(1982):1555.

Gibbons, E. *Stalking the Healthful Herbs.* New York: David McKay Co., 1970.

Gonzales, E. R. "Medical news: Vitamin E relieves most cystic breast disease; may alter lipids and hormones." *Journal of the American Medical Association* 244(1980):1077.

——. "Sperm swim singly after vitamin C therapy." *Journal of the American Medical Association* 249(1983):2747.

Goodman, D. S. "Vitamin A metabolism." *Federation Proceedings* 39(1980):2716-22.

——. "Vitamin A and retinoids in health and disease." *New England Journal of Medicine* 310(1984):1023-31.

Goodwin, J. S., et al. "Association between nutritional status and cognitive functioning in a healthy elderly population." *Journal of the American Medical Association* 249(1983):2917-2921.

Graham, S. "Toward a dietary prevention of cancer." *Epidemiology Review* 5(1983):38-50.

Graham, S., et al. "Diet in the epidemiology of cancer of the colon and rectum." *Journal of the National Cancer Institute* 61(1978):709-14.

——. "Dietary factors in the epidemiology of cancer of the larynx." *American Journal of Epidemiology* 113(1981):675-80.

Greenleaf, J. E. "Dehydration-induced drinking in humans." *Federation Proceedings* 41(1982):2509.

Greenleaf, J. E., Brock, P. J., et al. "Drinking and water balance during exercise and heat acclimation." *Journal of Applied Physiology* 54(1983):414.

233

Greenwald, P. "Manipulation of nutrients to prevent cancer." *Hospital Practice* 5(1984):119-134.

Greenwood, J. "Optimum vitamin C intake as a factor in the preservation of disc integrity." *Medical Annals of the District of Columbia* 33(1965):274-76.

Grieve, M. *A Modern Herbal.* New York: Dover Publications, Inc., 1971.

Griffin, A. C. "Role of selenium in the chemoprevention of cancer." *Advances in Cancer Research* 29(1979):419.

Haeger, K. "Long-time treatment of intermittent claudication with vitamin E." *American Journal of Clinical Nutrition* 27(1974):1179-81.

Hallberg, L. "Iron requirements and availability of dietary iron." *Experientia* 44(1983):223-44.

Halliwell, B. "Oxygen radicals: A commonsense look at their nature and medical importance." *Medical Biology* 62(1984):71-77.

Halliwell, B., and Gutteridge, J. M. C. "Oxygen toxicity, oxygen radicals, transition metals, and disease." *Biochemical Journal* 219(1984):1-14.

Hathcock, J. "Vitamin safety: A current appraisal." *Vitamin and Nutrition Information Service, Vitamin Issues* 5(1985):1-8.

Haussler, M. R., and McCain, T. A. "Basic and clinical concepts related to vitamin D metabolism and action." *New England Journal of Medicine* 297(1980):1041-50.

Hay, C. R. M., and Saynor, R. "Effect of fish oil on platelet kinetics in patients with ischemic heart disease." *Lancet* 2(1982):1269.

Heaney, R. P., et al. "Calcium nutrition and bone health in the elderly." *American Journal of Clinical Nutrition* 36(1982):986-1013.

Heidbreder, G., and Christopher, E. "Therapy of psoriasis with retinoid plus PUVA: Clinical and histologic data." *Archives of Dermatological Research* 264(1979):331-37.

Heinerman, J. "Capsicum, an energy food for active people." *The Herbalist* 2:22, 1980.

———. *The Science of Herbal Medicine.* Orem, Utah: Bi-World Publishers, 1983.

Hem, S. L., et al. "Evaluation of antacid suspensions containing aluminum hydroxide and magnesium hydroxide. *American Journal of Hospital Pharmacology* 39(1982):1825-30.

Hendler, S. S. *The Complete Guide to Anti-Aging Nutrients.* New York: Simon and Schuster, 1985.

Henningsen, N. C., et al. "Hypertension, potassium, and the kitchen." *Lancet* 1(1983):133.

Henzel, J. H., et al. "Zinc concentrations within healing wounds." *Archives of Surgery* 100(1970):349-57.

Herbert, V. "The vitamin craze." *Archives of Internal Medicine* 140 (1980):173.

———. "Spirulina and vitamin B12." *Journal of the American Medical Association* 248 (1982):3096.

———. "Toxicity of 25,000 IU vitamin A supplements in health food users." *American Journal of Clinical Nutrition* 36 (1982):185.

Hermann, W. J. "The effect of vitamin E on lipoprotein cholesterol distribution." *Annals of the New York Academy of Science* 393(1982):467-72.

Hermann, W. J. and Faucett, J. "Effect of tocopherol on HDL cholesterol." *American Journal Clinical Pathology* 72(1979):848.

Herold, E., et al. "Effect of vitamin E on human sexual functioning." *Sexual Behavior* 8(1979):397-403.

Herrmann, E. C., Jr., and Kucera, L. S. "Antiviral substances in plants of the mint family (Labiatae). Part III: Peppermint (*Mentha piperita*) and other mint plants." *Proceedings of the Society for Experimental Biology and Medicine* 124(1979): 27-34.

Heyden, S., et al. "The role of potassium manipulation in blood pressure control." *Arteriosclerosis* 3(1983):302-06.

Hikino, H., et al. "Antihepatotoxic actions of ginsenosides from *Panax ginseng* roots." *Planta Medica* 50(1985):62-64.

Hodges, R. E. "Vitamin C and cancer." *Nutrition Reviews* 40(1982):289-92.

Hodges, R. E., and Bleiler, R. E. "Factors affecting human antibody responses. Part III: Responses in pantothenic acid deficient men." *American Journal of Clinical Nutrition* 11(1962):85.

Hoffer, A. "Treatment of arthritis by nicotinic acid and nicotinamide." *Canadian Medical Association Journal* 81(1959):235.

Hooper, P. L., and Johnson, G. E. "Zinc lowers HDL cholesterol." *Journal of the American Medical Association* 244(1980):1960.

Hornsby, P. J. "The role of vitamin E in cellular energy metabolism in cultured adrenocortical cells." *Journal of Cellular Physiology* 112(1982):207-16.

Hornsby, P. J., and Gill, G. N. "Regulation of glutamine and pyruvate oxidation in cultured adrenocortical cells by cortisol, antioxidants, and oxygen: Effects on cell proliferation." *Journal of Cellular Physiology.* 109:(1981)111-20.

Horrobin, D. F., and Manku, M. S. "How do polyunsaturated fatty acids lower plasma cholesterol levels?" *Lipids* 18(1983):558.

Horvath, P. M., and Ip, C. "Synergistic effect of vitamin E and selenium in the chemoprevention of mammary carcinogenesis in rats." *Cancer Research* 43(1983):5335-37.

Horwitt, M. K. "Therapeutic uses of vitamin E in medicine." *Nutrition Reviews* 38(1980):105-13.

Hotz, W. "Nicotinic acid and its derivatives: A short survey." *Advances in Lipid Research* 20(1983):195-217.

Huton, C. W., et al. "Assessment of the zinc nutritional status of selected elderly subjects." *Journal of the American Dietetic Association* 82(1983):148-153.

Iacono, J. M., et al. "Reduction of blood pressure associated with high polyunsaturated fat diets that reduce blood cholesterol in man." *Preventive Medicine* 4(1975):426.

Iber, F. L., et al. "Thiamin in the elderly: Relation to alcoholism and to neurological degenerative disease." *American Journal of Clinical Nutrition* 36(1982):1067-69.

Innis, S. M., and Allardyce, D. B. "Possible biotin deficiency in adults receiving long-term total parenteral nutrition." *American Journal of Clinical Nutrition* 37(1983):185.

Iseri, L. T., and French, J. H. "Magnesium: Nature's physiologic calcium blocker." *American Heart Journal* 108(1984):188-93.

Isidori, A., et al. "A study of growth hormone release in man after oral administration of amino acids." *Current Medical Research and Opinion* 7(1981):475.

Ivy, M. and Elmer, G. "Nutritional supplements, mineral and vitamin products." In *Handbook of Non-Prescription Drugs.* Washington, D. C.: American Pharmaceutical Association, 1982.

Jacobs, M. M. "Effects of selenium on chemical carcinogens." *Preventive Medicine* 9(1980):362.

Jain, R. C., and Vyas, C. R. "Garlic in alloxan-induced diabetic rabbits." *American Journal of Clinical Nutrition* 28(1975):684.

Jansen, J. D. "Nutrition and cancer." *World Review of Nutrition and Diet* 39(1982):2-22.

235

Jenkins, D. J. A., et al. "Decrease in postprandial insulin and glucose concentrations by guar and pectin." *Annals of Internal Medicine* 86(1977):20.

Jie, Y. H., et al. "Immunomodulatory effects of *Panax ginseng* C. A. Meyer in the mouse." *Agents and Actions* 15(1984):385-391.

Kallner, A. B., and Hornig, D. H. "On the requirements of ascorbic acid in man: Steady state turnover in smokers." *American Journal of Clinical Nutrition* 34(1981):1347.

Kamath, S. K. "Taste acuity and aging." *American Journal of Clinical Nutrition* 36(1982):766.

Kane, J. P., et al. "Normalization of low-density-lipoprotein levels in heterozygous familial hypercholesterolemia with a combined drug regimen." *New England Journal of Medicine* 304(1981):251-58.

Kanofsky, J. D., et al. "Prevention of thromboembolic disease by vitamin E." (Letter) *New England Journal of Medicine* 305(1981):173-74.

Kasa, R. M. "Vitamin C: From scurvy to the common cold." *American Journal of Medical Technology* 49(1983):23-26.

Kay, R. M., et al. "The effect of pectin on serum cholesterol." *American Journal of Clinical Nutrition* 31(1978):562.

Keith, R. E., et al. "Lung function and treadmill performance of smoking and nonsmoking males receiving ascorbic acid supplements." *American Journal of Clinical Nutrition* 36:840-45, 1982.

Keys, J. D. *Chinese Herbs: Their Botany, Chemistry, and Pharmacodynamics.* Rutland, Vt.: Charles E. Tuttle Company, Inc., 1976.

Khan, A. R., and Qadeer, M. A. "Effect of guar gum on blood lipids." *American Journal of Clinical Nutrition* 34(1981):2446.

King, E. G., and Burns, J. J. "Second conference on vitamin C." *Annals of the New York Academy of Science* 258(1975):156.

Kingsbury, J. M. *Poisonous Plants of the United States and Canada.* Englewood Cliffs, N. J.: Prentice-Hall, Inc., 1977.

Kirby, R. W., and Anderson, J. W. "Oat-bran intake selectively lowers serum low-density lipoprotein cholesterol in hypercholesterolemic men." *American Journal of Clinical Nutrition* 34(1981):824.

Klevay, L. M. "Coronary heart disease: The zinc-copper hypothesis." *American Journal of Clinical Nutrition* 28(1975):764-74.

Kligman, A. M., et al. "Oral vitamin A in acne vulgaris: Preliminary reports." *International Journal of Dermatology* 20(1981):278-85.

Knapik, J. J., et al. "The effect of *Panax ginseng* on indices of substrate utilization during repeated, exhaustive exercise in man." *Federation Proceedings* 42(1983):336.

Kolata, G. "Cholesterol-heart disease link illuminated." *Science* 221(1983):1164.

Krochmal, A. and Krochmal, C. *A Guide to the Medicinal Plants of the United States.* New York: New York Times Book Co., 1979.

Kromhout, D., and Bosschieter, E. B. "Dietary fiber and 10-year mortality from coronary heart disease, cancer, and all causes." *Lancet* 2(1982):518.

Kumler, W. D. "Biochemical individuality and the case for supplemental vitamins." *American Pharmacist* 19(1979):498-51.

Kummet, T., et al. "Vitamin A: Evidence for its preventive role in human cancer." *Nutrition and Cancer* 5(1983):96-106.

Lamberg, L. "Zinc deficiency: When skin sends signals." *American Health* 1(1982):26.

Lane, H. W., et al. "Selenium content of selected foods." *Journal of the American Dietetic Association* 82(1983):24.

Langford, H. G. "Dietary potassium and hypertension: Epidemiologic data." *Annals of Internal Medicine* 98(1983):770-72.

Langford, H. G. "Potassium in hypertension." *Postgraduate Medicine* 73(1983):227.

Lee, C. J., et al. "Effects of supplementation of the diet with calcium and calcium-rich foods on bone density in elderly females with osteoporosis." *American Journal of Clinical Nutrition* 34(1981):819-23.

Lee, W. H. "For many health-beneficial reasons: Think zinc!" *American Druggist* 189(1984):64.

LeGardeur, B. Y. "Vitamins A, C, and E in relation to lung cancer incidence." *American Journal of Clinical Nutrition* 35(1982):851.

Leung, A. Y. *Encyclopedia of Common Natural Ingredients Used in Food, Drugs, and Cosmetics.* New York: John Wiley & Sons, 1980.

Leverett, D. H. "Fluorides and the changing prevalence of dental caries." *Science* 217(1982):26.

Levine, M. "New concepts in the biology and biochemistry of ascorbic acid." *New England Journal of Medicine* 314(1986):892-901.

Lewis, W. H., and Elvin-Lewis, M. P. F. *Medical Botany.* New York: John Wiley & Sons, 1977.

Li, C. P., and Li, R. C. "An introductory note to ginseng." *American Journal of Chinese Medicine* 1(1973):259.

Liebman, B. "Too much of a good thing is toxic." *Nutrition Action* 10(1983):6.

Lindenbaum, J. "Drugs and vitamin B12 and folate metabolism." *Current Concepts in Nutrition* 12(1983):73-87.

Liu, V. J. K., and Dowdy, R. "Effect of high-chromium-yeast extract on serum lipids, insulin, and glucose tolerance in older women." *Federation Proceedings* 36(1977):1123.

Liu, V. J. K., and Abernathy, R. P. "Chromium and insulin in young subjects with normal glucose tolerance." *American Journal of Clinical Nutrition* 35(1982):601.

Livingstone, P. E., and Jones, C. "Treatment of intermittent claudication with vitamin E." *Lancet* 2(1968):602-03.

Livingstone, S., et al. "Anticonvulsant drugs and vitamin D metabolism." *Journal of the American Medical Association* 224(1973):1634.

London, R. S., and Goldstein, P. J. "Medical management of mammary dysplasia." *Obstetrics and Gynecology* 59(1982):519.

Luhby, A. L., et al. "Vitamin B6 metabolism in users of oral contraceptive agents." *American Journal of Clinical Nutrition* 24(1971):684-93.

Lutz, J., and Linkswiter, H. M. "Calcium metabolism in postmenopausal and osteoporotic women consuming two levels of dietary protein." *American Journal of Clinical Nutrition* 34(1981):2178.

McCarron, D. A. "Calcium and magnesium nutrition in human hypertension." *Annals of Internal Medicine* 98(1983):800-05.

McCarron, D. A., et al. "Dietary calcium in human hypertension." *Science* 217(1982):267.

McCarty, M. F. "The therapeutic potential of glucose tolerance factor." *Medical Hypotheses* 6(1980):1177.

———. "Chromium and insulin." *American Journal of Clinical Nutrition* 36(1982):384.

———. "Salt and hypertension." *Lancet* 2(1984):689.

McConnell, K. P., et al. "The relationship of dietary selenium and breast cancer." *Journal of Surgical Oncology* 18(1980):67.

McLaren, D. S. "The luxus vitamins — A and B12." *American Journal of Clinical Nutrition* 34(1981):1611.

Maebashi, M., et al. "Lipid lowering effect of carnitine in patients with type IV hyperlipoproteinaemia." *Lancet* 2(1978):805.

Marshall, J., et al. "Diet in the epidemiology of oral cancer." *Nutrition and Cancer* 3(1982):145-49.

Massey, L. K., and Strang, M. M. "Soft drink consumption, phosphorus intake, and osteoporosis." *Journal of the American Dietetic Association* 80(1982):581.

Mayer, H., et al. "Retinoids, a new class of compounds with prophylactic and therapeutic effects in oncology and dermatology." *Experientia* 340(1978):1105-1246.

Mertz, W. "The essential trace elements." *Science* 213(1981):1332.

——. "Chromium: An essential micronutrient." *Contemporary Nutrition* 7(1982):3.

Mertz, W., ed. "Beltsville one-year dietary intake study." *American Journal of Clinical Nutrition* 40(1984):1323.

Mettlin, C., et al. "Vitamin A and lung cancer." *Journal of the National Cancer Institute* 62(1979):1435-38.

Michaelsson, G. "Effects of oral zinc and vitamin A in acne." *Archives for Dermatology* 113(1977):31.

Miller, J. D. "The new pollution: Ground water contamination." *Environment* 24(1982):8.

Millspaugh, C. *American Medicinal Plants*. New York: Dover Publications, Inc., 1974.

Mitscher, L. A., et al. "Antimicrobial agents from higher plants: Antimicrobial isoflavinoids and related substances from *Glycyrrhiza glabra* L. Var. typica." *Journal of Natural Products* 43(1980):259-60.

Mock, D. M., et al. "Biotin deficiency: An unusual complication of parenteral alimentation." *New England Journal of Medicine* 304(1981):820-23.

Mohsenin, V., et al. "Effect of ascorbic acid on response to methacholine challenge in asthmatic subjects." *American Review of Respiratory Disease* 127(1983):143-47.

Monagan, D. "The iodine scare." *American Health* 1(1982):26.

Moore, M. *Medicinal Plants of the Mountain West*. Santa Fe, N. M.: The Museum of New Mexico Press, 1979.

Morton, J. F. *Major Medicinal Plants: Botany, Culture, and Uses*. Springfield, Ill.: Charles C. Thomas, Publishers, 1977.

Muller, D. R., and Hayes, K. C. "Vitamin excess and toxicity." *Nutritional Toxicology* 1(1982):81-83.

Murphy, E. W., et al. "Nutrient content of spices and herbs." *Journal of the American Dietetic Association* 72(1978):176.

National Research Council. *Diet, Nutrition, and Cancer*. Washington, D.C.: National Academy of Sciences, 1982.

——. *Recommended Dietary Allowances*. 10th ed. Washington, D.C.: National Academy of Sciences, 1985.

Natow, A. B., and Heslin, J. A. *Megadoses: Vitamins as Drugs*. New York: Simon and Schuster, 1985.

Neuman, J. L., et al. "Riboflavin deficiency in women taking oral contraceptive agents." *American Journal of Clinical Nutrition* 31(1978):247-49.

Newberne, P. M., and Suphakarn, V. "Preventive role of vitamin A in colon carcinogenesis in rats." *Cancer* 40(1977):2553-56.

Nobbs, B. T. "Pyridoxal phosphate status in clinical depression." *Lancet* 1(1974):405.

Nockels, C. F. "Protective effects of supplemental vitamin E against infection." *Federation Proceedings* 38(9179):2134.

Oderda, G. M. "Iron and vitamin toxicities." *ENT Journal* 62(1983):84-87.

Offenbacher, E. G. "Beneficial effect of chromium-rich yeast on glucose tolerance and blood lipids." *Diabetes* 29(1980):219.

Ophir, O., et al. "Low blood pressure in vegetarians: The possible role of potassium." *American Journal of Clinical Nutrition* 37(1983):755-62.

Olson, J. A. "Adverse effects of large doses of vitamin A and retinoids." *Seminars in Oncology* 10(1983):290-93.

Olson, J. A., et al. "The function of vitamin A." *Federation Proceedings* 42(1983):2740-46.

Pal, B., and Mukherjie, S. "Chromium in nutrition." *Journal of Applied Nutrition* 30(1978):14-18.

Palmer, I. S., et al. "Selenium intake and urinary excretion in persons living near a high selenium area." *Journal of the American Dietetic Association* 82(1983):511.

Parfitt, A. M., et al. "Vitamin D and bone health in the elderly." *American Journal of Clinical Nutrition* 36 (supp. 5)(1982): 1014.

Parrot-Garcia, M., and McCarron, D. A. "Calcium and hypertension." *Nutrition Reviews* 42(1984):205.

Patty, I., et al. "Controlled trial of vitamin A therapy in gastric ulcer." *Lancet* 2(1982):876.

Pauling, Linus. *Vitamin C and the Common Cold.* San Francisco: W. H. Freeman & Co., 1970.

———. *Vitamin C, the Common Cold, and the Flu.* San Francisco: W. H. Freeman & Co., 1976.

Peto, R., et al. "Can dietary beta carotene materially reduce human cancer rates?" *Nature* 290(1981):201-08.

Pinsky, M. J. "Treatment of intermittent claudication with alpha-tocopherol." *Journal of the American Podiatric Association* 70(1980):454.

Pories, W. J., et al. "Acceleration of wound healing in man with zinc sulphate given by mouth." *Lancet* 1(1969):1069.

Prasad, A. S. "Zinc deficiency in human subjects." *Progress in Clinical Biology Research* 129(1983):1-33.

Prien, E. L., and Gershoff, S. F. "Magnesium oxide-pyridoxine therapy for recurrent calcium oxalate calculi." *Journal of Urology* 112(1974):509-12.

Rabinowitz, M. B., et al. "Comparison of chromium status in diabetic and normal men." *Metabolism* 29(1980):355.

Rasmussen, H. "Cellular calcium metabolism." *Annals of Internal Medicine* 98(1983):809-16.

Ray, T. K., et al. "Long-term effects of dietary fiber on glucose tolerance and gastric emptying in noninsulin-dependent diabetic patients." *American Journal of Clinical Nutrition* 37(1983):376.

Reinhold, J. G., et al. "Binding of iron by fiber of wheat and maize." *American Journal of Clinical Nutrition* 34(1981):1384.

Revolutionary Health Commitee of the Hunan Province, Fogarty International Center for Advanced Study in the Health Science, trans. *A Barefoot Doctor's Manual.* Bethesda, Md.: U. S. Department of Health, Education, and Welfare, National Institutes of Health, Public Health Service, 1974.

Riales, R., and Albrink, M. J. "Effect of chromium chloride supplementation on glucose tolerance and serum lipids, including HDL, of adult men." *American Journal of Clinical Nutrition* 34(1981):2670.

Rinke, C. "Vitamin C for bronchospasm." *Journal of the American Medical Association* 245(1981):548.

Ritchason, J. *The Little Herb Encyclopedia.* Rev. ed. Orem, Utah: Bi-World Publishers, 1982.

Rivlin, R. S. "Misuse of hair analysis for nutritional assessment." *American Journal of Medicine* 75(1983):489-93.

Roberts, H. J. "Toxicity of vitamin E." *Journal of the American Medical Association* 246(1981):129.

——. "Potential toxicity due to dolomite and bone meal." *Southern Medical Journal* 76(1983):556-59.

Roe, D. A. "Nutritional concerns in the alcoholic." *Journal of the American Dietetic Association* 78(1981):17.

——. "Nutrient and drug interactions." *Nutrition Reviews* 42(1984):141-43.

Rose, J. *Herbs & Things: Jeanne Rose's Herbal.* New York: Grosset & Dunlap, 1972.

Rosenberg, I. H., and Solomons, N. W. "Biological availability of minerals and trace elements: A nutritional overview." *American Journal of Clinical Nutrition* 35(1982):781.

——. "Folate nutrition in the elderly." *American Journal of Clinical Nutrition* 36(1982):1060-1066.

Rosenhauer, G., et al. "Effect of combined clofibrate-nicotinic acid treatment in ischemic heart disease." *Atherosclerosis* 38(1980):129.

Rossi, C. S., and Siliprandi, N. "Effect of carnitine on serum HDL-cholesterol" Report of two cases." *Johns Hopkins Medical Journal* 150(1982):51-53.

Rudman, D., and Williams, P. J. "Megadose vitamins: Use and misuse." *New England Journal of Medicine* 309(1983):488-89.

Russell, R. M., and Naccarto, D. V. "Current perspectives on trace elements." *Drug Therapy* 10(1982):115-25.

——. "Zinc and the special senses." *Annals of Internal Medicine* 99(1983):227-39.

Ryding, A., and Odegaard, B. "Prophylactic effect of dietary fiber in duodenal ulcer disease." *Lancet* 2(1982):736, 1982.

Salonen, J. T., et al. "Association between serum selenium and the risk of cancer." *American Journal of Epidemiology* 120(1984):342.

Sambaiah, K., and Satyanarayana, M. N. "Hypocholesterolemic effect of red pepper and capsaicin." *Indian Journal of Experimental Biology* 18(1980):898-899.

Sandstead, H. H. "Copper bioavailability and requirements." *American Journal of Clinical Nutrition* 35(1982):809.

Sandstead, H. H., and Darby, S. J. "Human zinc deficiency: Endocrine manifestations and response to treatment." *American Journal of Clinical Nutrition* 20(1979):422.

——. "Zinc nutrition in the elderly in relation to taste acuity, immune response, and wound healing." *American Journal of Clinical Nutrition* 36(1982):1046-59.

Saynor, R., and Verel, D. "Eicosapentaenoic acid, bleeding time, and serum lipids." *Lancet* 2(1982):272.

Schauenberg, P. and Paris, F. *Guide to Medicinal Plants.* New Canaan, Conn.: Keats Publishing, Inc., 1977.

Schaumberg, H., et al. "Sensory neuropathy from pyridoxine abuse: A new megavitamin syndrome." *New England Journal of Medicine* 309(1983):445-48.

Schorah, C. J., et al. "The effect of vitamin C supplements on body weight, serum proteins, and general health of an elderly population." *American Journal of Clinical Nutrition* 34(1981):871.

Schrauzer, G. N. "Selenium in medicine." *Bioinorganic Chemistry* 6(1979):114.

Schrauzer, G. N., and White, D. A. "Selenium in human nutrition: Dietary intake and effects of supplementation." *Bioinorganic Chemistry* 8(1978):303-18.

Schrauzer, G. N., White, D. A., and Schneider, C. J. "Cancer mortality correlation studies. Part III: Statistical associations with dietary selenium." *Bioinorganic Chemistry* 7(1977):23-24.

Schroeder, H. A., and Tipton, I. H. "Abnormal trace metals in man's chromium." *Journal of Chronic Disease* 15(1962):941.

Schultz, F. H., Jr., et al. "A possible effect of ginseng on serum HDL cholesterol." *Federation Proceedings* 39(1980):554.

Scott, M. L. "Advances in our misunderstanding of vitamin E." *Federation Proceedings* 39(1980):2736-39.

Seifter, E., et al. "Arginine: An essential amino acid for injured rats." *Surgery* 90(1981):244.

———. "Impaired wound healing in streptozotocin diabetes: Prevention by supplemental vitamin A." *Annals of Surgery* 194(1981):42-50.

Shamburger, R. J., and Willis, R. E. "Selenium in the diet and cancer." *Cleveland Clinic Quarterly* 39(1972):119.

Shekelle, R. B., et al. "Vitamin A and C consumption and mortality rates." *Lancet* 2(1981):1185.

Shohet, S. B., et al. "Vitamin E and blood cell function." *Annals of the New York Academy of Science* 3(1983):59-62.

Siegel, R. K. "Ginseng abuse syndrome." *Journal of the American Medical Association* 241(1979):1614.

Silberner, J. "Cell aging: A process of oxidation?" *Science News* 129(1986):249.

Silverman, H. M., Romano, J. A., and Elmer, G. *The Vitamin Book: A No-Nonsense Consumer Guide.* New York: Bantam Books, Inc., 1985.

Simpson, K. M., et al. "The inhibitory effect of bran on iron absorption." *American Journal of Clinical Nutrition* 34(1981):1469.

Singh, V. K., et al. "Combined treatment of mice with *Panax ginseng* extract and interferon inducer." *Planta Medica* 47(1983):234-36.

Skalka, H. W., and Prechal, J. T. "Cataracts and riboflavin deficiency." *American Journal of Clinical Nutrition* 34(1981):861.

Slovik, D. M. "The vitamin D endocrine system, calcium metabolism, and osteoporosis." *Special Topics in Endocrinology and Metabolism* 5(1983):83-148.

Sly, D. F. "Garlic: A clove a day keeps the doctor away?" *Professional Nutrition* 14(1982):7.

Smith, A. H. *Relationship between vitamin A and lung cancer.* National Cancer Institute Monograph 62:165-66, 1982.

Solomons, N. W. "Biological availability of zinc in humans." *American Journal of Clinical Nutrition* 35(1982):1048.

———. "Mineral interactions in the diet." *Contemporary Nutrition* 7(1982):1-3.

Sommer, A. "Increased mortality in children with mild vitamin A deficiency." *Lancet* 2(1983):585-88.

Spannhake, C., et al. "Vitamin C: New tricks for an old dog." *American Review of Respiratory Disease* 127(1983):139-40.

Spencer, H., and Osis, D. "Effect of small doses of aluminum-containing antacids on calcium and phosphorus metabolism." *American Journal of Clinical Nutrition* 36(1982):32-40.

———. "Calcium requirements in humans: Report of original data and a review." *Clinical Orthopedics* 184(1984):270-80.

Stadtman, T. C. "Biological function of selenium." *Nutrition Reviews* 35(1977):161-66.

Stamier, J., et al. "Clofibrate and niacin in coronary heart disease." *Journal of the American Medical Association* 231(1975):360-81.

Stampfer, M. J., and Hennekens, C. H. "Carotenes, carrots, and white blood cells." *Lancet* 2(1982):615.

Stanton, J. L. "Vitamin usage: Rampant or reasonable?" *Vitamin and Nutrition Information Service, Vitamin Issues* 3(1983):1-5.

Stich, H. F., et al. "Chromosome aberrations in mammalian cells exposed to vitamin C and multiple vitamin pills." *Food and Cosmetic Toxicology* 18(1980):497.

Sugarman, A. A., and Clark, C. G. "Jaundice following the administration of niacin." *Journal of the American Medical Association* 228(1979):202.

Suttie, J. W. "The metabolic role of vitamin K." *Federation Proceedings* 39(1980):2730-35,.

Takeda, A., Yonezawa, M., and Katoh, N. "Restoration of radiation injury by ginseng. Part I: Responses of X-irradiated mice to ginseng extract." *Journal of Radiation Research* 22(1981):323-35.

Tannenbaum, S. R. "N-nitroso compounds: A perspective on human exposure." *Lancet* 1(1983):629-32.

Taylor, V. E. *The Honest Herbal.* Philadelphia: George F. Stickley Co., 1982.

Thomson, W. A. R., ed. *Medicines from the Earth: A Guide to Healing Plants.* Maidenhead, Eng.: McGraw-Hill Book Co., Ltd., 1983.

Thorngern, M., and Gustafson, A. "Effects of 11-week increase in dietary EPA." *Lancet* 2(1981):1190.

Ting, S., et al. "Effects of ascorbic acid on pulmonary functions in mild asthma." *Journal of Asthma* 20(1983):39-42.

Trader, J., et al. "Vitamin B12 deficiency in strict vegetarians." *New England Journal of Medicine* 299(1978):1319-20.

Treasure, J., and Ploth, D. "The role of dietary potassium in the treatment of hypertension." *Hypertension* 5(1983):864-72.

Treichel, J. A. "Vitamin C for the cervix." *Science News* 123(1983):23.

Tsang, D., et al. "Ginseng saponins: Influence on neurotransmitter uptake in rat brain synaptosomes." *Planta Medica* 50(1985):221-224.

Vahouny, G. V. "Dietary fiber, lipid metabolism, and atherosclerosis." *Federation Proceedings* 41(1982):2801.

Van Gent, C. M., et al. "Effect on serum lipid levels of ingesting omega-3 fatty acids of fish oil concentrate." *Lancet* 1(1979):1249-50.

Vogel, V. J. *American Indian Medicine.* Oklahoma City: University of Oklahoma Press, 1970.

Von Lossonczy, T. O., et al. "Effect of fish diet on serum lipids in healthy human subjects." *American Journal of Clinical Nutrition* 31(1978):1340-46.

Ward, P. A., et al. "Evidence for a role of hydroxyl radicals in complement and neutrophil-dependent tissue injury." *Journal of Clinical Investigation* 72(1983):789-801.

Wargovich, M. J., et al. "Calcium ameliorates the toxic effect of deoxycholic acid on colonic epithelium." *Carcinogenesis* 4(1983):1205.

Wattenberg, L. W., et al. "Dietary constituents altering responses to chemical carcinogens." *Federation Proceedings* 35(1976):1327-31.

Weiner, M. A. *Earth Medicine—Earth Foods.* New York: Macmillan, 1972.

——. *Weiner's Herbal.* New York: Stein and Day, 1980.

Weininger, J., and King, J. C. "Effect of oral contraceptive agents on ascorbic acid metabolism." *American Journal of Clinical Nutrition* 35(1982):1408.

Wilber, J. A. "The role of diet in the treatment of high blood pressure." *Journal of the American Dietetic Association* 80(1982):25.

Willett, W. C., and MacMahon, B. "Diet and cancer: An overview." *New England Journal of Medicine* 310(1984):633-38.

——. "Prediagnostic serum selenium and risk of cancer." *Lancet* 2(1983):130.

——. "Selenium and cancer." *Lancet* 2(1983):130-34.

——. "The relation of vitamins A and E and carotenoids to the risk of cancer." *New England Journal of Medicine* 310(1984):430-34.

Williams, J. "Iron deficiency treatment." *Western Journal of Medicine* 134(1981):496.

Williams, S. R. *Nutrition and Diet Therapy*. 5th ed. St. Louis, Mo.: Times Mirror/Mosby College Publishing, 1985.

Winter, S. L., and Boyer, J. L. "Hepatic toxicity from large doses of vitamin B3 (nicotinamide)." *New England Journal of Medicine* 20(1971):1180-82.

Wolf, G. "Is dietary beta-carotene an anti-cancer agent?" *Nutrition Reviews* 40(1982):257.

Worobec, S., and LaChine, A. "Dangers of orally administered para-aminobenzoic acid." *Journal of the American Medical Association* 241(1984):2348.

Wren, R. C., ed. *Potter's New Cyclopaedia of Medicinal Herbs and Preparations*. New York: Harper & Row, 1972.

Wurtman, R. J. "Behavioral effects of nutrients." *Lancet* 5/21(1983):1145.

Yacowitz, H., et al. "effects of oral calcium upon serum lipids in man." *British Medical Journal* 1(1965):1352.

Yamamoto, M., et al. "Serum HDL-cholesterol-increasing and fatty liver-improving actions of *Panax ginseng* in high-cholesterol-diet-fed rats, with clinical effect on hyperlipidemia in man." *American Journal of Chinese Medicine* 11(1983):96-101.

Yang, G., et al. "Selenium toxicity in China." *American Journal of Clinical Nutrition* 37(1983):872-881.

Yeung, H. W., et al. "Immunopharmacology of Chinese medicine. Part I: Ginseng-induced immunosuppression in virus-infected mice." *American Journal of Chinese Medicine* 10(1982):44-54.

Yokozawa, T., and Oura, H. "Effect of ginseng saponin on serine dehydratase activity in rat liver." *Chemical and Pharmaceutical Bulletin* 27(1979):2494-95.

Yokozawa, T., Kobayashi, T., Kawai, A., Oura, H., and Kawashima, Y. "Effect of ginseng saponin on liver glycogen content." *Chemical and Pharmaceutical Bulletin* 24(1976):3202.

——. "Effect of ginseng principle of pyruvate kinase activity in rat liver." *Chemical and Pharmaceutical Bulletin* 27(1979):419.

——. "Hyperlipidemia-improving effects of ginsenoside-Rb2 in cholesterol-fed rats." *Chemical and Pharmaceutical Bulletin* 33(1985):722-29.

Yonesawa, M., et al. "Restoration of radiation injury by ginseng. Part IV: Stimulation of recoveries in CFU and megakaryocyte counts related to the prevention of occult blood appearance in X-irradiated mice." *Journal of Radiation Research* 26(1985):436-42.

Young, V. R., et al. "Selenium bioavailability with reference to human nutrition." *American Journal of Clinical Nutrition* 35(1982):1076.

Yun, T. K., et al. "Anticarcinogenic effect of long-term oral administration of red ginseng on newborn mice exposed to various chemical carcinogens." *Cancer Detection and Prevention* 6(1983):515-525.

Zemel, M. B. "Phosphates and calcium." *Journal of the American Dietetic Association* 81(1982):606.

INDEX

bleeding gums, 198
blood clotting:
    EPA (eicosapentaenoic acid), 89
    manganese and, 73
    vitamin E and, 53
    vitamin K and, 55
    white willow and, 131
blood loss during menopause, 209
blood loss during menstruation, 209
blood pressure, *see* high blood pressure
bloodshot eyes, 201
boils, 172, 216
bone loss, 209, 212
    see also osteoporosis
bone structure, *see* skeletal system
botanicals, how to use, 22-23
breast disorders, 53, 81, 192, 209
breasts, 192
bronchitis, 192
    catnip and, 105, 192
    licorice and, 121
bruises, 193
    vitamin K and, 55
burns, 193
    comfrey and, 109, 193

caffeine use, 193-194
calcium, 58-59
    alcohol use and, 59, 188
    blood pressure and, 59, 71, 146, 176, 205
    bone loss and, 77, 181, 209
    cancer and, 59, 140, 194, 195
    cardiovascular disease and, 59, 146
    cramps and, 207, 210, 211
    exercise and, 158
    iron and, 170, 213
    magnesium and, 71, 141, 176
    nervousness and, 176, 211
    osteoporosis and, 59, 209, 212
    phosphorus and, 59, 77
    pollution, protection against, and, 140, 213
    potassium and, 79, 159
    pregnancy and, 59, 213
    sodium and, 159, 176, 205
    stress and, 176, 205, 207, 211
    vitamin D and, 51, 59
cancer, 194-195
    Anti-Aging Program and, 138-142

    calcium and, 59, 140, 194, 195
    fiber and, 91, 140, 194, 195
    garlic and, 111
    iron and, 69
    molybdenum and, 75
    of the breast, 81, 140, 192
    of the cervix, 31, 49, 141, 194
    of the colon, 140, 141, 181, 194, 195
    of the skin, 170, 217
    selenium and, 81, 140, 194
    smoking and, 216-217
    vitamin A and, 31, 141, 194
    vitamin C and, 49, 141, 194-195, 196
    vitamin E and, 53, 194-195
capsicum, *see* cayenne
cardiovascular disease, *see* heart disease
carnitine, *see* L-carnitine
cataracts, 49, 201
catnip, 104-105
    as tranquilizer, 105, 177, 191, 207, 210, 212
    asthma and, 191
    bronchitis and, 105, 192
    insomnia and, 207
    menstrual cramps and, 105, 210
cayenne, 106-107
    arthritis and, 107, 190
    as anticoagulant, 107, 148
    asthma and, 191
    backache and, 191
    congestion and, 196
    cough and, 196-197
    hangover and,107, 189
    headache and, 107, 154, 203, 210
    indigestion and, 107, 206
    licorice and, 107, 121, 191, 196, 197
    migraine and, 210
    sinusitis and, 215
    sore throat and, 107, 197
cervical dysplasia, 31, 49, 141, 194
chills, 196, 219
cholesterol, blood, or serum, 17, 18, 25, 37, 61, 63, 89, 91, 95, 111, 113, 115, 123, 145-148, 204
choline, 18
chromium, 60-61
    cardiovascular disease and, 61, 146

246

247

edema, 200-201
    juniper berries and, 119, 201
    sodium and, 83, 201
    water and, 99, 200-201
EPA (eicosapentaenoic acid), 88-89
    as anticoagulant, 89, 148
    diabetes and, 89, 199
    cholesterol levels and, 89, 148
    triglyceride levels and, 89, 148
estrogen, 208-209
exercise:
    calcium and, 158
    chromium and, 61, 158
    comfrey and, 160-161
    Fitness Program and, 156-161
    ginseng and, 161
    iron and, 158-159
    L-arginine and, 160
    L-carnitine and, 95, 160
    magnesium and, 71, 159
    potassium and, 79
    riboflavin and, 35
    vitamin C and, 159
    water and, 99, 159-160
eye disorders, 201
eyestrain, 201

fatigue, 201-202
    ginseng and, 115, 154, 202
    licorice and, 121, 202
fats, dietary, 123, 145, 148
fats, blood or serum, see cholesterol,
        blood, or serum; triglycerides
fever, 131, 197
fiber, 90-91
    as detoxifier, 91, 140, 152, 165,
        171
    cancer and, 91, 140, 194, 195
    cardiovascular disease and, 91, 147,
        204
    cholesterol, blood, or serum, and,
        91, 147
    constipation and, 91, 197
    diabetes and, 91, 199
    diverticulitis and, 91, 196
    flatulence and, 202
    hemorrhoids and, 91, 205
    high blood pressure and, 91, 147
    varicose veins and, 218
    weight loss and, 91, 180, 181, 182

fibrocystic condition, 53, 192
fish oils, see EPA
flatulence, 202
    ginger and, 113, 202
flu, 202
    peppermint and, 127, 202
    white willow and, 131, 202
fluorine, 64-65
    osteoporosis and, 65, 212
    tooth decay and, 65, 198
folic acid, 44-45
    alcohol use and, 45, 188
    anemia and, 45, 189, 212
    smoking and, 43, 217
    vitamin B12 and, 43
forgetfulness, 202-203

garlic, 110-111
    bronchitis and, 192
    cardiovascular disease and, 111, 147
    common cold and, 111, 164, 196
    immune system and, 111, 164,
        192, 196, 215
    sinusitis and, 215
ginger, 112-113
    cardiovascular disease and, 113, 147
    chills and, 196, 219
    flatulence and, 113, 202
    indigestion and, 113, 206
    nausea and, 113, 211
ginseng, 114-115
    aging and, 115, 188, 198, 203
    as stimulant, 115, 154, 161, 177,
        194, 198, 202, 203, 206
    blood pressure and, 115, 147, 206
    cardiovascular disease and, 115, 147
    convalescence and, 166, 197
    depression and, 115, 198
    exercise and, 161
    fatigue and, 115, 154, 202
    immune system and, 115, 166
    pregnant women and, 115, 213
glucose metabolism:
    chromium and, 61, 199
    diabetes and, 199
    EPA and, 89, 199
    fiber and, 91, 199
glucose tolerance factor, see glucose
        metabolism
goiter, 67

goldenseal, 116-117
   acne and, 216
   as detoxifier, 117, 152, 164-165,
      189
   boils and, 216
   cold sores and, 195
   diarrhea and, 117, 199
   hay fever and, 203
   healing tissue and, 117, 195, 204,
      205
   hemorrhoids and, 205
   immune system and, 164-165
   pregnant women and, 117, 213
   sinusitis and, 214-215
gout, molybdenum and, 75
GTF (glucose tolerance factor), *see*
     glucose metabolism

hair, 168-172
hay fever, 203
headache, 203
   cayenne and, 107, 154, 203
   valerian and, 129, 203
   white willow and, 131, 203
   see also migraine
healing wounds, 203-204
   cayenne and, 107
   comfrey and, 109, 172, 195, 197,
     205, 218, 204
   folic acid and, 45
   garlic and, 111
   goldenseal and, 117, 195, 204, 205
   L-arginine with L-lysine and, 93,
     204
   vitamin A and, 31, 197, 204
   vitamin C and, 49, 195, 197, 203,
     217
   vitamin E and, 53, 171, 196, 204,
     217, 218
   yellow dock and, 133
   zinc and, 85, 171, 195, 197, 203,
     218
heart disease, 204-205
   calcium and, 59, 146
   Cardiovascular Program and,
     144-149
   cayenne and, 107, 148
   choline and, 18
   chromium and, 61, 146
   copper and, 63

   EPA and, 89, 148
   fiber and, 91, 147, 204
   garlic and, 111, 147
   ginger and, 113, 147
   ginseng and, 115, 147
   L-carnitine and, 95, 147, 204
   lecithin and, 18
   magnesium and, 71, 146
   niacin and, 37, 148, 204-205
   olive oil and, 123, 148
   selenium and, 81, 146
   vitamin E and, 146
   white willow and, 131, 149, 205
hemochromatosis, 69
hemoglobin, 31, 41, 45, 63, 69
hemopoiesis, 43
hemorrhoids, 91, 205
hepatitis, 208
herbs, *see* botanicals
herpes virus, 93, 127, 195, 214
hGH (human growth hormone), 93,
     160, 165, 181
high blood pressure, 205-206
   calcium and, 59, 146, 176, 205
   Cardiovascular Program and,
     144-149
   chromium and, 61
   fiber and, 91, 147
   ginseng and, 115, 147, 206
   magnesium and, 71
   potassium and, 79
   sodium and, 83, 176, 205
hot flashes, 209
human growth hormone, *see* hGH
hypertension, *see* high blood pressure

immune system:
   aging and, 85, 187
   calcium and, 59
   EPA and, 45
   garlic and, 111, 164, 192, 196, 215
   ginseng and, 115, 166
   goldenseal and, 164-165
   Immune-System Program and,
     162-166
   iron and, 69, 164
   L-arginine with L-lysine and, 93,
     165-166
   pantothenic acid and, 39
   selenium and, 81

MaxEPA, *see* EPA
megaloblastic anemia, 45, 212
Meniere's disease, 200
menopause, 208-209
menstrual cramps, 210
menstruation, 209-210
    angelica and, 103, 210
    catnip and, 105, 210
    parsley and, 125, 210
migraine, 210
    magnesium and, 71, 210
molybdenum, 74-75
mood elevators, *see* stimulants
motion sickness, 210-211
    peppermint and, 127, 211
mouth ulcers, 121, 198
multiple-vitamin/mineral formula:
    choosing a, 15-16, 19, 21, 187,
        223-227
    in Anti-Aging Program, 140
    in Detox Program, 152
    in Fitness Program, 158
    in Immune-System Program, 164
    in Skin & Hair Program, 170
    in Stress Program, 176
    in Weight-Loss Program, 180-181
muscle cramps or spasms, 211
    exercise and, 159
    see also backache
myoinositol, *see* inositol

nausea, 211
    cayenne and, 107
    ginger and, 113, 211
    peppermint and, 127, 154, 211
nervousness, 211-212
    calcium and, 176, 211
    catnip and, 105, 177, 212
    magnesium and, 176, 211
    valerian and, 129, 154, 177,
        211-212
    vitamin C and, 176, 211
niacin, 36-37
    alcohol use and, 37, 188
    cardiovascular disease and, 37, 148,
        204-205
    water and, 148, 205
nicotinic acid, *see* niacin
night blindness, 31, 201
night vision, *see* night blindness

nitrosamines, 49, 53, 75, 141, 194

olive oil, 122-123
    as detoxifier, 123, 152, 153, 171,
        182
    cardiovascular disease and, 123, 148
    constipation and, 123, 197
    dandruff and, 123, 171, 216
    skin disorders and, 123, 171, 216
omega-3 fatty acids, *see* EPA
oral-contraceptive use, 212
    vitamin B6 and, 41, 212
osteomalacia, 51
osteoporosis, 51, 58-59, 65, 77, 212
    calcium and, 59, 209, 212
    fluorine and, 65, 212
    manganese and, 73
    phosphorus and, 77
    vitamin D and, 51, 209, 212

PABA (para-aminobenzoic acid), 16,
    18-19, 45, 217
pantothenic acid, 38-39
    arthritis and, 39, 190
    healing tissue and, 39, 193, 204
parsley, 124-125
    as detoxifier, 125, 153, 171
    as diuretic, 125, 153, 171, 210
    menstruation and, 125, 210
pellagra, 37
peppermint, 126-127
    as appetite suppressant, 127, 180
    bladder disorders and, 192
    bleeding gums and, 198
    flu and, 127, 202
    motion sickness and, 127, 211
    nausea and, 127, 154, 211
pernicious anemia, 43
phenylalanine, 17
phlebitis, 212-213
phosphorus, 76-77
    calcium and, 59, 77
PMS, *see* premenstrual syndrome
poison ivy, 216
poison oak, 216
pollution, protection against, 213
    calcium and, 140, 213
    copper and, 63
    fiber and, 140
    L-cysteine and, 97, 142